The Master Musicians

Bartók

Series edited by Stanley Sadie

The Master Musicians

Bartók

Paul Griffiths

**With eight pages of photographs, one map and
seventy-nine music examples**

J.M. Dent & Sons Ltd
London & Melbourne

First published 1984
© Text, Paul Griffiths

Made and printed in Great Britain by
Biddles Ltd, Guildford for
J.M. Dent & Sons Ltd
Aldine House   33 Welbeck Street   London W1M 8LX

This book is set in 10/12 pt VIP Sabon by
Inforum Ltd, Portsmouth

Music examples set by Tabitha Collingbourne

British Library Cataloguing in Publication Data

Griffiths, Paul
    Bartok. — (The Master musicians series)
    1. Bartok, Bela   2. Composers — Hungary
    — Biography
    I. Title   II. Series
    780'.92'4   ML410.B26

    ISBN 0–460–03182–1

for John Tyrrell

Acknowledgments

Photographs

The author and publishers are grateful to Ferenc Bónis for lending prints and allowing the reproduction of photographs which appear in his book, *Béla Bartók, His Life in Pictures and Documents*, Corvina, Budapest, 1981.

Music examples

Quotations from Bartók's works are included by permission of the following publishers.
Boosey & Hawkes: Exx. 2–4, 7–11, 14, 31, 34, 37–8, 48–9 and 64–79.
Editio Musica Budapest: Exx. 1, 5–6, 12–13 and 15–22.
Universal Edition (excluding U.S.A.): 10, 23–30, 32–3, 35–6, 39–47, 51–60 and 63. In the U.S.A. copyright in these works (apart from Ex. 29) is controlled by *Boosey & Hawkes*.

Preface

Bartók would be astonished, no doubt pleased and perhaps also, given his reserve, slightly embarrassed at the scale of his posthumous reputation. Hardly a month passes without some new recording of interest or without some important contribution to scholarship: partly thanks to the complete recorded edition published by Hungaroton, the Bartók discography far exceeds that for any other musician of our century, while the literature on the composer is immense. The present book, therefore, stands on many shoulders.

Since that is so, some justification is perhaps needed for an addition to the library of monographs, documentary compilations, critical articles, analyses and sleeve notes covering every aspect of Bartók's life and work. But justification comes from the very activity of Bartók studies, for this book has been able to profit from scores, recordings and documentation not available to earlier general writers on the composer. Also, I have attempted, because that is the way I see Bartók, to show the importance of everything he created from his early twenties onwards, and not to favour any of the particular faces he chose to put on view, whether the constructivist of the late twenties or the folksong arranger, the wild genius of *The Miraculous Mandarin* or the superb artist of the Concerto for Orchestra. Finally, Bartók is so various a composer as to provide ample room for any number of individual points of view.

One cannot foresee that such viewpoints will become any less diverse or less positive, but one can hope that the next author of a Master Musicians book on Bartók will be able to benefit from some volumes, at least, in a complete critical edition. The division of Bartók's manuscripts and other material between Budapest and New York has so far stood in the way of this project, but a set of authoritative scores, taking note of variant readings in different autographs and recordings, would have a value that ought to outweigh any difficulty.

Meanwhile this book owes much to the catalogue of works established by Lázló Somfai and Vera Lampert for their article in *The New Grove*. Among fellow woodcutters in that institution I had the good fortune to meet this book's dedicatee, John Tyrrell, whose work on Janáček needs no praise here. Since Bartók and Janáček must have known of each other's work, and probably met, both he and I have been searching for some recorded expression of appreciation on either part, but without success. May this volume stand, then, as a proxy remedy.

Lower Heyford   Paul Griffiths
5 October 1983

Footnote references are to the most accessible sources in English, where such exist.

Contents

List of illustrations

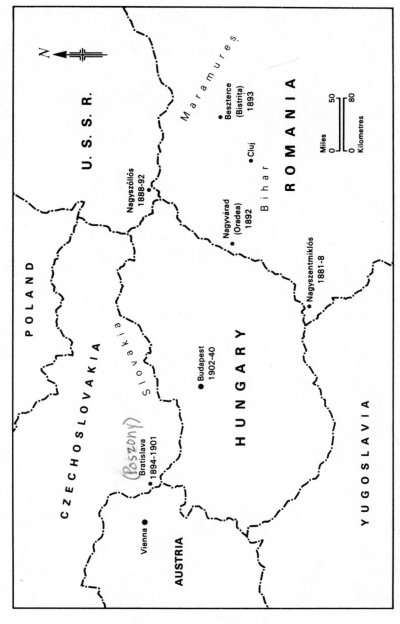

Places where Bartók lived and worked (modern national boundaries)

1
Childhood and youth

Artistic genius can appear only where there are special qualities of mind and experience, but it depends too on time and place. No better exemplary case could be found than that of Béla Bartók. He was born on 25 March 1881, right in the middle of a period extraordinarily productive of composers: Schoenberg and Ives were boys of six, Stravinsky was to arrive the next year, Berg, Webern and Varèse soon after. Just as important, he was born a Hungarian, though the town of his birth, Nagyszentmiklós (literally Great St Michael) in the far south-east of the territory settled by the Magyars, is now just within the borders of Romania and bears the name Sinnîcolau Mare.

Nagyszentmiklós at the time of Bartók's birth had a population of around 10,000 and a certain importance as a stage on the route between Szeged and Timişoara, but was otherwise unexceptional among the many small towns of the Habsburg empire. As elsewhere in Hungary, the agricultural college was a centre of new ideas, under the directorship of the composer's grandfather János Bartók (1817/18–1877) and then of his father, also Béla (1855–88). Béla Bartók senior would seem to have been a rather remarkable man. Taking over the agricultural college at the age of 21, he threw himself into his work with intellectual vigour and enthusiasm, and yet found time too for artistic pursuits: he kept a diary of his thoughts and activities written up in fine style, and he was a keen musician, playing the piano, composing dances and taking his cello to the concerts of the local music league, which he founded. On 5 April 1880 he married Paula Voit (1857–1939), a schoolteacher and also a pianist.

The composer was their first child and was christened Béla Victor János after his father, his grandfather and his godfather, Victor Schreyer, a lawyer. For information about his early life we are reliant on his own autobiographical sketch[1] and on the reminis-

---

[1] 'The Life of Béla Bartók', *Tempo*, no. 13 (1949), 3–6.

cences of his mother, set down forty years later for the benefit of her grandson.[2] Time and affection might be expected to have gilded her memories, but in fact what she records about Bartók's childhood musical talent is not so very prodigious. At the age of eighteen months, we are told, he could recognise a favourite tune, at three he could accompany his mother on a drum, and at four he could pick out forty folksongs with one finger at the piano: more formal lessons with his mother began when he was five. Paula Bartók also recalled that a smallpox inoculation in infancy had brought him up in a rash which lasted until he was five, and that until it was gone he would hide himself from people: here it is tempting to find the root of his later self-consciousness and reserve.

One might speculate, too, about the effect on the boy when his father died at the age of thirty-two after a long period of illness. Bartók was then seven, his sister Elza three, and his mother returned to piano teaching while her unmarried sister Irma Voit came to help with the house and children. A year later, in 1889, Paula Bartók obtained a schoolteaching post in another small town, Nagyszőllős in the north-east corner of the country (it is now incorporated in the Soviet Union as Vinogradov), and there the family remained for three years, during which time Bartók's musical gifts began to flower and to be recognised. His first compositions date from 1890 and 1891: dances and other small piano pieces of no importance. Christian Altdörfer, an organist and composer visiting the town from Sopron in 1890, predicted a great future for the boy, and the next year his mother took him to Budapest to be seen by Károly Aggházy (1855–1918), a piano professor at the National Conservatory and one of the outstanding Hungarian composers in the generation after Liszt. Aggházy was impressed, and would have accepted Bartók there and then as a pupil. His mother, however, decided on normal schooling, and so in the autumn of the same year, 1891, he was sent to stay with another aunt, Emma Voit, widow of his mother's elder brother, and attend the Gymnasium in Nagyvárad, there being no such institution in Nagyszőllős.

Nagyvárad, still on the eastern fringes of Hungary, was a bigger town than Bartók had known hitherto: Michael Haydn and Dittersdorf had been there in the service of the bishop (to them it was

---

[2] In János Demény, ed.: *Bartók Béla levelei*, ii (Budapest, 1951), 203–17.

Grosswardein; as part of present-day Romania it is Oradea). But Bartók was not happy there. He seems to have been the victim of favouritism among his teachers, who preferred the children of wealthier families, and in April 1892 he was brought back to Nagyszőllős, where on 1 May he gave his first public recital, his programme including the first movement of Beethoven's 'Waldstein' sonata and his own *A Duna folyása* ('The course of the Danube'). Playing for about twenty minutes, this is the longest of his childhood compositions, though it falls into little sections no more ambitious than his other pieces and is of interest only as a clue to the eleven-year-old child's patriotic feeling: on the model of Smetana's *Vltava*, but in an altogether simpler way, the piece follows the course of the Danube from its source to the sea, and finds the river jubilantly entering Hungary to a polka and leaving with a turn into the minor.

In Nagyszőllős it went down rather well. Paula Bartók was given leave of absence for a year from her teaching post so that she could take the family right across the country to Bratislava (as it is now known, being within Czechoslovakia; to Hungarians it was Pozsony, and to Germans Pressburg), one of the most important cities of the empire, lying on the Danube sixty miles from Vienna. Only twenty-five years before Franz Josef had been crowned there as King of Hungary, to a mass by Liszt, and there was an active musical life befitting a city so near the imperial capital. Bartók also had the opportunity to study with László Erkel, son of the great pioneer of Hungarian opera, Ferenc Erkel. But his mother failed to find a position, and the family had to move back over to the east of the country, to another small town where she could get work: Bistriţa (Beszterce to Hungarians), now deep in the territory of Romania.

To the twelve-year-old Bartók this brought an abrupt change: the opera and orchestral concerts of Bratislava were replaced by sonata evenings with a local forester who could play the fiddle. However, in April 1894, after only a few months in Bistriţa, Paula Bartók gained a post in Bratislava. The family could move back to the big city, Bartók resume his studies with László Erkel and his education at the Catholic Gymnasium.

He was at an impressionable age, and it is not surprising that he should have been drawn to admire and emulate an older contemporary at the Gymnasium whose musical talent was already well evident: Ernő Dohnányi. Dohnányi's allegiances were westwards to

3

the Vienna of Brahms, who in this summer of 1894 was writing his op. 120 clarinet sonatas. Naturally Bartók began to look in the same direction. In Bratislava he set out on a new series of opus numbers (the old one had reached to 31 works since 1890, all for piano) and a new seriousness. Instead of little dances he wrote sonatas, though at first his models were a century old: Mozart in the F major piano sonata op. 3 (1895), Beethoven in the G minor piano sonata op. 1 (1894) and the C minor violin sonata op. 5 (1895). Of course it would be absurd to look for very much in these efforts of a boy of thirteen or fourteen. Most other composers would have taken care to destroy or lose such juvenilia, and the fact that Bartók retained them is merely evidence of his scrupulously systematic nature, which seems to have been inherited from his mother. Looking at the case more generally, the time was not right for the flourishing of boyhood geniuses like Mendelssohn or Britten, let alone Mozart. Among composers belonging roughly to Bartók's generation, Schoenberg, Stravinsky, Sibelius, Debussy, Ives and Ravel all produced nothing distinctive until they were in their mid-twenties, and the same is true of Bartók.

Meanwhile there were ten more years of waiting. Nothing survives from the year 1896, in which Bartók turned fifteen and began to study with a German teacher, Anton Hyrtl, after László Erkel's death. By 1897–8 he had made a great advance, very much in the direction of Brahms, who looms large behind the A major violin sonata op. 17 (1897), the C minor piano quartet op. 20 (1898) and the F major string quartet, apparently written after Bartók had abandoned this second sequence of opus numbers but also dating from 1898: all three scores bear the proud signature 'Bela von Bartok', and testify to the young composer's ambition to enter the Austro-German mainstream, as Dohnányi already had. There is also the evidence of his belated first vocal composition, a set of three lieder from 1898 including, quite oddly, an unprepossessing setting of a Heine lyric famously set by Schumann, 'Im wunderschönen Monat Mai'. At the same time, however, he would have been aware of the gradual renascence of Hungarian nationalism. He played at school occasions celebrating in 1896 the millenary of the Magyars' arrival in modern Hungary and in 1898 the fiftieth anniversary of the insurrection led by Lajos Kossuth. Nor were these his only opportunities to perform in public: he took part in domestic chamber music parties, he appeared at other school concerts (playing Tausig and

4

Liszt) and he played the organ at school mass on Sundays.

After finishing at the Gymnasium in the summer of 1899 he might well have been expected to continue his musical education in Vienna. Indeed, this was expected: on 8 December 1898 he went with his mother to the Vienna Conservatory, where he was seen by Hans Schmitt and promised a free place for the next academic year. During the Christmas holiday, however, he changed his mind. His idol Dohnányi five years before had taken the unconventional course of continuing his training within Hungary, at the Budapest Academy of Music, and he determined to do likewise. In January 1899 he and his mother had an interview with István Thomán, the principal piano teacher at the academy, who gave the Bartóks the impression that the boy would be admitted without having to sit any examination. All looked bright, but then the next month Bartók became suddenly ill with a pulmonary condition that was to recur through his student years, and he was unable to touch the piano during his illness and a period of convalescence with his mother in Carinthia in the summer (though he did complete the Gymnasium course). He was therefore quite unprepared when he arrived at the academy in September to find that he was required to play for the staff before being accepted. In the event, though, his performance was eminently satisfactory, and for the first time in his life he was installed in the heartland of Hungary, in Budapest.

It would be possible to exaggerate the importance of this, at least initially. The teaching of composition at the academy was still biassed towards the solid German tradition: Robert Volkmann had been succeeded in the chief post by another German, Hans Koessler, a cousin of Reger and follower of Brahms in his own hefty works. He was not much impressed by the young Bartók, whose creative talent might indeed have seemed modest by comparison with the recent memory of Dohnányi, for Dohnányi had published his op. 1, a piano quintet in C minor (1895), while still at the academy, and had it complimented by Brahms himself. Bartók was discouraged by Koessler's lack of enthusiasm for his work, but he found a much more sympathetic mentor in Thomán, who not only took care of his pianism but also helped him in other ways, giving him scores, securing him concert tickets and drawing him out to discuss what he had heard. Nevertheless, the repertory he studied with Thomán was nothing unusual. Thomán had been a pupil of Liszt, and works by Liszt figured among those Bartók was learning, but the bulk of his time was spent with the more mainstream classics: Bach, Beethoven, Schumann, Chopin and Brahms.

In the library and the opera-house, though, he was discovering something new: Wagner. It is a remarkable witness to the Vienna-centred prejudice against Wagner that Bartók in Bratislava, half a century after *Lohengrin*, had had no opportunity to see any of the music dramas on the stage. All he seems to have known was Liszt's transcription of the *Tannhäuser* overture. Budapest, however, was another matter. Ödön Mihalovich, director of the academy in succession to Liszt, was an ardent Wagnerian, one of whose operas was a realisation of Wagner's scenario *Wieland der Schmied*. He had been influential in securing the appointment of Gustav Mahler as director of the Budapest Opera, and though Mahler was there only from 1888 to 1891, the seeds had been sown for a strong Wagner tradition. Around the age of nineteen, therefore, Bartók came into contact for the first time with the *Ring, Tristan* and *Die Meistersinger*, and was bowled over: he writes in astonishment to his mother that 'there are a lot of instruments' in *Das Rheingold*, though adds that his orchestration teacher, Ferenc Xaver Szabó, is said to write for orchestras so large he needs sixty staves on his manuscript pages.

Nothing so ambitious was yet to come from his own pen. 'I got rid of the Brahmsian style, but did not succeed, *via* Wagner and Liszt, in finding the new way so ardently desired',[3] he said in retrospective explanation, though perhaps Koessler's attitude was as important in damping his creative spark. In 1899 he began a piano quintet, but Koessler found his ideas valueless and advised him to try simpler things. He took the hint. During the next two years his only serious compositions seem to have been pieces addressed to one of his fellow students, Felicitas Fábián, he casting himself as Schumann to her Clara.[4] There was a set of six *Liebeslieder* (1900) to poems by Rückert, Lenau and Goethe, one of them incorporating a theme by Fábián. Another theme by her he took as the basis for a set of twelve variations for piano (1900–1), and in a scherzo for piano in B flat minor (1900) he combined his initials with hers, the theme beginning 'F–F–B♭–B♭'.

[3] 'The Life of Béla Bartók', 3.
[4] See Ferenc Bónis: *Béla Bartók: his Life in Pictures and Documents* (Budapest, 1972, 2/1981), 53, for photographs of Fábián and of Bartók's autograph of his FFBB scherzo.

Otherwise our information about Bartók's personal life at this time is meagre. In October 1899, after he had been at the academy only a month, his landlady had to send for his mother because he was ill once more – possibly, one might guess, in reaction to losing the cossetting of his mother and aunt Irma, the home where he alone must have carried the family's hopes. Irma Voit duly came to the capital to look after him; later he moved into a flat with aunt Emma. The charming suggestion came from one of the academy teachers that he ought to study law instead, his constitution being too frail for music, but this was firmly resisted by the young composer. Nevertheless, next summer, on the very day before he and his mother were due to leave their holiday accommodation in Styria, he went down with a high fever diagnosed as pneumonia, and though the two of them were able to return to Bratislava in September, it seemed advisable that Bartók should spend the winter of 1900–1 in a warmer climate, so his mother took him to Merano in the Italian tyrol from November until early spring. It was there that he wrote the scherzo and variations for Fábián, away from the doubting Koessler. There too he gained a lot of weight (photographs of 1901 show a quite uncharacteristically plump Bartók[5]), as well as enough strength to go back to the academy.

After this his bouts of illness disappeared as his confidence and success grew. At the beginning of his third year at the academy, in September 1901, he received the Liszt Scholarship; his finances were further helped by a few piano pupils and the odd paid performance. On 21 October he played in public at the academy for the first time, performing Liszt's B minor sonata, and on 14 December he received his first fee, for playing at a casino: this was carefully kept a secret from mother until she could be surprised with the purse at Christmas. And in the next term, on 12 February 1902, came an experience that at last stirred his long-dormant creative powers. 'From . . . stagnation I was aroused as by a lightning stroke by the first performance in Budapest of *Thus Spake Zarathustra* . . . I threw myself into a study of Strauss's scores and began again to compose.'[6]

No less important, though, was his growing awareness of himself as a Hungarian, an awareness shared by many in Budapest in

[5] See Bónis, 54–6.
[6] 'The Life of Béla Bartók', 4.

the early years of the century, and it is this rather than Strauss's influence that marks what seems to have been his first work of 1902, a set of four songs to folksy poems by Lajos Pósa. These were his first settings of Hungarian words, and after them there would be no more German lieder: in the first three even the tempo markings were in Hungarian. The second and fourth are merry numbers, answering two songs of a more soulful character, of which no. 3, 'Nincs olyan bú' ('There is no greater sorrow'), is the pick of the set, with its moments of harmonic and melodic bareness. But at twenty-one Bartók was still far from entering into his own musical territory. 'I don't know of any Hungarian song better than these,' he wrote to his mother the next year, '– which isn't saying too much, as there are extremely few Hungarian songs.'[7]

He was also occupied with the Hungarianness of the music of his admired Dohnányi. Like everyone else in Budapest, he was strongly impressed by the appearance of Dohnányi's First Symphony in D minor (1900–1), which he played at the salon of Emma Gruber, musical patroness, amateur composer and later the wife of Zoltán Kodály. But he disagreed with a critic who detected a certain musical nationalism in the work, except that he found the adagio second movement 'definitely Hungarian (gipsy-like)' – an association of ideas that had plentiful support in Liszt and Brahms but that he himself would very soon disclaim. At the same time his letters to his mother were becoming distinctly testy over the subject of identifying with Hungarian aspirations: she must persist in speaking Magyar at home and in shops, whatever the difficulties, and she must have his sister (now Hungarianised as 'Böske') come in national dress to his celebratory homecoming recital in Nagyszentmiklós, fixed for 13 April 1903.[8]

Apart from Emma Gruber, the circle of his important musical acquaintanceship in Budapest was also enlarging in 1902 to include the Arányis. Adila Arányi, later Fachiri, was a violin student at the academy, and both she and her sister Jelly were to become violinists of international repute: Holst's Double Concerto of 1929 was written for them. In all likelihood it was for Adila that in November 1902 Bartók sketched out a duo for violins, with themes that could

[7] János Demény, ed.: *Béla Bartók: Letters* (London, 1971), 25.
[8] Ibid., 21–31.

be combined with their retrograde inversions:[9] the medium was one to which he would return three decades later in his set of Forty-four Duos; the manifest contrapuntal ingenuity was to be a more constant presence. That same month, too, he wrote an Andante for violin and piano, and sent to Adila a couple of postcards with themes from Strauss's *Don Quixote* arranged for solo violin.

At the same time he was completing his first work of obvious Straussian reach, a symphony in E flat, the heroic key not only of Beethoven's 'Eroica' symphony but also of Strauss's *Ein Heldenleben*. This was his first large-scale work since the sonatas, quartets and quintet of his Bratislava years, and it became an outpouring of everything he had been storing up while coming to terms with Wagner, Liszt and Strauss. Nor was Brahms yet forgotten: that much is evident from the scherzo, which was by every consent the most successful movement and the only one he orchestrated (it had a performance in Budapest on 29 February 1904, another in 1905, and was then forgotten until 1961). But Strauss was in the ascendant. Bartók while working on his symphony made a piano transcription of *Ein Heldenleben*, remarkably enough, and played it before an audience of academy staff on 22 December 1903. Just five weeks later he performed it in Vienna under the auspices of the Tonkünstlerverein, and gained great critical attention.

He was now nearing the end of his time at the academy. On 8 June 1903 he took part in a recital there with other departing students, his contributions being two piano pieces he had recently played in Nagyszentmiklós (the Fantasy no. 1 and the Study – then Sonata – for the left hand, both written early in 1903) and the third movement of his violin sonata, then in progress. Also on the programme were pieces by Emmerich Kálmán, subsequently a master of the operetta, but it was Bartók and not Kálmán who was hailed three and a half weeks later in the Budapest musical-theatrical weekly *Zenevilág* as a 'phenomenal young genuis, whose name today is known only to a few, but who – and this is our firm belief – is destined to play a great and brilliant role in the history of Hungarian music'.[10]

If one considers the works Bartók had written so far, this was a

---

[9] See reproduction in Bónis, 59.
[10] Ibid., 62.

piece of astonishing foresight. The two piano pieces, joined during the year by a second Fantasy and a Scherzo to make a set of four, dip their toes in the languorous decoration and rich harmonic colouring of Liszt's Hungarian music, but do not find there anything to impel them through more than a few bars at a time. The violin sonata shares the same gipsy ancestry, but shows it more ostentatiously, partly because the medium allows an evocation of impassioned gipsy fiddling to an accompaniment in which the jangling tones of the cimbalom can be heard:

Ex. 1

Violin Sonata (1903)

This, however, is from the slow second movement which Bartók did not write until August-September 1903, when he was spending a month with Dohnányi and his wife in Gmunden, Upper Austria: all the *Zenevilág* correspondent had heard of the sonata was its excessively long finale.

Bartók's purpose in staying with the Dohnányis was to take further piano lessons with his elder colleague, but he found the possibility of a close relationship excluded by Dohnányi's 'unforgivable sin': he was not patriotic enough. Dohnányi also had no high opinion of the new orchestral work which Bartók had written between April and August that year, and which, along with the scherzo from the 1902 symphony, he was writing out in fair copy. This was *Kossuth*, the first full creative embodiment of the purpose he gave himself in a letter to his mother from Gmunden: 'Everyone, on reaching maturity, has to set himself a goal and must direct all his work and actions towards this. For my own part, all my life, in every sphere, always and in every way, I shall have one objective: the good of Hungary and the Hungarian nation.'[11]

Kossuth suggests that Bartók's ambition was not just to be a Hungarian composer but to be the outstanding Hungarian composer of his time, for in it he claimed for himself the right to a musical treatment of the most momentous event in recent Hungarian history: the revolution of 1848–9. The symphony is in ten linked sections, all but one of them bearing explanatory headings,[12] and the obvious model for it was again *Ein Heldenleben*, Strauss's heroic self replaced at the centre by the Hungarian patriot:

Ex. 2

Kossuth: main theme

This Kossuth theme, announced as above in the opening section, is threaded through the work, appropriately transformed to meet

[11] Demény (1971), 29.
[12] For the work's programme see ibid., 35–7.

whatever the needs of the programme may be at the time; vigorous in B major on trumpets and trombones when he recalls his country's glorious past (section 3), expressively extended in C major on divided cellos and double basses when he dejectedly remembers that those times are over (section 4), reduced to a busy repeating figure when he decides to prepare for combat (section 6), made into a fortissimo summons on all eight horns with string support when he calls on the Magyars to take up arms (section 7), and returning to A minor as a funeral march when the battle is over and the cause is lost (section 9):

Ex. 3
Kossuth: funeral March

The chromatic ornament, the double-dotted rhythm and the triplets here are standard Hungarianisms taken over from Liszt, who also provided Bartók with models of theme transformation in his *Faust Symphony*, which eight years later, in an article written to celebrate Liszt's centenary, Bartók was to praise for 'its host of wonderful thoughts and the planned development of the diabolic irony (Mephisto) which first appeared in the fugato of the sonata', adding in a footnote that 'Liszt was the first to express irony by means of music'.[13] But not the last. In the eighth section of *Kossuth*, for which he left the listener to supply a title, Bartók uses Liszt's weapons of distortion to caricature the Austrian imperial hymn, taking it from Haydn's confident G major through the diabolical interval of a tritone into malevolent C sharp minor:

---

[13] 'Liszt's Music and our Contemporary Public', in Todd Crow, ed.: *Bartók Studies* (Detroit, 1976), 122–3.

Ex. 4

Kossuth: battle sequence

During the course of this section, the longest in the symphony, the parody hymn is grotesquely inflated with all the forces of the huge orchestra Bartók uses, an orchestra bigger than any he was ever to need again (it is almost identical with the ensemble required for *Ein Heldenleben*), and so is depicted the oppressive might of the Austrian forces which, with the help of Russia, put down Kossuth's revolt.

The daring of the 22-year-old Bartók in guying the national anthem is rather amazing: it is as if a young Irish composer at the time had written a Daniel O'Connell symphony parodying 'God Save the King'. Not unsurprisingly, there was trouble when the work was put into rehearsal by the Budapest Philharmonic in preparation for the first performance in the city on 13 January 1904. Some members of the orchestra refused to play the eighth section, and eventually five players declined to appear. Nevertheless, and equally expectably, the symphony scored an immense success with the Hungarian public and critics, and Bartók was now firmly placed with Dohnányi among, as one paper put it, 'the most significant masters of Hungarian music'.

Five weeks later, on 18 February 1904, *Kossuth* brought Bartók his first orchestral performance abroad, in Manchester. The venue was not quite as odd as might appear. Hans Richter was conductor of the Hallé Orchestra at the time, and kept in touch with musical life in his native Hungary. Bartók seems to have been brought to his attention by János Batka, a musical amateur living in Bratislava who had known the young composer from boyhood, and it was in Bratislava, in June 1903, that he heard Bartók play *Kossuth* (it had yet to be orchestrated). By July the Manchester engagement had been fixed: *Kossuth* was to be played, and Bartók would also appear as a soloist, in Volkmann's Handel Variations and Liszt's *Rhapsodie espagnole*, the latter with orchestral accompaniment by Busoni. In the event, as an encore, he also played a scherzo of his own, probably the one he had written the previous summer. The demand for an encore, however, would seem to have been occasioned more by Bartók's skills as a pianist than by his composition. The *Manchester Guardian* critic found the battle music of *Kossuth* wearisome and the abuse of the 'noble anthem' inexcusable,[14] and though Bartók met Richter again in Bayreuth the following summer and played him his new Scherzo for piano and orchestra, no further invitation was forthcoming. Nor was there a revival of *Kossuth* in Hungary, for by the time it could have become a national monument, with the achievement of Hungarian independence in 1918, Bartók's style had moved on enormously.

Meanwhile he was making a name for himself in Berlin, where he had gone in October 1903, after the month with the Dohnányis. Thomán had provided an introduction to the pianist Leopold Godowsky, who looked after him, and he began to build a career as a virtuoso: on 4 November he played Beethoven's 'Emperor' Concerto in Vienna; on 14 December he gave a solo recital in Berlin, including three of the four piano pieces he had written during the year; on 22 January he repeated this programme in Bratislava; on 25 January in Budapest he gave the first complete performance of his Violin Sonata with Jenő Hubay, the violinist and composer whom he would have known as head of the violin department at the academy; and on 3 February he played the same work with Rudolf Fitzner in Vienna, soon before leaving for Manchester. Then, while in London on his way back to Berlin, he gained a promise from the firm of Broadwood for six concerts in England during the following season.

His next major composition was the Piano Quintet (1903–4), his third essay in a medium to which he was drawn no doubt by Dohnányi's example, and also by the fact that a quintet provided a pianist-composer with something in which he could show himself off doubly at chamber recitals. It is an unequivocally late-Romantic combination (after Schumann's invention of the genre in his op. 44, the great examples are those of Brahms, Franck, Reger and Fauré), and Bartók's is an unequivocally late-Romantic piece. There are four movements, the first an allegro with an andante introduction that sentimentalises Brahms, the second a scherzo dancing on ostinatos, the third a big adagio and the last another lively dance. Once more, as in the Violin Sonata and *Kossuth*, the Hungarian tone comes from

[14] Review reprinted in Lajos Lesznai: *Bartók* (London, 1973), 208–11.

the kind of gipsy music Bartók could have heard equally well in the cafés of Budapest or in Liszt, while other influences on the quintet, besides those of Brahms and presumably Dohnányi, include the theme-transformation technique he had already learned from Liszt and Strauss. One might point to other connections – there are, for instance, some Debussy-like passages near the start of the adagio – but these are probably fortuitous similarities bound to occur in a work so much of its time. Essentially the quintet is Hungarian Brahms slightly modernised. There are technical features that hindsight might want to relate to the later Bartók, like the transformation of themes from movement to movement, or the fugato of the finale, or the combination of bowed with percussed strings (already adumbrated in the Violin Sonata, and perhaps exploited there with more of a will, at least in such passages as Ex. 1). However, none of these is peculiarly Bartókian, and in no way can the quintet be seen as prophetic: after a performance in 1921, the only performance in which he took part after 1910, he was infuriated that it was preferred to his more characteristic music.

By the time Bartók was completing this work, in July 1904, he had withdrawn to the country, to Gerlicepuszta in the district of Gömör. There he met the poet Kálmán Harsányi, who very much shared his nationalist outlook: he had already set a poem by Harsányi, 'Est' ('Evening'), as a song and (differently) as a partsong in March 1903. In August he left his retreat to visit Bayreuth, where he met Richter and saw *Parsifal*, and in September he was occupied by the recent appearance in print of his Four Piano Pieces of the previous year, published by Ferencz Bard, who also in 1904 brought out the Pósa songs: these were his two first works to be printed. But the most important experience of that summer in the country was his discovery of folksong, not the commercialised music he had encountered in the cities but real folksong, on the voice of a young girl.

2
Folksong studied

The song that Bartók heard in Gerlicepuszta was this:[1]

Ex. 5
Hungarian folksong as notated by Bartók in 1904

It was sung by Lidi Dósa, who was eighteen and a nursemaid with a Budapest family on holiday in the same house where Bartók was staying, but who was by origin a Székely, a Hungarian from Transylvania. Much later, after years of collecting and research, Bartók was to find this a particularly interesting tune, apparently starting out as a Hungarian composed song of folk type, then taken over and adapted by Slovak peasants, next borrowed by Hungarian peasants and further changed – and finally, one might add, collected by a Hungarian composer, given a simple piano accompaniment and published on 15 February 1905 in a magazine, *Magyar Lant*. For the moment, though, his curiosity was aesthetic rather than scientific and historical. Peasant music was not, as Liszt had supposed, a crude simplification of the flamboyant music of the gipsy bands; it was, rather, a natural indigenous culture, its freshness encapsulated in Lidi Dósa's Dorian melody. For Bartók the discovery was like finding a wild Guelder after years of believing that the only roses were Hybrid Teas.

[1] Béla Bartók: *The Hungarian Folk Song*, ed. Benjamin Suchoff (Albany, New York, 1981), 281.

16

Quite how this would affect his own music he did not yet see. For two or three years he continued to pursue his career as a pianist and composer very much as he had in 1903–4, while collecting folk music was a completely separate sideline, though pursued with increasing relish and activity. On 26 December 1904 he wrote to his sister: 'I have a new plan now, to collect the finest examples of Hungarian folksongs and to raise them to the level of works of art with the best possible piano accompaniment. Such a collection would serve the purpose of acquainting the outside world with Hungarian folk music. Our own good Hungarians . . . are much more satisfied with the usual gipsy slop'[2] – clearly he had already formed the view that authentic peasant music was more valuable than the 'Hungarian' music of the towns. During the next summer he made more folksong notations while staying with his sister, who had married one Emil von Oláh Tóth and settled in Vésztő in the district of Békés. In December he wrote a set of children's songs for their son, with the punning title *A kicsi 'tót'-nak* ('To the Little "Slovak" ').

Meanwhile his enthusiasm for folksong had been stimulated by his encounter with Kodály, who was also a pupil of Koessler at the academy, but whom he appears not to have met before the autumn of 1905, when they were both at Emma Gruber's. By then Kodály was at work on a dissertation on Hungarian folksong, and he introduced Bartók to the technique of collecting on gramophone records, which Béla Vikár had been doing in Hungary since 1896. In the summer of 1906 Bartók and Kodály set out on separate collecting expeditions in various parts of Hungary, and pooled their resources to publish in December a thin volume of twenty folksongs with piano accompaniment, the first ten arranged by Bartók and the second ten by Kodály. They seem to have chosen songs they had themselves collected (an exception is no. 8, which Bartók took from Vikár's collection), and their aim in presenting their material was, as Kodály's postface had it, 'so that the Hungarian general public might get acquainted with and acquire a liking for folksong'. Deliberately, therefore, the arrangements were made as simple as possible, the piano nearly always doubling the vocal line and, particularly in Bartók's arrangements, touching in only a discreet and fresh harmony. The perfect elegance of this approach is best shown in no.

[2] Quoted in József Ujfalussy: *Béla Bartók* (Budapest, 1971), 60.

17

3a, where the additions could hardly be more unassuming yet apt:

Ex. 6
Hungarian Folksongs (1906): no. 3a

The cover of the volume was in the same simple taste, with just the title in Hungarian lettering and a band of peasant-style decoration in yellow-orange, but the 'Hungarian general public' failed to respond to these musical wild flowers. It took until 1938 before the printing of 1500 copies was sold out, and then Bartók and Kodály brought out a second edition with some alterations to accord with intervening research: most notably, one of Bartók's numbers had been discovered to be a composed song, and so was excised.

The failure of the *Hungarian Folksongs* as a commercial enterprise put paid to plans for a second volume (Bartók had already arranged another ten songs in anticipation), but in no way did it dampen the two young composers' eagerness to collect more. In the summer of the next year, 1907, Bartók at last set out, as he had long wanted to, for the Székely country of Transylvania, and there visited the districts of Csík, Gyergyó and Kolozs. Writing to the young violinist Stefi Geyer, the person closest to him at the time, he recounted in humorous dialogue form the difficulties experienced by a folksong collector faced by a woman who thinks to impress the gentleman with art songs or hymns,[3] but on a picture postcard to his pupil Etelka Freund on 17 August 1907 he announced: 'I have made a rather strange discovery while collecting folksongs. I have found examples of Székely tunes which I had believed were now lost.'[4]

Almost certainly this 'strange discovery' was that of pentatonic tunes, which Bartók identified as products of the oldest style of Hungarian folk music, dating back to a time when the Magyars lived on the banks of the Volga rather than those of the Danube (he was later delighted to find certain similarities with songs still then sung by populations in the Soviet Union). Some evidence of this style had already been collected: Bartók himself drew attention to the pentatony present in the background of such songs as that quoted in Ex. 6. But in Transylvania he found pentatonic tunes surviving in an ancient state, along with equally primitive material conditions on which he remarked to his mother: 'in the streets of Bánffy-Hunyad the filth and litter is quite Moroccan without any of the amenities imported there for the sake of Europeans.'[5] But he was not downcast. The hardships were cheerfully borne in the elation of discovery, and Bartók's feelings while collecting are well conveyed in a later reminiscence:[6]

> In order to secure musical material uninfluenced by urban culture, we had to travel to villages as far as possible removed from urban cultural centres and lines of communication. There were many such villages at that time in Hungary. In order to obtain older songs – songs perhaps centuries old – we had to turn to old people, old women in particular, whom, quite naturally, it was difficult to get to sing. They were ashamed to sing before a strange gentleman; they were afraid of being laughed at and mocked by the villagers; and they were also afraid of the phonograph (with which we did most of our work), as they had never in their life seen such a 'monster'. We had to live in the most wretched villages, under the most primitive conditions, as it were, and to make friends of the peasants and win their confidence. And this last, in particular, was not always easy, for in previous times

[3] Demény (1971), 70–4.
[4] Ibid., 74–5.
[5] Ibid., 69.
[6] 'The Folk Songs of Hungary', in Benjamin Suchoff, ed.: *Béla Bartók Essays* (London, 1976), 332.

the peasant class had been too thoroughly exploited by the gentry, and, in consequence, was full of suspicion where those who appeared to belong to this class were concerned. Yet, despite all this, I must admit that our arduous labour in this field gave us greater pleasure than any other. Those days which I spent in the villages among the peasants were the happiest days of my life.

Bartók came back from Transylvania having ordered elaborately painted furniture for his new Budapest flat,[7] and bringing with him a fund of folktunes. Before the year of 1907 was out he had arranged three of them for recorder and piano, these later adapted to piano solo as Three Hungarian Folksongs from the Csík District, and also set five for voice and piano (this group was to be published together with a triptych of soldiers' songs as Eight Hungarian Folksongs: the Csík songs are nos. 1–5). The song arrangements are quite different in style from those of the previous year: they were intended for public performance rather than private delectation (the latter had already been shown to be a vain hope), and so the piano is not an anxious shadow of the voice but a complement to it, enjoying the thumping dance rhythms of the third and fifth songs, and enjoying too the seventh chords that Bartók finds a natural support to the pentatonic melodies. Sometimes, indeed, the pentatony is so wholeheartedly embraced by the accompaniment that its bows to more normal practice are a concession one might well regret, especially at the end of the first song, where the A major arpeggios seem an unnecessary preparation for the cadence and the final chord of E major is quite out of place:

Ex. 7
Eight Hungarian Folksongs: no. 1

[7] See Plate 3.

Bartók described the arranging of a peasant melody as 'the mounting of a jewel',[8] and it was an art he was on the point of mastering when he made the group of Csík songs: the breakthrough was to come in 1908–9, and it was to come through the challenge of being simple, writing eighty-five little folksong transcriptions *For Children*, as the title of these volumes has it. Half of these tiny pieces were based on Hungarian tunes, including many Bartók had collected in Békés and in the musically fecund village of Felsőireg, where he recorded 307 tunes in 1907. The other half were Slovak, collected among Slovak communities along what is now the border territory between Hungary and Czechoslovakia. *For Children* was an undertaking of what might appear small ambition, created in order to encourage an appreciation of folksong, a keyboard dexterity and a fineness of taste among the very young, but the best of the pieces achieve those purposes while also being small masterpieces of perfection and grace, where the folktune is not grandly upholstered or excessively adorned but simply allowed to be:

Ex. 8
For Children: vol. 1 no. 2

[8] 'The Relation between Contemporary Hungarian Art Music and Folk Music', in *Essays*, 351.

A further important feature of *For Children* was its openness to the music of a people òther than the Magyars. Bartók had started out with the intention of bringing Hungarian folk music to the notice of the outside world, but he quickly found he could not ignore the musical cultures of neighbouring populations, in particular the Slovaks to the north and the Romanians to the east. He visited Slovakian villages every year between 1906 and 1909, and was impressed by something the Hungarians had already lost: the reserving of particular songs for particular occasions and purposes. This functioning of music he found to be maintained even more strongly among the Romanians, whom he visited first in the summer of 1909, going to the Bihar district of Transylvania, whither he returned in February 1910 and again at Christmas 1910. The last visit was necessary in order for him to collect Christmas carols, for the Romanians were not inclined to sing their music out of season: he was sometimes told that no lament could be performed because no one had died recently.

Bartók found this deeply satisfying. He must have been aware of the irony that the conditions most propitious for the preserving of an ancient musical practice were also those that left the people most deprived. He was later to recall the 'medieval' state of Romanian Transylvania before the first world war: 'there are entire villages with illiterate inhabitants, communities which are not linked by any railways or roads; here, most of the time the people can provide for their own daily wants, never leaving their native habitats except for unavoidable travel as arises from service in the army or in occasional appearances in court.'[9] But at the same time there is a note of longing in his conviction 'that in ancient times (and even today in the Rumanian regions I have just mentioned [Transylvania]) music must undoubtedly have been a communal occupation. Here, an important event in Man's life – the celebration of Christmas, harvesting, a wedding, death, and so forth – cannot and must not take place unless it is accompanied by specific traditional rituals.'[10]

Here among the Romanians Bartók the folksong collector became Bartók the ethnomusicologist. In 1908 he had published an article on Transylvanian ballads, with his own transcriptions of

[9] 'Romanian Folk Music', in *Essays*, 119.
[10] Ibid., 120.

material collected in Csík, but in Hungary he could find no interest in any larger enterprise. By contrast, the Romanian Academy of Sciences in Bucharest was willing to publish his Bihar collection, and in 1913 this was duly brought out, with transcriptions of 371 songs.[11] An important link between Bartók and the Romanian Academy was the Romanian composer and conductor Dumitru Kiriac, to whom Bartók wrote first in 1910, mentioning that: 'at first I used to take a Rumanian student with me to write down the songs, but now I can do this myself, and I think my rendering of the local dialect is more accurate – my companion often used to modify it (the practice of those who want above all things to correct the people).'[12] The trust here in the value of peasant ways is entirely typical, as is Bartók's thoroughness in equipping himself with the linguistic tools for his task.

If the Székelys had given him a first hint of ancient folk music, the Romanians provided far more, and from now on his collecting was very much centred on them. Especially important was the material he collected in the district of Maramureş in north-west Transylvania in the short period of 5–17 March 1913, for there he discovered the *hora lunga*, or 'long song', a style of highly elaborate and extended vocal lines, evidently connected with Asian music. Immediately he conceived the wish to check this discovery against folk music of direct Eastern origin, for which purpose in the summer of 1913 he went to the old town of Biskra in Algeria to collect Arab music. There indeed he found similarities with the music of Maramureş, and had he been able to travel as far as Kampuchea he would have found there too a similar form of ornamented melody.

The outbreak of the first world war brought disruptions that made it hard for Bartók to continue his work in Romania, but he was able to return to the Slovaks, in the Zólyom district, in 1915, and he was allowed too to collect songs from soldiers: hence the three soldiers' songs that found their way into the set of Eight Hungarian Folksongs, and hence too the five Slovak Folksongs for male chorus, a beautiful little group expressive more of the pity of war than of bellicosity and unified by the use of the same music in the fourth number as in the first:

---

[11] *Cântece popolare româneşti din comitatul Bihor (Ungaria)* (Bucharest, 1913).
[12] Demény (1971), 102.

Ex. 9
Slovak Folksongs: no. 1

These songs show the simplicity of Bartók's technique of arrangement at its most spontaneous: the melody is totally absorbed into its
new context without any fuss. In an earlier group for male voices, the
Four Old Hungarian Folksongs (1910, with two more songs from his
Csík collection), Bartók had achieved the same effect by keeping very
much to block harmony; the set of Four Slovak Folksongs for mixed
chorus and piano (?1916) shows again the Slovaks' love of the
Lydian mode and its tritone fourth (cf. Ex. 9), though the genre of
choral folksong with piano is an unfortunate one, never repeated in
Bartók's later years.

For all that Bartók detested the war (if nothing else, it took his
peasant singers away from their home villages, and so away from his
gramophone), for all, too, that he despised the imperial régime, he
contributed both groups of soldiers' songs, the choral and the solo
(the latter with himself accompanying), to a concert before the
Queen-Empress in Vienna on 12 January 1918. At least, as he wrote
to a Romanian colleague, 'there was an opportunity for "real"
Hungarian folksongs to be heard by those few Viennese musicians
who accidentally dropped into that company of pluto-aristocrats.'[13]

Several other arrangements emerged from the war period. The
Romanian collections were the source of songs and choruses that
Bartók arranged but never published; he did, however, publish piano
transcriptions of seven Romanian Folkdances (to be distinguished
from the Two Romanian Dances of 1909–10, which were original
compositions based on folk music) and twenty Romanian Christmas
Carols. Both sets date from 1915, in which year appeared also the

---

[13] Ibid., 137.

Sonatina for piano, whose three short movements are similarly based on Romanian material from the Transylvanian tours. All these works put into effect the principles of *For Children*, placing each folktune in an apt and slender context which may be varied for one or two repetitions to create a small strophic form. The Romanian Folkdances, so lively and exotic, quickly became one of Bartók's most popular works, whether in the original form, in his own orchestration of 1917 or in other versions, but it is the set of Christmas Carols that required of him the more scrupulous care. One must forget all about 'While Shepherds Watched': as Bartók himself was pleased to note, the Romanian *colinda* was an ancient form, about a third of the examples he collected having entirely pagan texts, and most exhibiting the odd mixture of modes and sometimes also metres that give Romanian music its special flavour, and that attracted Bartók to it:

Ex. 10
Romanian Christmas Carols: series 2, no. 3

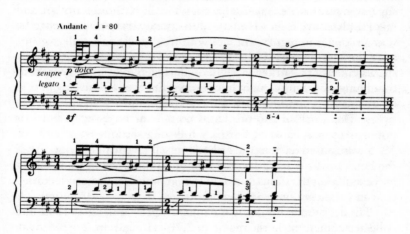

Bartók's predominant attention during the war years to Slovak and Romanian music was designed to give a voice to the minorities who were being ignored in the floodtide of imperial patriotism, and in the case of the Romanian works to express uninterrupted solidarity with a people whose government in Bucharest was on the opposing side in the conflict (the non-Transylvanian parts of

Romania – Moldavia and Wallachia – formed an independent country outside the empire). However, there was at the same time another Magyar work, the Fifteen Hungarian Peasant Songs (1914–18), which matters of arrangement and ordering make into more of a 'work' than a collection. One is even invited to consider the set as a sonata, with a slow first movement ('Four Old Tunes'), a scherzo (called so, setting its tune in a tiny ABA pattern), a slow movement (a theme and eight variations on a ballad, 'Angoli Borbála', which Bartók himself collected in Vésztő in 1918) and a finale (nine 'Old Dance Tunes'). These are still all peasant melodies, but Bartók's intervention now goes much further than it had in *For Children*, and the piece is an entirely suitable concert item.

In the Fifteen Hungarian Peasant Songs the distinction between arrangement and original composition is beginning to break down, and the process was to be continued in Bartók's next folksong work for piano, which he carefully entitled Eight Improvisations on Hungarian Peasant Songs (1920). As for straightforward arrangements, he simply stopped making them. Several reasons could be suggested for this: he may just have felt that he had done enough, and he may also have been less inclined to create arrangements when he was no longer in regular contact with folk music as a collector, for after the war he ceased his expeditions except for one not entirely successful visit to Turkey in 1936, undertaken to test the hypothesis that Hungarian music might have been influenced by the long period of Turkish occupation during the sixteenth and seventeenth centuries. This Turkish trip produced no new arrangements, but it is noteworthy that most of Bartók's folksong settings from 1904 to 1918 were based on material he had himself recently collected. After the First World War he devoted himself to the work of transcribing and classifying the songs and dances that had already been recorded instead of setting out to collect more.

His decision to do this was eminently practical. By 1918 he had collected something in the region of 2,700 Hungarian, 2,500 Slovak and 3,500 Romanian melodies; there were also about 5,000 other Hungarian tunes collected by Kodály, Vikár and others. So far Bartók had published only his Bihar collection: plans to publish the Maramureş material had been frustrated by the war. There was, therefore, a great deal of scholarly work to be done, and unlike other composers who have interested themselves in folksong (Vaughan Williams, for example), Bartók had the temperament for sorting and analysing as much as for collecting and arranging, for deciding on questions of taxonomy – which tunes were variants of others, which independent – as diligently as he did in his equally passionate collecting of insects.

It was already obvious that there were two basic kinds of song: those of flexible speech-like rhythm ('parlando rubato' in Bartók's terminology) and those which had taken on the more decisive metres of dancing (his 'tempo giusto'). From his earliest sets of arrangements Bartók had made use of this dichotomy in building larger forms, having slower parlando numbers followed by brighter dance-like pieces in balance and contrast, as in the Csík songs for piano and for voice and piano, or the Four Old Hungarian Folksongs for male chorus. He also came at an early date to recognise three categories of melodies cutting across the song-dance divergence. First there were the 'old style' melodies, retaining an evident basis in pentatony, and distinguished also by a mid-point cadence onto the flattened third and by what Bartók called a 'non-architectural' structure, not rounded off by a return in the last line to the music of the opening. Melodies of his 'new style' did have this feature besides being most commonly in the Dorian, Aeolian or major modes, and having a mid-point cadence onto the fifth or the tonic. The largest class, however, was that of 'other tunes', which did not fit either pattern, and which Bartók supposed to show the cross-fertilisation of 'old style' and 'new style', and to show also the influence of neighbouring peoples. He certainly did not regret this mixing. Indeed, he thought it a great strength of eastern European folk music that different musical-linguistic groups – Hungarians, Slovaks, Romanians and the rest – had been able to enrich each other's music. By contrast, in his view, the music of the Arabs of Biskra had been left in a primitive condition by their isolation from foreign contact, and when the notion of 'racial purity' suddenly and grotesquely became a public issue, in the 1930s, he was firm to assert that musical cultures positively gained from being mongrel.

Nevertheless, the rich and heterogeneous collection of folk-songs that had been obtained from the Magyars left him with fearsome problems of classification, which he sought to address by adapting the system established by the Finnish composer and ethnomusicologist Ilmari Krohn. The criteria were, in order of importance, first the number of text lines per stanza (four, three or two), then the pitch on which the tune has its main internal point of rest, then the pitches of other line endings, then the number of syllables per line, and finally the compass of the whole tune. This was the system Bartók used in his first serious study of Magyar folk music, *Hungarian Folksong*, completed in October 1921 and published in 1924, containing 320 tunes arranged in order. The much larger project of publishing an ordered corpus of the whole Hungarian folk-song repertory then occupied his thoughts until in 1934 he was granted a commission from the Hungarian Academy of Sciences to undertake this. However, the work was not completed by the time he left Budapest in 1940, and when the *Corpus musicae popularis hungaricae* eventually began to be published – in 1951, six years after Bartók's death – it was in accordance with quite different, and indeed inconsistent systems of classification. Meanwhile, in America, Bartók had found a new ethnomusicological task in the work of notating and classifying a large recorded archive of Yugoslav folk music collected in 1934–5 by Milman Parry and deposited at Columbia University.

Bartók's work on folk music – Hungarian, Slovak, Romanian, Yugoslav and other – fills more than a dozen posthumously published volumes, sufficient to have guaranteed him remembrance as one of the outstanding ethnomusicologists even if he had never written a note of original music. But of course composing was the centre of his life, at least as viewed in retrospect: posterity values him above all else as a composer, and so naturally his other activities have come to be seen as adjuncts. In the case of his folksong research, though, the connection with his creative work was an intimate one, in terms not only of material influence but of entire approach: for instance, the period of active collecting and arranging, between 1904 and 1918, was also the period when Bartók's original music seems most immediate and uncontrolled, a direct 'arrangement' of musical discoveries he was collecting from within his own mind, whereas after 1918 his music became more analytic, just as his work on folk music did.

In conflict with this pattern is a group of folksong arrangements made between 1929 and 1933, more than ten years after Bartók's last previous sets of this kind. But though these are not 'improvisations' on peasant music, neither are they tactful settings in the earlier manner. The superb set of four Hungarian Folksongs for mixed chorus (1930) is no longer homophonic but filled with a musical intelligence working under and around the folktunes, the first, slow song rippling with imitative tendrils in a rich eight-part texture, the quick third and fourth numbers briskly undercut with real counterpoint (the slow-slow-fast-fast pattern is repeated from the first choral folksongs of 1910). Something of this style crops up too in the Székely Songs for male chorus (1932), but these are a good deal simpler: they also, curiously, avoid songs Bartók had himself collected, whereas the 1930 set looks back to his summers of 1906–7. Other folksong works from this brief but intense revival include orchestrations of the Sonatina (as *Transylvanian Dances*), of the Ballad and most of the dances from the Fifteen Hungarian Peasant Songs, and of a mixed bunch of piano pieces from 1908–11 (as *Hungarian Pictures*). However, Bartók's major effort apart from the 1930 choruses was the book of Twenty Hungarian Folksongs for voice and piano (1929). This is a collection and not a cycle, divided as it is into four sections: 'Sad Songs', 'Dance Songs', 'Diverse Songs' and 'New-Style Songs'. But it is not simply a book of arrangements. The piano accompaniments are technically much more challenging than in the 1907–17 group, and there is now no attempt to fit irregular material into the major-minor system, as may be indicated by a comparison of Ex. 7 above with the ending of another slow song, no. 2, from the 1929 collection, where the harmony is in open conflict with the mode of the song until in the postlude it settles on a chord made up of the mode's principal notes, $F - G - B^\flat - C - D$:

Ex. 11

Twenty Hungarian Folksongs: no. 2

The intention now is not just to complement the folktune but openly to set it in relief, by divergences of melody, harmony and rhythm, just as happens too in the choral folksongs of 1930 and 1932.

The message is clear. The songs of the peasants cannot be simply transferred to the concert hall or drawing room, as one might construe Bartók's aim to have been in his arrangements of 1904–18. It is an affectation to suppose that folk art can be displayed in a formal environment (the rustic furniture in the city flat), and a patronising affectation. The composer who really values folk music will absorb its essences of rhythm, modality, texture and so on, as Bartók began to do in his original music from soon after his first encounter with real Hungarian folk music, or if he takes complete melodies, he will make sure that they enter art music dressed for the occasion, as is the case in the arrangements of 1929–32. The solo volume condescends not at all but is fully a book of art songs, and the arrangements for mixed chorus are as richly textured and carefully formed as Bartók's original choral works of the same period (the *Cantata profana*, no less, was composed in the same year of 1930).

If we can interpret Bartók's work as an arranger as paralleling his understanding of folksong – first a period of close involvement and direct transcription, then a time of analysis and deeper creative connections – it is tempting to see too a larger significance in the change. Before 1918 Bartók was perhaps seduced by the Rousseau-esque idea of peasant life as natural and unquestionably preferable to city life, just as he found peasant song infinitely more valuable than the music of the street cafés: his 1931 definition of folk music insists, in italics, that it *'actually is nothing but the outcome of changes wrought by a natural force whose operation is unconscious in man'*.[14] The First World War, however, made it clear that any vision of natural man in harmony with his environment was optimistic in the extreme and could not be simply conveyed in a folksong arrangement without an appearance of naivety. The war was also the extreme and raw expression of other changes that were to destroy the kinds of society in which folksong could flourish. As Bartók recalled a quarter century after his last expedition: 'I had the great privilege to be a close observer of an as yet homogeneous, but unfortunately rapidly disappearing social structure, expressing itself in music.'[15]

[14] 'What is Folk Music?', in *Essays*, 6.
[15] 'Folk Song Research in Eastern Europe', in *Essays*, 34.

3

Romantic interludes

During that summer of 1904 when he first heard a true peasant song, Bartók was also giving his attention to music of a very different sort: the Rhapsody for piano that he dedicated to Emma Gruber and dignified as his op. 1 in his third and definitive sequence of such numberings. The work has a rather complicated history. It was composed as a piano solo, apparently between October 1904, when Bartók was still in Gerlicepuszta, and December the same year, by which time he was back in Bratislava: this information is given on the manuscript. However, there is also a version for piano and orchestra with an added introduction, possibly written in the same year but certainly before 15 November 1909, when Bartók gave the first performance of this version in Budapest; a two-piano form of the same version dates from 1905. Finally there is a shortened form, consisting only of the opening slow section, which was the text used when the work was first published in 1907.

The complete Rhapsody consists of this adagio followed by a quick section in the csardas manner, and so takes over the slow-fast pattern favoured by Hungarian gipsy musicians. It also takes over a great deal of their style, at least as interpreted by Liszt, whose Hungarian rhapsodies obviously provided the model. The piano writing is splendidly grand, with massive chords, great runs and charging octaves, and the music makes play with the languid, soulful ornaments and other clichés of the supposed Hungarian style. Even so, the Lisztian character of the Rhapsody can be overestimated. The dominant voice sounding confidently from its pages is that of the young Bartók, the Bartók of *Kossuth*, the Violin Sonata and the Piano Quintet. To some extent the personality is compromised by the virtuoso medium – and it is curious that Bartók, unlike most other pianist-composers, developed most rapidly when not writing for his own instrument. However, there are passages that look way ahead to *The Miraculous Mandarin* and beyond, passages such as the episode of chromatic counterpoint for low winds (figure 6 in the orchestrated version), or the many-voiced canon coming soon afterwards and taking the basic motif of the slow section, with all its tawdry Hungarianisms, into a whole new realm of musical discourse:

Ex. 12
Rhapsody op. 1

There are other features that appear no less Bartókian, like the ironic amplification and grace-note decoration of the trivial fast theme, or the derivation of that theme from an idea introduced in the slow section, but here Bartók is displaying his debts to Liszt.

Because it was quickly and then repeatedly published, and because Bartók himself continued to play it occasionally (the last

time was in 1936), the Rhapsody became one of the best known of his early works, and still it overshadows his other piece for piano and orchestra of this period, the Scherzo op. 2. This is unfortunate. Despite its modest title, the Scherzo is an ambitious composition lasting half as long again as the seventeen-minute Rhapsody, and it also contains clearer indications of the composer Bartók was to become: it reaches beyond Lisztian irony towards the cold grotesqueness of *The Wooden Prince*. And yet it would seem to have been written before the Rhapsody, in July–August 1904, since Bartók was able to play it to Richter when he met him in Bayreuth that summer (and what a decisive summer it was, with the visit to

Bayreuth, the embarking on two big virtuoso works for piano and orchestra, and the first recognition of real folk music). The later opus number of the Scherzo may record the fact that its orchestration was completed after that of the Rhapsody; in any event, it was neither published nor performed until 1961.

In October 1904 Bartók returned from his momentous summer retreat, and the next month he took part in the first performance of his Piano Quintet, in Vienna, where he spent the first few months of 1905. During that time he wrote his op. 3, a work again boldly conceived on a large scale, like everything he had written since 1903: the Violin Sonata, *Kossuth*, the Piano Quintet, the Rhapsody, the Scherzo. It was an orchestral suite in five movements, in the grand and glowing key of E major. By calling the piece a suite Bartók relieved himself of the problem of writing a sonata allegro (the first movement is rather a sort of rondo), and of course there were Romantic precedents for the form in Tchaikovsky and others. There were also precedents, not least in Beethoven's *Pastoral* symphony, for the five-movement structure which one might otherwise be tempted to see as adumbrating similar symmetrical forms in the much later Fourth and Fifth Quartets and the Concerto for Orchestra. In truth, there is not a lot in the First Suite that sounds like the later Bartók. The jolly, clear-cut polyphony of the outer movements springs out of *Die Meistersinger*, and the general atmosphere of comfortable relaxation with a national tang suggests that Bartók might have become a Hungarian Dvořák. However, this only makes the few forward-looking moments all the more startling: the complex texture of divisi strings in the second movement, for instance, which stares ahead through Bartók to Ligeti, or the first attempt, in the middle of the scherzo (third movement), at a sound image that will reappear in the middle of the Concerto for Orchestra, one of cadences chromatically clinched in the brass within a rich chordal texture.

Of course, to look for traces of the older composer in works he wrote when he was twenty-three and twenty-four is to judge those works by very partial criteria. The Rhapsody and the Scherzo can be enjoyed more wholly as products of the Hungarian school written within nineteen years of Liszt's death, the First Suite as a juvenile exercise by a composer of as much confidence as polish. For indeed the suite is the most inexperienced of these works despite its later date. Some of the movements show their structural joins, and some are repetitive (Bartók himself advised several cuts). Moreover, the device of thematic unification is so over-used that one begins to wonder why the composer cannot think of some idea that does not start with a step down a fourth and back up again:

Ex. 13
Suite no. 1 op. 3

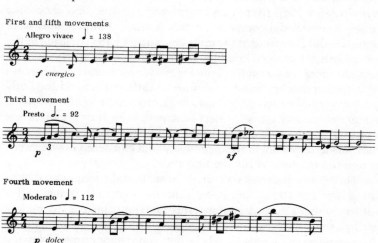

This thematic metamorphosis is perhaps the single Lisztian feature in a work that has left the very Lisztian territory of the Rhapsody and the Scherzo for more anonymous ground.

The summer of 1905 was occupied with folksong collecting and also with preparations for the Rubinstein Competition, to be held in Paris in August. Bartók entered both as pianist and as composer, and was not surprised to lose the piano prize to Wilhelm Backhaus. But he was infuriated that the judges gave no composition prize but instead awarded certificates of merit to a certain Attilio Brugnoli and himself, placing Brugnoli's name first: 'I may say that Brugnoli's pieces are absolutely worthless conglomerations. It is quite scandalous that the jury could not see how much better my works are', he wrote to his mother,[1] the works by which he was judged being the

[1] Demény (1971), 45.

Rhapsody and the Violin Sonata (he had submitted the Piano Quintet, but that was deemed too difficult for the quartet to learn in time).

However, the stay in Paris, which continued for some weeks after the competition, was by no means wasted. Bartók seems not to have made any important musical acquaintances, which is not altogether surprising given his youth: Debussy he was to meet on a second visit to Paris four years later, by which time he had become himself a substantial composer. But non-musical impressions were legion. He did the round of the museums and galleries (Murillo at the Louvre struck him very forcibly) and he was prettily scandalised by the night spots (one wonders how far his adventures went: he writes to his mother that 'men and women are so different in mind and body that it may not be such a bad idea after all to demand from women a greater degree of chastity'[2]). After Budapest, even after Vienna, Paris appeared to him a vastly beautiful and also a dangerously exotic place: his letters home have the naivety of a cloistered maiden aunt visiting the metropolis for the first time.

These same letters, however, indicate that the long stay abroad was giving the young composer time to think. He writes to his mother of his conclusion that 'spiritual loneliness is to be my destiny', that it is vain for him to search for 'the ideal companion'.[3] To one who would gladly have been that companion, Irmy Jurkovics, he confides his thoughts in more detail. Jurkovics was a judge's daughter in his home town of Nagyszentmiklós, and he had evidently gained her adulation and that of her sister through his recital there in 1903: he dedicated the Fantasy no. 2 to the two of them. The Paris letter to her[4] must be part of a larger correspondence, for in it he takes issue with some suggestion of hers about national contributions to music, and insists that the German (represented by Bach, Beethoven, Schubert and Wagner) is by far the weightiest. Liszt is next to these big four, but otherwise Hungary's great achievement he sees already as being in folk music, 'vastly superior' to that of other nations 'as regards force of expression and variety'. A 'real Hungarian music' on the concert platform is still a project for the future, and he leaves no doubt that he will play a major part in creating it (his

[2] Ibid., 53.
[3] Ibid., 53.
[4] Ibid., 47–52.

artistic self-confidence is out of all proportion to his naivety in the ways of the world). Also to Jurkovics he writes of himself as 'a follower of Nietzsche', crudely atheistical and intent, so he says, on striving for the 'highest degree of indifference'.

In November 1905 Bartók made his return journey to Manchester to play Liszt's *Totentanz*, and in March–April 1906 there was another distant journey, to Spain and Portugal as accompanist to the boy violinist Ferenc Vecsey. Bartók spent his twenty-fifth birthday in Madrid and also visited Lisbon, Coimbra, Oporto and Barcelona, besides making a short trip to north Africa, but the place that delighted him most was Venice, where he stayed on his way home. Otherwise his travels were mainly within Hungary to collect folk music, and they were assiduous. For roughly two years, between the summer of 1905 and that of 1907, he composed nothing: the Second Suite for orchestra, begun soon after the First in Vienna, was left awaiting completion while Bartók put his energies into collecting folksongs and winning subscribers for the volume he published with Kodály in December 1906. In November that year he writes to his colleague Lajos Dietl that he has 'hardly practised for the last six months', and that now he must for a forthcoming recital, when he would 'far rather have spent my time collecting as many more songs as possible'.[5] Another revealing comment comes in a letter of the same year to his Aunt Irma, when, in discussing humorously his iconoclastic behaviour in the bourgeois household of the Vecseys – he intends to shock them by wearing a summer shirt and worn shoes to dinner – he makes a comment that will return again in his letters: 'I have a taste for dissonance'.[6]

That taste had already been exercised in the Rhapsody and the Scherzo, and also in what had been written of the Second Suite, Bartók's op. 4. A quarter of a century later he would draw attention to the fact that the third movement of this work ends with an F sharp minor triad to which the flattened seventh is added, but so far the composition had not been able to proceed beyond the challenge of that moment. Somewhat less rampantly confident than the First Suite, for a smaller orchestra and cast in the diametrically opposed tonality of B flat major, the suite begins with a Comodo of gentle

[5] Ibid., 68.
[6] Ibid., 66.

improvisational play around motifs introduced by the pair of harps, sounding distinctly Bartókian in the way the metrical changes snap home the modal cadences. As usual in early Bartók, though, it is the scherzo that seems most characteristic: here it is an Allegro scherzando with a passage of fugal development that considers its theme with obstinate intensiveness and ends with splashes of tritones. The Andante then begins with a long bass clarinet melody (the tendency for thematic material to be presented in the bass register gives the whole work a masculine feel), and it is the melodic importance of the seventh chord in this theme that justifies the final chord.

It is possible that Bartók intended to complete the suite symmetrically, as he had the First Suite, but in the event he finished it with a fourth movement that serves both as second scherzo and as return to the Comodo motion and B flat major tonality of the first movement. That was in the summer of 1907, when he was discovering the ancient pentatonic tunes of Transylvania: the very postcard to Etelka Freund alluding to this, in all probability, also conveys the information that the finale of the 'Serenade', as it was then called, 'is waiting to be orchestrated on this 800-metre-high plateau'[7]. As if to confirm the coincidence, the movement is largely based on a pentatonic tune:

Ex. 14
Suite no. 2 op. 4: fourth movement

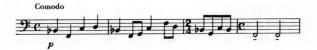

However, there are movements in Dvořák that are no less pentatonic, and the finale of the Second Suite is not really a breakthrough into a new musical world: it is still heavy with the inheritance of Wagner and Strauss. The work nevertheless remained important to its composer, who generally was distressed when his early compositions were accorded favour or used, in the way that Schoenberg's *Verklärte Nacht* was used, as a yardstick against which to denigrate

[7] Ibid., 74–5.

later pieces. He revised the work in 1920 and again in 1943, tightening its structure; and in 1941 he made a version for two pianos, to add to the repertory he could play with his wife. So this early composition became also one of the very last he worked on.

Possibly this had something to do not just with the work's intrinsic quality but also with the happy revelation of peasant life and music Bartók had enjoyed in Transylvania. In September 1907 he had to return to Budapest to take up the teaching post he had inherited from István Thomán at the Academy of Music that January: he was now the dashing young Professor Bartók, living in a flat with his peasant furniture and with his mother, who had moved in soon after his appointment to the academy, and at the age of twenty-five he evidently had what would now be called 'charisma', at least as far as his young women students were concerned. Indeed, this had already been proved in his relationships with the Arányi and Jurkovics sisters and with Etelka Freund, and in 1907 he gained two pupils and young admirers in the sisters Herma and Márta Ziegler, of whom Márta, then in her fifteenth year, gained his special attention: in 1908 she became the subject of his 'Portrait of a Girl', published as the first of the Sketches op. 9b for piano, and in 1909 he married her, privately, almost secretly.

Márta Bartók is an enigmatic figure. The few photographs of a simple, smiling girl[8] say nothing; even the date of her marriage is a matter of doubt. Whatever qualities she may have possessed as a musician, she seems to have made no public appearances after her marriage to Bartók: within about a year, on 22 August 1910, she had given birth to a son, Béla Bartók jr. Thirteen years later, when she would still have been only about thirty, Bartók divorced her to marry another young student. Her later life is as obscure as everything else about her. The young Béla grew up to become an engineer and, after the second world war, technical adviser to Hungarian State Railways. How much he and his mother saw of Bartók after the break-up of the family remains unclear, though certainly the composer wrote to his son from America during the war.

It seems plain that something deep in Bartók's personality wanted a wife who would not be in any sense an intellectual equal, would be happy to leave him in mental solitude. We have already found him despairing of meeting 'the ideal companion', and right at

[8] See Plate 6.

the time Márta entered his life he was drawing away from a close friendship with the last human being in whom he was to confide: Stefi Geyer.[9] Two letters to her of September 1907[10] take up from the one he wrote to Irmy Jurkovics two years earlier, for again the main subject is atheism, though now expressed with much more maturity. Bartók says that as a child he was 'a devoted Catholic' but by the time he was twenty-two he had become 'a new man – an atheist', 'greatly influenced' in this by 'my studies of astronomy, the works of a Danish writer [who must surely be Kierkegaard], an acquaintance, and, above all, by my own meditations'. It is clear that Geyer did not share his beliefs, was on the contrary scandalised by them, and that this contributed to the ending of the relationship. One wishes she could have responded to his missionary zeal on behalf of Nietzsche by pointing out that atheism was, by his own logical standards, quite as inadmissible as Christian belief, being beyond proof. On the other hand, in dispensing with Christianity Bartók would appear to have found the road cleared towards internal self-reliance, and perhaps this had an effect on his music, for his 'conversion' dates precisely from the year of the Symphony and the Violin Sonata. This may be, though, merely a coincidence due to the importance to him, at once musically and philosophically, of *Also sprach Zarathustra*, Strauss's and Nietzsche's.

The second of his intimate letters to Geyer includes a discussion of suicide, which he seems to regard as a justifiable, perhaps even an inevitable act once the goal of Nietzschean independence has been achieved. Geyer has evidently given her view that the suicide is a coward, and Bartók flicks over their vast disagreements in his mind before turning his thoughts elsewhere. 'After reading your letter,' he writes, 'I sat down to the piano – I have a sad misgiving that I shall never find any consolation in life save in music. And yet –'. What follows is a manuscript shred of an adagio, which eventually grew into the thirteenth of the Fourteen Bagatelles op. 6 for piano, dated May 1908. This piece is marked Lento funebre, and unlike all the preceding pieces in this set it has a title too, '(Elle est morte –)', written also in Hungarian over the theme that in the letter Bartók calls Stefi's 'Leitmotiv', a five-note figure consisting of a rising major arpeggio with interpolated seventh, though perhaps he could also

[9] See Plate 5.
[10] Demény (1971), 75–87.

have been thinking still of Felicitas Fábián, who had died prematurely in 1905. And so after a dozen little studies of various kinds – including Hungarian folksong arrangements, some speculative essays in new harmonic formations and tests of ostinato patterns – the fateful no. 13 of the volume is a memorial to the lost beloved, and the meaning of the last piece, a nightmare presto entitled 'Valse (Ma mie qui danse –)' and turning Stefi's 'Leitmotiv' from an expressive sigh into a quick cackle, can only be that Bartók is visited by her ghost.

It is not surprising that the same motif is much to the fore in the concerto which Bartók wrote for Geyer, but which she never played – which indeed the composer never mentioned later (the second concerto he wrote in the 1930s he called simply 'Violin Concerto'), and which was not heard until after Geyer's death. Or at least, the second of its two movements had to wait until then. The first Bartók had re-used in 1911 as the first of the *Two Portraits* op. 5 for orchestra, with no change except for a shortening of the final appoggiatura and the addition of a title, 'One Ideal'. The other *Portrait*, 'One Grotesque', was an orchestrated version of the frenzied waltz that concludes the Bagatelles. In both, therefore, the main feature portrayed is the Stefi theme, first as the gateway to a melody introduced by the solo violin without accompaniment, then as a noisome shriek in the high woodwind:

Ex. 15
Two Portraits op. 5

The pairing of a slow movement with a fast antithesis is very Bartókian, and has occurred before, notably in the Rhapsody, but of course its origins lie in Liszt, who provides the model too for the gross distortion Bartók practises on his material. The negation of 'One Grotesque' is the negation of the Mephistopheles movement from the *Faust Symphony*.

Naturally the original Violin Concerto, now often called 'no. 1' to distinguish it from its successor, does something rather different in its second movement. Instead of the gargoyle dance that replaced it, Bartók originally provided a rondo of gawky humour and secret significance, the latter most ostentatiously presented towards the end, where a little A major fanfare in the pair of flutes is placed in quotation marks and given as footnote a place and a date: Jászberény, 28 June 1907. What happened there on that day remains as mysterious as so much in Bartók's life, and the mystery is deepened rather than mitigated by the fact that the tune is so toy-like: it would be easier to explain a great surge of passion with the same annotation. In any event, three days later Bartók began the concerto, which he completed in Budapest on 5 February 1908, and so the period of composition extended over the time of his revealing letters to Geyer.

The first movement, later the 'Ideal' *Portrait*, is a meditation on the Stefi theme quoted above, in which the solo violin attracts to itself a progressive entwining of independent string lines, reminding one of a reference in one of the Geyer letters to Reger. This influence may at first seem surprising, but for a young composer in 1907 who felt his music moving in directions where Strauss could no longer be of help, Reger must have seemed a beacon of encouragement, simply because there was so little else: Debussy's music was apparently quite unknown to Bartók, despite his French trip of 1905, until Kodály brought back some scores from Paris in the summer of 1907, and nothing of Schoenberg was published until that year. Here in the Violin Concerto the Regerian polyphony leads to a homophonic climax, no less Reger-like, before settling into B minor, relative minor of the movement's D major tonality. There is a middle section much concerned with another motif from the opening string polyphony, and after this has run its course the soloist leads the way back to the original melody, sweetly played two octaves up.

This Stefi theme, rarely out of earshot in the first movement, is only a passing presence in the finale, though the rondo theme starts out again from a triad, this time minor. The key is also changed, to

the subdominant, G major, and one of the movement's many per-
plexing gestures is the fierce ending on unadorned octave Gs
throughout the orchestra. If the first movement expresses Bartók's
love for Stefi, it does so in an 'ideal' way indeed; the language is that
of the romantic slow movement, and the only surprise is that it
should come first rather than in the middle of the work (the key
scheme too suggests that this was an affair that had a decisive end but
no real beginning). The second movement, by contrast, is less expressively direct and yet it appears, by virtue of its puzzles, to be
speaking more personally.

In addition to its appearances in this concerto and in the
Bagatelles, Stefi's motif is also worked into the 'Dedication' that
stands as an extra page before the set published as Ten Easy Pieces
for piano, just as it dominates the two pieces that come after the
straight dozen of Bagatelles. The Ten Easy Pieces are dated the
month after the Bagatelles, June 1908, and though the absence of an
opus number might suggest they are inconsiderable, in fact they are
not all conspicuously easy, and as studies in compositional technique
and folksong setting they stand with the Bagatelles. It is presumably
to both sets that Bartók is referring when he writes to Delius in 1910
of 'little piano pieces written somewhat later [than the Second Suite]
as a consequence of the peculiar mood I was in at the time, one which
will probably never recur'.[11]

There can be no doubt that this 'peculiar mood' had much to do
with the widely dissimilar musical impulses to which Bartók was
subject in and around 1908: folksong, the still potent presence of
Liszt, the waning passion for Strauss and passing enthusiasm for
Reger, the new discovery of Debussy. To consider only the crucially
important influence of folksong, it appears that until the first half of
1908 Bartók had regarded his ethnomusicological work as rather
separate from his creative activity. On the one hand there would be
folksong arrangements for voice and piano, akin to those made for
the 1906 volume, and on the other there would be big abstract
compositions: suites and concertos. But the coexistence of folksong
arrangements with original compositions in the sets of Bagatelles
and Easy Pieces indicates that the barrier was beginning to break
down, and that folksong was not to be so effectively compart-
mentalised.

[11] Ibid., 105.

At the same time, it is easy to imagine how Bartók might have been in a 'peculiar mood' in the first half of 1908 for more personal reasons, caught as he was between Stefi Geyer and Márta Ziegler. The evidence is there in the music, most especially in the first movement of the Violin Concerto, that the Stefi side of him was a composer commanding the vast musical and intellectual resources of late Romanticism. Even in February 1908, the month the Violin Concerto was finished, he could sit down and write music that develops straight out of the most bravura Liszt, this in the first of the Two Elegies op. 8b:

Ex. 16
Two Elegies op. 8b: no. 1

It is tempting to guess what kind of composer Bartók might have become if he had gone on in this manner: perhaps a sort of Schoenberg, tempestuous and convoluted, no doubt giving vent at some point to his Nietzschean independence of thought in some oratorio or opera.

But it was not to be. Almost exactly contemporary with the Elegy just quoted is the first of the Sketches op. 9b, the portrait of Márta Ziegler which shows a quite different composer:

Ex. 17
Sketches op. 9b: no. 1

Rhetoric is abandoned for a capricious dance of motif, variously harmonised as the piece proceeds. The portrait captures the freshness and youth of its subject, but the portraitist stands apart and offers several possible harmonic interpretations, none with any great certainty. If Stefi promised a career within the noble central European tradition, Márta beckoned Bartók towards a less secure future. But it was to her voice that he listened. Stefi's theme disappeared from his music, vaporised in high treble chords in the 'Dedication' to the Ten Easy Pieces, and the new, unstable, folksong-derived accents of Márta became the ones he was to follow. The decision could not, however, be absolute. In the pieces eventually brought together in the *Two Portraits* Stefi had stirred him both to passionate ardour and to its common corollary of violent destructiveness. Feelings so intense were not to be forgotten.

4
Folksong applied

As a Gymnasium scholar Bartók would have been aware of Herder's belief that the culture of a country has and must have a national identity. As a Hungarian he would have known that the Magyar language itself owed its survival and development to the work of Ferencz Kazinczy (1759–1831) and other writers around the beginning of the nineteenth century, who established a modern tongue on the basis of the speech of the peasants at a time when the everyday language of the nobility and the educated classes was German or French. Whether consciously in emulation of this model or not, Bartók and Kodály found themselves around 1908 discovering in folk music a source for the creation of that genuinely Hungarian art music which had already been Bartók's aim for several years. And so the paths of composition and ethnomusicology conjoined.

Perhaps this would not have happened, though, if Bartók had not found that the Hungarian peasants were telling him the same things he was learning at the same time from Debussy: the ratification from Paris of new harmonic and rhythmic explorings helped him to make use of what he was recording in the villages of Hungary. The outcome of that was, as he later recalled, 'of decisive influence upon my work, because it freed me from the tyrannical role of the major and minor keys. The greater part of the collected treasure, and the more valuable part, was in old ecclesiastical or old Greek modes, or based on more primitive (pentatonic) scales, and the melodies were full of the most free and varied rhythmic phrases and changes of tempi, played both *rubato* and *giusto*. It became clear to me that the old modes, which had been forgotten in our music, had lost nothing of their vigour.'[1]

The creative result of this insight is already very evident in the two collections for piano written in the early summer of 1908, the

[1] 'The Life of Béla Bartók', *Tempo*, no. 13 (1949), 4–5.

Bagatelles and the Ten Easy Pieces, in both of which folksong arrangements appear for the first time alongside original compositions. Even more significant than companionship, though, is marriage, and in both these sets Bartók weds his creative to his ethnomusicologist self. Sometimes it is a matter of writing original music in folk style, as in the beguiling 'Evening in the Country', no. 5 of the Easy Pieces, where a simple ABABA form is made up of ballad and dance tunes in the pentatonic manner of the Transylvanians, the repeats being differently harmonised in the way of the song transcriptions published in *For Children* at the same time. But on other occasions, and they are in the majority, the folksong influence goes deeper: Bartók does not imitate his peasant material but rather analyses it, and uses what he discovers.

The threefold value of folk music – as subject for arrangement, imitation or analysis – was certainly something he was conscious of in those terms,[2] and he liked to contrast his own approach with that of Kodály (not of course with any pejorative intention: he was too close to Kodály not to have a profound admiration for him). Where Kodály restricted himself to Hungarian music, he, Bartók, had studied and used the music of Slovaks, Romanians and others. And where Kodály was fond of using folk themes in concert works (as for instance in his 'Peacock' Variations), his own preference was for writing freshly on the basis of folk music, and indeed he only used peasant melodies in pieces that are declaredly arrangements, like nos. 1, 3, 6 and 8 of the Easy Pieces.

Where the approach is more analytic, it may be difficult to tell what Bartók is taking from folk music and what from Debussy. And indeed there may be no point in seeking to make the distinction, since both influences were working on him at the same time, and in the same direction. Among the Easy Pieces, for example, no. 4 'Sostenuto' sounds very Debussian when it interchanges chords of A minor and C sharp minor. On the other hand, no. 2 'Torment', has some connection with the recently discovered Slovak folk music in its insistence on the Lydian tritone, the tune accompanied by a chromatic ostinato that leaves the music nowhere to rest:

[2] See for example 'Harvard Lectures', *Essays*, 354–92.

Ex. 18
Ten Easy Pieces: no. 2

The Bagatelles, as befits their more professional nature, explore similar ground more fully, though the range of musical and practical difficulty is wide. The third of them, for instance, is a straightforward piece that like 'Torment' has a chromatic repeating pattern heard as background to a modal melody, and the first is an utterly simple but also wholly extraordinary little essay in unresolved bitonality, the right hand playing in E major and the left in C Phrygian. Curiously Bartók's own description of the key is 'C major', in a letter[3] where he also ignores the unmistakable modalities of nos. 4, 5 and 7, besides giving keys to pieces that have only a very uncertain and shifting relation with major-minor tonality: no. 12, for example, which certainly ends in Bartók's key of B minor, but which has travelled through some very strange, even Schoenbergian territory before this point.

Since Schoenberg's op. 11 piano pieces were not written until the next year, there is no question of his influence on Bartók, and the passing coincidence needs indeed no other explanation than that both composers were reacting to the same musical pressures at the same time. While Bartók was writing his Bagatelles and Easy Pieces, Schoenberg was just beginning to test the waters of atonality in his song cycle *Das Buch der hängenden Gärten* and the finale of his Second Quartet. And that latter work, moving from heavily beset F sharp minor into the new air of atonal liberation, takes a very different course from the one Bartók was pursuing in his quartet of this period, his First, op. 7, though in Bartók's case the course is no less emblematic. The first movement is a Lento whose main business

[3] Demény (1971), 98.

is with Reger-influenced polyphony of a kind familiar from the 1907–8 Violin Concerto, but now sounding at times distinctly like the Schoenberg of *Verklärte Nacht*. Then comes a twilight Allegretto in sonata form, dancing and spectral, emerging from the first movement to form with it a slow-fast pair which again suggests a connection with the early Violin Concerto. The finale, though, is in a different country altogether, the country of the Hungarian peasants, and it becomes clear that for Bartók, unlike Schoenberg, the collapse of the old order is to make way for something new, rustic and lusty. For Kodály, speaking in 1921 and therefore during Bartók's lifetime, the programme is 'a man's return to life after travelling to the very borders of non-existence'. For Bartók it was a departure from the musical world called into being by Stefi Geyer and an arrival at an application of folk music only glimpsed in the Bagatelles and Easy Pieces.

The First Quartet took an unusually long time to reach this form: Bartók seems to have begun it in the summer of 1907, at the height of his relationship with Geyer, but he did not complete it until January 1909, according to a note of relieved achievement in a letter.[4] The first movement he described as a funeral dirge,[5] though without explaining that the very opening is a modification of Stefi's theme, turned from D major into F minor, and from positive ascent into the double calamity of two falling sixths:

Ex. 19

String Quartet no. 1 op. 7: first movement

This canonic relation between the two violins soon breaks down, but the music continues on its way as two straying, unsupported lines – a sound quite unprecedented in the quartet literature and admirably

[4] Ibid., 94.
[5] Quoted in Stephen Walsh: *Bartók Chamber Music* (London, 1982), 11.

qualified to introduce a cycle (eventually of six quartets, if we may briefly look ahead thirty years) that is the densest contribution to the medium since Beethoven's. When the viola and the cello join in, it is to repeat the opening down an octave and then to take their own places in the texture of four independent parts, a texture in which particular keys are only briefly attained. There is a middle section, with the viola straining costively at falling semitones and the ensemble making later a rustle of parallel triads, and then the polyphony is taken up once more, raised an octave in an apotheosis that turns out to be the prelude to the Allegretto. Here again the falling semitone is important, and indeed after the Stefi motif has been atomised in the opening bars, the quartet builds itself a new theme, through stages marked below by the viola interlude from the first movement, the main subject of the second movement and the principal, almost omnipresent idea of the finale:

Ex. 20
String Quartet no. 1 op. 7

Other notable features of the second movement include the whole-tone scale, presented quite straightforwardly as a scale, and the use of ostinato figures to act as stabilising agents in music not much governed any more by key (a phenomenon to be observed also in Schoenberg, Berg, Webern and Stravinsky). These ostinatos had already been introduced in the central portion of the first movement, but it is in the finale that they really come into their own. Whether it is a matter of insistently repeated notes, as at first, or of pounding two-note steps, the effect is a widening of the quartet's range no less than in the opening violin duet, and a widening into hard-edged, fiercely dynamic territory where Bartók was to go again and again for many of his most characteristic quartet inventions. It is a decisive homecoming, and all the more so for arriving after two movements of a suspended, improvisatory kind.

In form the finale is again a sort of sonata, prefaced by an introduction made up of chordal summonses separating recitatives from the cello and the first violin. However, the movement is also galvanised by an element of variation so intense that it sometimes amounts to parody. Much of what can be regarded as the development section, for example, is a fugato where the abrupt principal theme is teased into a playful grazioso subject, and before this passage the theme has taken on another mask, as the melody for a quasi-operatic banal accompaniment in G sharp minor. This is very Bartókian. So too is the recasting of the driving second theme (semiquaver fall three times repeated, followed by a drop of a minor third) to make an impassioned adagio lament, or the quick replacement of this same idea by its inversion. No doubt Bartók was by his musical nature attracted by the variation principle – this had been evident in *Kossuth* – but no doubt too his work with folk music, which was turning from a hobby into a scientific pursuit during the time he was writing the First Quartet, accentuated the natural taste. For part of his task as an ethnomusicologist was to track variants, to decide whether a tune collected from one village was an independent creation or an altered version of a melody from another. Putting this analytic operation into reverse provided the mental apparatus for the variational cunning displayed in the finale of the First Quartet and many later scores.

Also traceable to folk music, of course, is the rhythmic energy of this music: its fast pulsations and its vigorous syncopations of the common time that is the prevailing metre (both are introduced in the first few bars), and also the freely flowing changes of metre that occur when Bartók develops the second part of his principal theme, a garland of anapaests (quaver-quaver-crotchet units). Along with these very different rhythmic types there are also, accordingly, contrasts of harmonic character. The chromatic opening theme subsides in its anapaests into Aeolian A minor, but by the end the anapaestic music has come to chart out a whole-tone scale, preparatory to a final four bars of blazing, saturated A-centredness, A clashing supremely in the last chords with just its fifth, E, and its fifth's fifth, B, the note which the second movement had eventually decided was its tonic.

Three and a half weeks before completing this work, on 2 January 1909, Bartók had at the invitation of Busoni conducted the scherzo from his Second Suite in Berlin. He was pleased with the result: 'I believe I did it well – at least, everything not only "came out", but it sounded brilliant too', he wrote to Etelka Freund.[6] However, he was never to conduct again, and in the twentieth century, when almost every outstanding composer has conducted his or her works from time to time (Berg is perhaps the only other major exception), Bartók's quick disappearance from the podium is cause for comment. He surely could have conducted had he wished: his disinclination must have been temperamental rather than enforced, and this would go along with everything else we know of his privateness and reticence.

Others, though, were beginning to become active on his behalf. In the same year of 1909 there were performances in Budapest of both suites, both being played complete for the first time, of the Rhapsody in its concerto form and of the first *Portrait*. There was also a festival of Hungarian music organised by Sándor Kovács in Paris in January 1909, and in December Bartók was himself again in that city, meeting d'Indy to no avail but apparently not seeking out the composer who had recently come to take a prominent place in his musical world: Debussy. In many ways more significant than any earlier performances, however, were two concerts given in Budapest on 17 and 19 March 1910, evenings devoted to the music of Kodály and Bartók respectively. The orchestral concerts of the previous year must have been ironic successes for Bartók, coming after he had composed himself into a new style with his First Quartet: now at last that new voice was being heard alongside the old, the First Quartet in its première performance balanced by the Piano Quintet of only four years before, the Bagatelles by one of the fantasies of 1903. Not for the last time, it was the older music that was preferred, but a start had been made, and a valuable association struck up with the young Waldbauer Quartet, formed for these concerts and destined to give the first performances of Bartók's next three quartets as well. And even if audiences in Budapest were hostile, Bartók was extending his reputation abroad: in May 1910 he was in Zurich to play his Rhapsody in its concert form for the Allgemeiner Deutscher

---

[6] Demény (1951), ii, 87.

Musikverein, and it was on that occasion that he made the acquaintance of his fellow Nietzschean and fellow folksong enthusiast Delius,
to whom he wrote warmly on several occasions.[7]

Meanwhile he was returning his creative attention to piano
music, and with prolific results. As an offshoot from his teaching
work he began a series of instructive editions, and there were also the
eighty-five folksong arrangements of *For Children*, written in 1908
and 1909. At the same time there were more ambitious pieces,
composed variously between 1908 and 1911, and published as five
sets under the opus numbers 8 and 9: the Two Romanian Dances op.
8a, the *Two Elegies* op. 8b, the *Three Burlesques* op. 8c, the *Four
Dirges* op. 9a and the seven *Sketches* op. 9b. Of these, the Romanian
Dances are vigorous tributes to the majestic musical strength Bartók
had discovered during his first Romanian expedition in the summer
of 1909. They are big pieces, filled out with repetitive phraseology
and with borrowings from Romanian peasant rhythms and modality.
For example, the second of them, dated 1910, is based on the
favourite Romanian scale of a Lydian bottom half and a Mixolydian
top, a scale sometimes known as the 'acoustic scale' because it is
closer than the normal diatonic scales to the notes represented early
in the overtone series:

Ex. 21
Two Romanian Dances op. 8a: no. 2

This scale was to be important to Bartók for the rest of his life, but
the Romanian Dances, in which it makes its debut, were to remain
his first and last attempts at a synthetic folk music.

Equally without successors were the *Elegies*, last flamboyant

[7] Demény (1971), 104ff.

products of his post-Lisztian self (the much vaunted 'aleatory' device of the second, where the player can choose how many little accompanying scale patterns to fit into the bar, is merely a matter of practical efficiency). The *Sketches* also contain a farewell to Romantic bravura in their middle item, a cuckoo in a nest of more natural, simple pieces. These include the portrait of Márta already mentioned (no. 1), a Romanian folksong characteristically presented three times with different, each time economical harmonic support (no. 5), a robustly tritonal piece in Wallachian style, with the scalar embellishments Bartók had noted among that people[8] (no. 6), and three inquisitive essays in new harmony along the lines of the Bagatelles. No. 2, entitled '(See-saw . . .)', is delicately bitonal; no. 3 has the slipping instability of the first piece as it plays constant variations of harmony on a little motif; and no. 7 makes much of the two opposing whole-note scales. In his preface to the revised edition of 1945 Bartók stubbornly described this piece as being in B major, against 'those who like to label all music they do not understand as "atonal" music', but in truth this tonality, Mixolydian in any case, has been lost after the first three bars.

The other two sets of pieces from 1908–11, the *Dirges* and the *Burlesques*, are altogether more unified in style and expressive character. It is not surprising that they should also be more wholly within Bartók's individual world: indeed, if the Romanian Dances represent him at his most characteristically positive, embracing life as it presents itself in the form of peasant rhythms, then the *Dirges* and the *Burlesques* show his equally characteristic negative side and its alternatives of impersonal lament and snappish irony.

The *Dirges* of their nature are slow, allowing room for the resonance of the wide-spread but essentially quite simple harmonies of which they are constructed: octaves, fifths and triads are by far the commonest chords, often much doubled, as most toweringly in the middle of the third piece, where triple octaves alternate with piles of fifths repeated through three octaves. However, the melodies of these grave organa are not so simple, and the effect of the transparent but never firmly rooted harmony is not to compromise the tune by making it fit a definite key. In the second piece, for instance, the opening phrase is given just in octaves, following Bartók's practice in

[8] Ibid., 95.

the folksong arrangement that was the first of the Easy Pieces. The melody uses only six notes, and in typical Magyar fashion is impregnated with fourths:

Ex. 22
Four Dirges op. 9: no. 2

The scale, though, remains undecided, and only the addition of sustained C sharps to the second phrase, a slight variation of the first, indicates the probability of Dorian C sharp. Thereafter the phrase is further twisted before returning to its initial shape, and all the time new notes are progressively added to the accompaniment, until it has become a spray of pentatonic arpeggios. So the piece ends. The other three are structurally a little more complicated, but the elements are much the same, and so too is the coolness with which Bartók works on what he perhaps considered as equivalents to the mourning songs he was discovering among the peasants: not splashy self-indulgent 'elegies', like the pair of 1908–9, but expressions of a socially accepted passing.

After the last comes the dateline 'Budapest 1910', which perhaps refers to the group as a whole; certainly the more personal *Burlesques* were written at different times throughout this piano-centred period, the first in November 1908, the third in 1910 and the last in May 1911. Like the first of the *Sketches*, the first *Burlesque* is dedicated to Márta, but a little less flatteringly, for the piece has the title 'Quarrel'. This is variously interpreted in the music: as a presto alternation of the hands in imitation, as an overlapping of triple and quadruple metre, and as a salting of octaves with biting major seconds. On the large scale the piece is an argument on the subject of a six-note idea made up of semitones and a tritone, a subject which is of course abrasively non-tonal. It therefore seems a cheat when Bartók ends the piece with octave Cs (the case is similar to that of the first of the Eight Hungarian Folksongs, already mentioned), but perhaps there is a further irony here and one is meant to find the patching-up artificial and unconvincing. Whether or not this is a record of some domestic scene, it is tempting to see the second

Burlesque, 'A bit drunk', as an insight into the realities of folksong collecting. The theme is a peasant-style tune played at first in triads, but 'in an unsteady rhythm', as the score requires, and with the hiccoughs of dissonant appoggiaturas. After this comes a finale to the set that is necessarily more abstract, since it lacks a title, but that suggests the armoury scene in *Bluebeard's Castle* by its semitone clashes and its rush up and down the Lydian scale through a tritone.

The Romanian Dances, the *Dirges* and the *Burlesques* together embody the appearance of a new Bartók, forged in the spirit of folk music. There is nothing now, even in the parallel chords of the *Dirges*, that sounds like Debussy, nor is there anything, even in the chromaticism of the first *Burlesque*, that sounds at all like Schoenberg: such recent affiliations and correspondences have already been put away, and so too have the constructional speculations of such things as the second Easy Piece, with its symmetrical pitch movements above and below a central axis. The only echoes to remain are those of folk music, and as has been seen they are multiple, relating to melodic structure, modality, rhythm and form. Bartók had succeeded, so soon, in his aim of creating a musical style that was at once personal and national, and when twenty years later he came to orchestrate a set of *Hungarian Pictures*, he could justly take his material largely from his own compositions, choosing 'An Evening with the Székely' and 'Bear Dance' from the Ten Easy Pieces, the second *Dirge*, the middle *Burlesque* and, as a final piece of 'real' folk music, a number from *For Children*.

Meanwhile, alongside some of these piano pieces, he had in August 1910 completed a new orchestral work, the *Two Pictures* op. 10. As one might expect, this is another diptych of contrast like the *Two Portraits*, though there is now no motivic connection, and instead of the second movement being a distorted reflection of the first it is simply something quite other. The opening movement, whose title is variously translated as 'In full flower' or 'Blossoming', is an opulent image of natural effulgence, and is usually taken to be Bartók's most Debussian piece, though in fact by now the impressionism is very much his own (it will return soon in the first pages of the ballet *The Wooden Prince*). The announcing of falling modal lines over vibrant ostinato backcloths, for example, has been part of his repertory since the Bagatelles and the Easy Pieces, and the themes have a more graspable presence than ever they do in Debussy. In any event, the handling of the orchestra still owes at least as much to

Strauss as it does to the French composer.

The companion piece, 'Village dance', is different. Like the recent Romanian Dances for piano, it is of course a refraction of folk music, but now without any direct model: this is not any particular village, but rather an ideal village abstracted from what Bartók had heard in his travels of the last few years throughout Hungary, Slovakia and Romania, a village to which he was to return in similar dance movements in his Second Quartet, Dance Suite, Music for Strings, Percussion and Celesta, and other works long in the future, and which he had already caught sight of in the First Quartet's finale. In form the movement is a rondo, or perhaps a scherzo with two trios, of which the second, with espressive woodwind dropping over a bed of A flat in harps and strings, brings a moment of expectant rest to interrupt the tempestuous rush of quavers elsewhere. Quite in contrast with the first movement, this second more generally exhibits a clear-cut, block-style handling of the orchestra, with woodwind answering strings at the start, and with an extraordinary winding up of the ensemble as one massive machine as the final return of the opening material is prepared.

By the time of his thirtieth birthday, in March 1911, Bartók could look back on achievements of various kinds. He was the respected professor of piano at the Budapest Academy, with growing lists of instructive publications and adoring pupils. In collaboration with Kodály he had made a tremendous start in the business of collecting central European folk music, even if there were few buyers as yet for their little collection of arrangements. He was married, with a baby son. Above all, he had established a style that fitted the ideals he had set himself seven and a half years before, those of serving 'the good of Hungary and the Hungarian nation', and he could look back on an acknowledged output of six big orchestral scores, a quartet and many piano pieces of various kinds. Several of these works, moreover, had already appeared in print, and even though his name might be little known abroad, even though audiences at home were backward, he felt confident. That much is clear from the photographs of an unusually self-assured and well dressed Bartók that date from this time.[9] It is no less clear from the music.

[9] See Bónis, 97.

5

Bluebeard's Castle and The Wooden Prince

In the month of his thirtieth birthday Bartók set out on a new creative project, larger than any he had undertaken before: the composition of the opera *Bluebeard's Castle*, 'my first vocal composition, as well as my first composition for the stage'.[1] So it was. Until now his output of vocal music had been limited to a dozen or so early songs, various other minor items and some folksong arrangements, most of these last intended for joint publication with Kodály. For Bartók now to break this habit of silence, of allowing his musical thoughts no verbal expression, must indicate some special compulsion, especially when the 'first vocal composition' is not just a song but an opera. Perhaps he thought that through this genre he might more easily make contact with the Hungarian public. Perhaps he was attracted merely by the announcement of a national competition for one-act operas. Perhaps he felt ready for a challenge. Perhaps, too, the subject was of more than ordinary interest to him.

That might seem surprising, since to English ears the name 'Bluebeard' is associated with the horrifying crimes of child rape and murder attributed to Gilles de Retz, fifteenth-century Marshal of France. However, the legendary tradition behind Bartók's opera is rather different. It begins with Perrault and culminates in Maeterlinck's libretto for the opera *Ariane et Barbe-Bleue* (1907) of Dukas, and it is a myth not so much of murder as of that thirst for information with which human beings are cursed. Bluebeard's new wife is given the keys to seven doors (in Maeterlinck-Dukas; only one in Perrault), with instructions that she must not use them. While he is away she does so, and thereby discovers that he has had previous wives whom he has killed (Perrault) or locked away (Maeterlinck-Dukas). She then is rescued by her brothers (Perrault) or departs of her own accord having failed to persuade the other wives to leave (Maeterlinck-Dukas).

Quoted in Ujfalussy, 104.

In *Ariane et Barbe-Bleue* these episodes are only part of a larger action involving the peasantry of Bluebeard's realm, but in Bartók's opera the unlocking of the seven doors is all that happens, and it gains a new profundity from having Bluebeard present while his young wife (Judith) unlocks the doors, and from making her silently at the end join her predecessors. Because Bluebeard is there, the unlocking is not just an act of childish furtiveness but one that engages the two characters in a shifting dialogue of pleading and restraint. But of course there is also a practical need for Bluebeard to remain, since now that attention has been focussed exclusively on the serial unlocking, without him there would be nobody for Judith to sing to, and therefore no opera. At the same time Bluebeard's presence squashes our fantasies about him, and the opera dispenses with any criminal past to show him as a wholly admirable man whose treatment of Judith is always gentle and considerate. He wants only what is best for them both, as he sees it, and that is a relationship in which the doors on other things remain closed.

The responsibility for this new interpretation of the Bluebeard story belongs to the librettist, Béla Balázs, for apparently the text was written before a note of the music, and indeed, according to Balázs's own account,[2] he offered it for setting by either Bartók or Kodály. Three years younger than his eventual composer, Balázs was one of the rising young Hungarian poets of his time, influenced, as so many were throughout Europe, by the general current of symbolism. But he was influenced too by the ballads and lyrics that his musician friends were collecting among the peasants. To quote his later reminiscences of how *Bluebeard's Castle* was composed, he was looking for a Hungarian style of drama. 'I wanted to magnify the dramatic *fluidum* of the Székely folk ballads for the stage. And I wanted to depict a modern soul in the primary colours of folk-song.'[3]

In other words, his intentions were exactly analogous to those of Bartók, who might well, therefore, have been attracted as much by the style of Balázs's libretto as by the substance. That style, though, raised certain difficulties. In imitation of the old ballads Balázs had written the entire text in eight-syllable lines, which might have caused severe metrical monotony if Bartók had elected to set the

[2] Ibid., 104.
[3] Ibid., 109.

verse as straight verse. Instead he varied the pattern to suit the rhythms of speech, and the score is an extraordinary showcase of how a rhythmic unit of eight notes can be treated with flexibility, at the simplest extreme as two bars of 2/4, which remains the standard throughout, or in a range of more complex expressions. Here, for instance, are two extracts from the opening dialogue, exhibiting a typical contrast between the plainness of Bluebeard's speech in rhythm and tonality (Dorian D) and the prettification of Judith's:

Ex. 23
Duke Bluebeard's Castle op. 11

In both cases, however, the setting intimately fits the music of the Magyar language with its initial stresses and propensity to descending melodies (fully realised in Hungarian folksong), which makes it exceptionally difficult to produce an adequate translation of the libretto: in English the short trochaic lines generate a stilted mechanical rhythm that is at odds with Bartók's.

This fluid setting of the text obviously owes much to the composer's experience of folk music, and of course it is from that source too that he draws the modality in which *Bluebeard's Castle*, particularly the music of Bluebeard himself, is saturated. But as in the immediately preceding piano and orchestral music, the influence of

Debussy was also important, working in parallel with that of folk music. *Pelléas* may have much more of monotone chant, whereas the Magyar words of *Bluebeard's Castle* tend to suggest rather falling scales or gentle arcs, but in both operas the music only very rarely takes on a melodic profile of its own, and in both operas these rare moments are specially significant: in Bartók's opera the most notable comes at the point where Bluebeard is enraptured after Judith has opened two of the seven doors, perhaps trying to weaken her resolve to go on and open the others, or perhaps giving voice to a melancholy satisfaction that the curse is again working itself out.

Bartók leaves this crucial matter of interpretation to be decided by his performers, for what he sets is the text, not the underlying intentions. There is, in other words, a moral distance between the composer and his creatures, and it is not at all clear from the score whether Bluebeard begins with the idea that he can enjoy a new, untainted life with Judith provided he keeps his past a secret, or whether he knows himself all along to be the victim of an inevitable cycle in which his wife will come to know him and therefore be lost to him. The only thing that is certain is that the cycle is indeed inevitable, whether or not Bluebeard knows it to be, for the opera is grounded in a tonal scheme of departure from the opening F sharp and return thither by steps of a minor third, first to D sharp/E flat (second and fourth doors), then to C (fifth door) and then to A (sixth door) before the final sinking into F sharp again.

In its five-part mirror symmetry the opera thus enshrines a kind of form to which Bartók was attracted all through his life, from the First Suite to the Concerto for Orchestra. But of course the five main pillars of the work are surrounded by subsidiary centres, and the progression through a diminished-seventh chord, $F^\sharp - D^\sharp - C - A - F^\sharp$, is not at all as crude a structural device as might appear from this superficial description: if the opera is to engage our attention as a fable of human relationship, it could hardly be otherwise. And indeed *Bluebeard's Castle* does so engage our attention, making the spoken prologue more than redundant, with its teasing questions about whether the stage lies within or outside the 'curtain' of our eyelashes. What is nice about the prologue is that it alerts the audience to the fact that this is but the latest incarnation of an ancient myth, but since the speaker departs after delivering his few stanzas at the start, the work is not constantly being made into an object as happens in Stravinsky's *Oedipus Rex*, and silence is a better prelude to it than portentous speech that overlaps the first stirrings of the orchestra, setting the scene of Bluebeard's grim castle in pentatonic F sharp minor.

The opening dialogue, quoted above, has Bluebeard declaring to Judith that they have reached his home and inviting her to reconsider her decision to come with him. She, however, insists warmly that she has made up her mind, and in doing so she adopts her new home harmonically, singing in Mixolydian F sharp. There is then a passionate embrace, which calls forth for the first time almost the whole of the large orchestra Bartók uses here, an ensemble larger than in any other of his works and requiring more than a hundred players. Bluebeard calls for the door to be bolted on the castle which is the orchestra, and the music shifts once more into austere pentatony, now centred on D sharp. This is the next step in the opera's master plan, but it is not sustained for very long. Judith notices that the walls of the castle are 'weeping' – symbolically, of course, they are the walls of Bluebeard's skull – and he sensitively offers her another opportunity to escape. He now sings in Lydian G major, a fifth above the C major that will stand for boundless space when the fifth door comes to be opened. She repeats her determination that she has come to stay, and sings in C sharp, a fifth above the F sharp that stands for gloomy enclosure. Each of them is, therefore, at this point on the dominant of one of the opera's opposed tonalities and equally opposed emotional situations.

Next Bluebeard turns his attention to Judith's motivation and bluntly asks her why she came. She can only fantasise about how she will warm and dry his castle for him, and again the two of them are as distant from each other tonally as they are in understanding: she answers his A with A flat. She also notices the seven locked doors and asks about them, which brings about a varied repeat of the previous interchange. Bluebeard simply states that nobody must see behind them; Judith becomes highly exercised about the changes she will bring, the light and air that she will let in if she can have the doors opened (Bluebeard asks her to remember the rumours about him, and the aside is cunningly placed in a different metre from that of Judith's apostrophe). She hammers on the first door and is answered by a sigh, which is not depicted in the music but left to be produced in answer to a stage direction demanding 'a cavernous sighing, as when the night wind sighs down endless, gloomy labyrinths'. Perhaps in hope, Bluebeard asks her if she is frightened, but she is not, and she repeats her request for the keys to the locked doors. Bluebeard capitulates and gives her the first key. As she opens the door, the sigh is heard once more.

After that, the hard glitter of xylophone and high woodwind, scurrying up and down scales through a tritone, presents an image of the torture chamber that lies behind the first door. The main pitch is A sharp, a fifth above the D sharp that dominates this section of the opera, and a stage direction asks for a red light to escape from the newly opened door: there will be similar effects when each of the next four doors is opened, each time a different colour being associated with a different harmony. It is hard to avoid seeking a comparison with such contemporaneous works as Skryabin's *Prometheus* (1908–10) and Schoenberg's *Die glückliche Hand* (1910–13), and indeed there does seem to have been a feeling, shared even by these very different composers, that tonal functions were becoming so dubious they needed support from an additional kind of perception. Judith is mesmerised by the horror of what she has uncovered, and appalled again when she notices the castle walls are stained with blood: here an intense minor second is sounded from the orchestra, and will appear again when Judith sees blood on the sights to greet her through the next four doors. The image is a simple one, but dramatically effective when it comes each time to pierce through a supposed harmonic stability, and also musically interesting when it gives Bartók the opportunity to display his skill in varying the character of a uniform device, as these instances may suggest:

Ex. 24
Duke Bluebeard's Castle op. 11

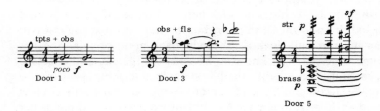

This first time, though, Judith turns from recognising blood to marvelling at the sunrise, and the music moves into brightly scored G sharp for a passage of false optimism. Inevitably the mood changes when Judith recalls her mission and once more calls for the keys. Bluebeard asks her why she wants them: 'Because I love you' is the simple answer, and the awful truth. And so, after repeating his warning, Bluebeard hands over another key and Judith rushes to open the second door. The light behind it is yellowish red, 'sombre, and disturbing to behold', according to the stage direction, and the tonality is D sharp, affirmed most positively by a trumpet fanfare: the scene that meets Judith's eyes is that of Bluebeard's armoury. Again there is the blood, and again, more resolutely than before, Judith turns to demand the rest of the keys. Bluebeard tries gently to warn her off, and when that does not work he rises to the exalted arioso already mentioned, but she is adamant that she must know his secrets because she loves him, and finally he gives her three more keys.

If the first two doors had shown Bluebeard in a bad light, bringing out the unpleasant sources of his power, the next three turn out to show the pleasures that power supports. First there is the jewelhouse, glittering in harps and celesta on a bed of D major, and suffused with a golden light. Of course the jewels are bloodstained, it appears, but this time Bluebeard turns Judith's attention from this and on to the next door, which gives on to Bluebeard's gardens, to E flat major warmly sustained, and to a bluish-green light. Here again Bluebeard hastens Judith on once she has noticed the blood on the blooms, and so we arrive at a rush at the fifth door and the burst of C major throughout the orchestra that accompanies its opening. This is the climactic centre of the opera, and it is one of those instances, not infrequent in the music of this period, where in a context of expanded and uncertain tonalities pure C major sounds majestically new (another example is the end of Schoenberg's *Gurrelieder*).

In contrast to his behaviour before, Bluebeard does not now rush Judith on to the sixth door, but instead says that the last two doors must remain locked. She will have none of this. She has become obsessed with knowing Bluebeard's secrets, and obsessed too, the music hints, with the blood she has seen everywhere: she gains the accompaniment of a moto perpetuo that keeps circling around an A^b – A minor second. Bluebeard gives in and hands her another key, which she turns, and once more there is a sigh, only this time it has come nearer and invaded the orchestra (it is a glissando in the lower strings with bassoons). When the fifth door was opened a dazzling white light had entered the hall, but the sixth brings a darkening and a change to A minor, next stage in the harmonic journey back to F sharp. There is a change, too, to a spectacle of a more symbolic nature: a lake of tears. Bluebeard now calls Judith to him for one last time, and there is a second embrace richly celebrated in the orchestra.

However, a new problem surfaces as Judith is led on not by inquisitiveness alone but also by jealousy. She asks about those whom Bluebeard loved before her, and though he realises that doubts of this kind are the sure way to disaster, he is powerless to dissuade her from pressing her questions. Inevitably she replaces his silence with fantasy, and guesses that he has murdered all his former wives. There is now no point in restraining her, and Bluebeard in cold hopelessness gives her the last key. She opens the seventh door, out of which troop the three former wives. In a second passage of elevated arioso Bluebeard addresses them as sources of his wealth and lands, and as the loves of his dawns, noons and evenings. Judith through all this can only give voice to her comparative unworthiness, but Bluebeard turns to her as the fairest of all, destined to reign over his nights once she has taken her place, as she must, with the rest. The wives, now four in number, go back in line behind the seventh door, and Bluebeard is left alone, in the pentatonic F sharp of his solitary castle, with an addition only to his memories.

Bluebeard's Castle did not win the competition for which it was submitted, and indeed had to wait almost another seven years before it was performed for the first time, in Budapest in 1918. Since then its revivals have been sporadic, partly because of the difficulty in pro-gramming it: in Hungary, and sometimes elsewhere too, this question has been answered by performing the opera on a triple bill with Bartók's two later one-act ballets, but while such a solution is eminently suitable artistically, it is impractical. In any event, there are other hindrances to a successful presentation of *Bluebeard's Castle* in the theatre, most notably its lack of action. In other media, however, this is a positive advantage, and it is not surprising that around the time of Bartók's centenary in 1981 his opera should have become one of his most frequently recorded works, for it is a piece that settles itself well within the theatre of the mind, which is, after all, where its real action unfolds.

Some of Bartók's frustration at the rejection of his opera may have found its way into his next work, written in the same year of

1911 but not published until 1918, and then soon widely regarded as one of the most notorious products of 'modern music': the Allegro barbaro for piano. It is said that in the title Bartók was flinging back the accusation of a French critic that he was a musical barbarian. In any event, the name well suits a piece that attacks the instrument with pounding rhythms and savage tritone and semitone dissonances:

Ex. 25
Allegro barbaro

Some of Bartók's earlier pieces had been written for the piano as a percussion instrument, but the emphasis here on a decisive uniform touch and on the clangorous middle and low registers justifies the piece's celebrity in the history of piano music, and indeed in the history of dynamic musical primitiveness in the years immediately preceding *The Rite of Spring*. Meanwhile the tonality of the piece, insisting on F sharp minor, is another, much harder face of the tonality of *Bluebeard's Castle*.

Apart from the opera and its keyboard aftermath, Bartók in 1911 was also much occupied with founding an organisation to promote new music in Hungary, the New Hungarian Music Association, often known by its Magyar acronym of UMZE. He had long been aware that the progress of Hungarian music would depend on the progressiveness of the Hungarian audience – his letter to Irmy Jurkovics from Paris in 1905[4] insists on this point – which may be why his Budapest society antedated by several years Schoenberg's Society for Private Musical Peformances in Vienna. Both, however, were attempts to tackle the same problem, that of creating a sym-

[4] Demény (1971), 50.

pathetic environment for the creation of new work in an age when fresh musical departures were still deemed important enough to arouse alarm and fierce criticism. After several months of planning, the new institution made its debut on 27 November 1911 with a recital in the Royal Hall, Budapest, including some of Bartók's and Kodály's folksong arrangements, and with Bartók playing eighteenth-century keyboard music: Scarlatti, Couperin and Rameau. This is intriguing early evidence of his interest in baroque music, which he was also publishing in his series of teaching editions, though the main purpose of UMZE was of course to present contemporary music by Hungarian and foreign composers. In the second concert, fifteen days later, Bartók played works by Debussy, Ravel and Leó Weiner, but he had no part in either of the next two concerts, early in 1912, which turned out to be the last the society presented, largely because, so it seems, the audience response was pitiful.

There was therefore no question of UMZE succeeding in its larger aim of establishing its own orchestra, an idea which Bartók apparently held dear. In March 1911 he had written to Delius about the plans for UMZE, remarking that if they did not succeed, 'I shall have to give up all hope, for many years to come, of hearing my things performed (the compositions I plan writing), for I prefer no concert at all to a poor one from which it is impossible for either the audience or the composer to learn anything.'[5] This suggests that the run of orchestral performances in 1909 had not been so successful. And granted the problems in knowing what compositions if any Bartók might have been projecting in the spring of 1911, it is hard to resist linking this declaration with the fate of his next orchestral work, and Four Pieces op. 12, written in 1912 but not orchestrated until 1921, and destined to be his last concert piece for orchestra until the Dance Suite was commissioned under the very different circumstances of 1923.

The Four Pieces continue that avoidance of the symphony which Bartók was to sustain to his death. He had already composed two works preferring the less ambitious title of 'suite'; 'Four Pieces' suggests a still looser association of the movements, as indeed is the case. The title suggests too the influence of Schoenberg, who had composed his Five Pieces op. 16 in 1909, and to be sure the first

[5] Ibid., 111.

piece, Preludio, is Bartók's most Schoenbergian orchestral composition – or perhaps his most Bergian, since the triad is still a prominent feature, and the piece begins and ends afloat on E major. On the smaller scale, though, the harmonic sense of the brief melodic ideas is often irresolute, and there is some feeling of Schoenberg's perpetual variation, even if the ending does plainly bring back the start.

After this comes a Scherzo that is a great deal more definite. Using the large *Bluebeard's Castle* orchestra, but with the notable addition of an Allegro barbaro piano at which four hands must stamp, this is the most mightily grotesque and noisy of Bartók's orchestral scherzos, following on from op. 2 and the second *Portrait*, and preparing the way for the more picturesque, and therefore milder, fourth dance of *The Wooden Prince*. In both these later examples Bartók might almost be emulating the achievement of Dukas in creating large-scale continuity from small-scale variation in *L'apprenti sorcier*: the stepwise increase in dynamism from one section to the next is similarly planned in all three works. However, Bartók works with much more savage materials than his French contemporary, and the Scherzo of op. 12 abounds in ostinatos, rude mechanical figures, effects of ostentatious bizarreness and harsh dissonances. Chords filled with tritones and semitone relations are common, much more so than in the corresponding section from *The Wooden Prince*, and the bald sound of tritones in the brass looks way ahead to Bartók's next ballet, *The Miraculous Mandarin*.

This Scherzo makes its way much more by aggressive rhythmic force than by harmonic movement, but it comes to a stop on B flat, a tritone removed from the E of the Preludio, and B flat minor is duly the principal key of the Intermezzo that follows. Like the Preludio, this is a moderately paced movement; it is also a moment of nostalgic calm, with its lilting siciliano rhythm at the beginning and end, resting the senses between the assaults of the Scherzo and of the final Marcia funebre, a funeral march more snarling than heroic, again loud and black with tritones, but coming to a conclusion in C sharp minor and therefore completing three corners of a diminished-seventh chord in the set as a whole. Partly because they require such an extravagant orchestra, without the dramatic excuse of *Bluebeard's Castle* and *The Wooden Prince*, the Four Pieces have remained among the least played and least known of Bartók's works, but in no other composition did he express his 'taste for dissonance' or his nihilism more blatantly.

Some light on his feelings at this time is shed by a letter of August 1913 addressed to a younger Hungarian composer, Géza Vilmos Zágon, in which he states that 'a year ago sentence of death was officially pronounced on me as a composer' and names Jenő Hubay among the 'musical leaders' antagonistic to him. 'Therefore', he goes on,

> I have resigned myself to write for my writing-desk only. So far as appearances abroad are concerned, all my efforts during the last eight years have proved to be in vain. I got tired of it, and a year ago I stopped pressing for that, too. If they want to perform something somewhere, they can take my published works and perform them without me; if they ask for a manuscript with a definite intention, I'll give it with pleasure. But I shall never take any steps myself; I've had enough of that during the last eight years. My public appearances are confined to *one sole field*: I will do anything to further my research work in musical folklore![6]

Thus it was. Earlier that year he had undertaken his important collecting trips in Maramureş and Algeria; also in 1913 his Bihar material was published, to be followed by several articles during the next few years. By contrast, after a spate of publications in 1912 (the First Suite, the *Sketches*, *Dirges*, *Burlesques* and *Pictures*), only one more work appeared in print before 1918: the *Two Portraits* in 1914. There was also only one important Bartók première during the years from 1912 to 1917, that of the *Two Pictures* in 1913, described by one Budapest paper as 'a pathological phenomenon rather than art'.[7] Even the flow of compositions for the writing-desk came to a standstill, and after the Four Pieces Bartók wrote nothing for two years apart from eighteen very easy piano pieces for a teaching manual he published with another Hungarian musician. He continued to teach at the academy of music, walking there from his flat in Rákoskeresztúr, where the family had moved in the spring of 1911 (*Bluebeard's Castle* was written from there, and all Bartók's major works until his next move in 1920), but otherwise he took no part in musical life in the city. 'I hardly ever go to Budapest these days', he wrote to his old Romanian friend Ion Buşiţia in August

---

[6] Ibid., 124.
[7] Quoted in Ujfalussy, 119.

1917,[8] apologising for his failure to send a photograph of the striking portrait done of him in 1913 by Róbert Béreny, with its high domed forehead and appraising expression.[9]

One further reason for Bartók's isolation and inactivity during these years was the outbreak of the First World War. As early as October 1914 he was writing to Father Bobál, parish priest in a Slovak village he had visited, saying that there was a good chance he would be rejected from military service on health grounds (as in fact happened: he weighed only forty-five kilograms), and wondering about 'those good little women, my singers, for they are all sure to have somebody involved in the war. I wonder if I'll ever collect songs there again!'[10] In fact, as we have seen, he was able to return to the Slovaks in 1915 and also to collect soldiers' songs, but he never got back to the Romanians, and this grieved him bitterly. To Buşiţia in May 1915 he wrote that 'nothing matters but to remain good friends with Romania', and that he was 'thrown into a state of depression by the war – a condition which, in my case, alternates with a kind of devil-may-care attitude':[11] here was an unusually explicit fragment of self-knowledge, an expression of the duality to be found also in the pairing of manic scherzo with calamitous funeral march in works from *Kossuth* to the Four Pieces.

In the same letter Bartók remarks, almost at the end, almost as if apologising for the fact, that he has 'even found the time – and ability – to do some composing: it seems that the Muses are not silent in modern war'. This return to creative life was marked at first by a great flowering of Romanian arrangements: the Sonatina, the Folk dances and the Christmas Carols for piano all date from 1915, as well as unpublished songs and choruses. But Bartók also started work that year on his Second String Quartet, and he had already in the middle months of 1914 made a start on his ballet *The Wooden Prince*, finished in the summer of 1916, orchestrated during the next autumn and winter, and produced for the first time at the Budapest Opera on 12 May 1917. This was the public event with which Bartók came out of his five-year retirement, and the success of the occasion was such that the previous slight was redeemed and the Opera House

[8] Demény (1971), 136.
[9] Reproduced in Bónis, 128, and on the present volume's dust-jacket.
[10] Demény (1971), 130.
[11] Ibid., 131.

made plans for a production of *Bluebeard's Castle*, to follow within little more than a year.

There is a sense in which the chronology of these premières is apt, for *The Wooden Prince* feels like an earlier work than *Bluebeard's Castle*. It is laxer and more spacious. The same enormous orchestra is used with less acuity, the harmony rests much more on simple modalities (most extraordinarily, the whole introductory passage of more than sixty bars uses only the notes of the C major triad with added augmented fourth to create a new version of the *Rheingold* prelude), and there is very little of the incisive musical detail that underlies the dialogue in the opera. To a great extent this must be because the scenario, again by Balázs, is this time much more a fairy tale than a psychological drama, though partly it is a matter of genre: not until *The Miraculous Mandarin*, significantly called a pantomime and not a ballet, was Bartók able to create a danced drama as accurate as his opera. Indeed, the plot of *The Wooden Prince*, as written into the published score, misses many of the nuances in Balázs's original libretto,[12] and this has led to difficulties of interpretation.

What the score indicates is a sequence of seven numbered dances, with prelude, postlude and interludes that are sometimes very substantial but not separately marked out. The scheme is as follows:

> Prelude, towards the end of which the curtain rises to show two tiny castles on hills, one girded by a stream and a forest. There is a fairy on stage, and a princess sitting among the trees.
> First dance: the princess in the forest. A prince emerges from one of the castles; the fairy gestures to the princess to return to her own castle, and eventually she does so.
> Interlude: the prince comes on his way, spies the princess spinning in her castle, and falls instantly in love with her. He decides to climb to her castle, but the fairy makes new gestures to cast a spell on the forest.
> Second dance: the trees stir themselves. The prince is appalled, then begins to fight his way through, and the trees come to rest again.
> Interlude: the prince now makes for the stream, but this too is magicked by the fairy.

[12] Published first in the Budapest literary magazine *Nyugat* (1912), 879–88; English translation in Crow, 101–10.

Third dance: the waves of the stream rise from their bed. The prince tries to continue on his way, but he has to give up, and then the waves return to their rightful place.

Interlude: the prince has another idea. He puts his cloak on his staff and waves it in the princess's direction. She does not notice. He then puts his crown on the staff, and this time her attention is caught, but not for long. Finally he cuts off his golden hair and adds that to the puppet. This time the princess is enchanted. She comes racing down from her castle; meanwhile the fairy makes her imperious gestures towards the bedecked staff and brings it to life. The princess arrives and takes hold of the wooden prince instead of the real one.

Fourth dance: the princess dances with the wooden prince and goes off with him.

Interlude: the prince is in the depths of despair. He falls asleep. The fairy now comes to him, and at her command every living thing comes to pay him homage. From three flowers she restores to him his cloak, crown and hair, then leads him away as king over everything, whereupon the princess reappears with the wooden prince, now looking the worse for wear.

Fifth dance: the princess tries to continue her dance with the run-down wooden prince, which finally collapses.

Interlude: the princess catches sight of the prince again.

Sixth dance: she tries to lure him towards her, but he keeps himself aloof.

Seventh dance: the princess tries to rush towards him, but the forest stands in her way.

Postlude: in her despair the princess casts off her own cloak and crown, and cuts off her hair. Now the prince comes to her and takes her in his arms, but as he does so, the transfigured beings return to their earlier form, and the curtain falls.

On the face of it, this is a seven-part symmetrical plan like that of *Bluebeard's Castle* (Balázs's scenario was differently organised into eight dances), with the outer elements in Lydian C instead of the opera's F sharp, and with the centre marked by the fourth dance, which by its heavy orchestration, abrupt ideas and repetitive force does indeed stand out from the rest of the ballet. However, Bartók himself considered three parts as 'clearly distinguishable', the first extending up to and including the fourth dance, the second bearing 'the typical characteristics of an inner movement', and the third beginning with the reappearance of the wooden prince in the fifth dance, after which the events of the first part are recapitulated in reverse.[13] This focusses attention on the interlude of sorrow and transfiguration, and on music which moves from C sharp minor tragedy recalling the tonality of the funeral march from op. 12 into luminous chromaticism which looks rather towards the Good Friday music in *Parsifal*, and which is, until the Shostakovich guying in the Concerto for Orchestra, the last occasion on which Bartók will suggest the atmosphere of another work.

Taken in conjunction with Balázs's libretto, this helps to make it clear that the plot of the ballet is not as wooden as its subject. The fairy does not suddenly change from hindering the prince to helping him. She has a purpose of her own – in Balázs she is 'a tall woman sheathed in a grey veil', a figure much more mysterious than a Christmas tree fairy – and it is her task to prevent the prince achieving human love. Once that has been done, in the central interlude, she can reveal to him the riddle of the living universe, but when despite her efforts he comes to clasp the princess in his arms, then he forsakes the power and knowledge he has gained. It is abundantly clear from Balázs's scenario that he saw the prince as a metaphor of the artist. He wins love for his art (the wooden replica) but finds himself spurned. Moreover, as the above interpretation suggests, he can gain love himself only by foregoing access to the secrets that his muse is ready to open to him. *The Wooden Prince* is not therefore a tale ending happily in love but rather a tragedy. That tragedy is indicated subtly in the orchestra when Bartók weaves back the transfiguration music briefly before the music sinks once more into the Lydian C from which it emerged, to give an ending that is as hopeless as that of *Bluebeard's Castle* in confirming the perpetual cycle of fate.

Nevertheless, the ballet is a feast of sound pictures that can command a greater scale than in the opera. The dance of the trees has hefty swirling modal scales in strings and woodwind, and iambic figures pounding home in brass and timpani, while the waves dance in stable Aeolian E, whose glowing harmony is overlaid by a melody falling from a pair of saxophones. The princess dances to flighty music that has something of the gipsy style about it: no doubt by this stage, though we are only a decade on from the op. 1 Rhapsody, Bartók uses that 'artificial' style to suggest the princess's suscepti-

---

[13] Quoted in Ujfalussy, 137.

bility to seduction by artifice. By contrast, the music for the prince is ruggedly hewn from the old modes: Mixolydian D when he first sets out, and Mixolydian B when he makes his determined bid to reach the princess (B major has been the key of his declaration of love). There are also places where Bartók mixes two modes so that all twelve notes are in play: towards the end of the prelude, for instance, the upper instruments play in Mixolydian A flat and the lower in Mixolydian C. The major third transposition gives this complementary relation, as does transposition by a minor second or a tritone, and whether used harmonically or melodically, this was to be an important technique in Bartók's armoury of devices for a modal mastery of chromaticism.

Naturally those devices are exposed much more starkly in the music associated with the wooden prince, which in its grotesquerie not only follows on from earlier works but casts forward to the distilled barbarity of a good deal of later Bartók. Music examples can indicate something of this, but they cannot unfortunately substitute for the sounds Bartók uses to suggest the stiff movements of the puppet, including the very direct use of wood itself in col legno playing on the strings or the prominent part assigned to the xylophone, whose clatters sound on alarmingly through pauses in the big climax to the fourth dance. Otherwise this movement makes its effect either by parodying ideas from elsewhere in the work (notably the prince's first theme), in the way Bartók had already inherited from Liszt and Strauss, or else – and here the only precedents were his own op. 12 pieces, the *Allegro barbaro* and a few other piano works – by wielding musical subjects that are inherently disruptive because inherently antagonistic to the diatonic system.

For example, one of the principal motifs turns an eminently tonal fifth into a notoriously atonal tritone:

Ex. 26
The Wooden Prince op. 13

Later this idea is softened, made diatonic, and as so often Bartók does this by redesigning it within the acoustic scale, whose use here, together with all the Mixolydian modality, confirms the Romanian inclination of his musical thinking during the war years:

Ex. 27
The Wooden Prince op. 13

Yet another derivative of the same motif – to which, indeed, a great deal of this dance can be related – shows Bartók seeming to work almost with calculated efficiency to ensure complete chromaticism. First he outlines one augmented triad, then slips down a semitone and fills in another (ignoring the C sharp here as a stepping stone):

Ex. 28
The Wooden Prince op. 13

If this theme is transposed down a tone, as happens in the music directly, then all twelve notes will have been sounded. It would probably be wrong, however, to see too much abstract speculation here. Always excepting the C sharp, the theme as given above is an expression of a mode alternating semitones and minor thirds: it is in Messiaen's terms a 'mode of limited transposition', though not one favoured by him, and for the Bartók analyst Ernő Lendvai it is the '1:3 model'. For Bartók, though, it was surely no more than a pair of augmented triads, and it would be unwise to see him experimenting with new modes when he was merely putting into effect the most obvious means of dividing the octave symmetrically and thereby denying diatonic sense: the means of the diminished-seventh chord, the tritone, the whole-tone scale and the augmented triad. Transposition of these elements may generate interesting modes, but in

Bartók the elements themselves remain rudely present, even when, as will happen during the next few years, such devices take on much more than the momentary importance they have in *The Wooden Prince*.

The speedy production of Bartók's first ballet was not due to enthusiasm for the music but rather for the subject. Miklós Count Bánffy, director of the Budapest Opera, drew illustrations for the book edition of Balázs's scenario and was keen to have the work staged to his own designs[14] irrespective of the score. The story goes that Balázs himself had to act as producer because the theatre's regular staff refused to cooperate, and that a guest conductor, the Italian Egisto Tango, had to be brought in to conduct when the Hungarian conductors attached to the Opera declined the task (though in fact Tango had been working at the Budapest Opera since 1912). It is enough to note that the première of *The Wooden Prince*, like that of *The Rite of Spring* four years before, was the kind of event around which legends accrete, and that it was undoubtedly an enormous success. For the first time since the *Two Pictures* of 1910, Bartók had composed orchestral music on a generous scale. Moreover, in the midst of a debilitating war the Budapest public was perhaps ready to salute a major Hungarian work, and in *The Wooden Prince* they sensed they had found what they were looking for (Bartók must have derived a certain ironic pleasure from the knowledge that much of the musical sap for the ballet came from the Romanians, who in 1916 had entered the war on the opposing side). A production of *Bluebeard's Castle* could not now be denied, and the Opera duly presented it on 24 May 1918,[15] once more under the baton of Tango, whom Bartók much admired for his willingness to study a score and rehearse it thoroughly.[16] Here at last the double bill was presented as Bartók intended. The third item for the programme was just around the corner.

[14] See Bónis, 124–7.
[15] For pictures of the set and costumes see Bónis, 130–1.
[16] Demény (1971), 133.

6

The approach of the Mandarin

Before arriving at *The Miraculous Mandarin* it is necessary to go back a little. So far it has been suggested here that the return of Bartók's creative drive in 1915 was occasioned by his contact with Romanian music, a contact which had intensified through the preparation of so many arrangements, by his diminished ability during the war to pursue his alternative work of folksong collecting, and perhaps also by the new favour shown him by musical authorities and audiences in Budapest. There was, however, a more personal spur that came to light only long after the composer's death.

How his relationship with his wife stood by 1915 it is impossible to judge. It may be significant that in 1914 she had gone with him for the first time on a folksong trip; or it may just be that young Béla was now, she felt, old enough at four to be left. *Bluebeard's Castle* is also an unreliable witness: did Bartók intend it for Márta as a metaphor of their own situation, or was the dedication merely the gesture of a loving husband inscribing to his wife his first large-scale masterpiece? One thing alone is clear, though highly uncertain in its detail. In the summer of 1915, while collecting folksongs in Slovakia with his wife and son, he made the acquaintance of a forester's daughter, Klára Gombossy, fifteen years old at the time.[1] Through her he met the teenage daughters of her piano teacher, Wanda and Ani Gleiman (yet another pair of young sisters), and they belonged among his friends for years, though the connection with Klára Gombossy was abruptly broken off in September 1916, after only a year. During that year, nevertheless, Bartók had returned decisively to composition, and Klára Gombossy's role in this reawakening is strongly suggested by one of its first fruits, the Five Songs op. 15 for voice and piano.

---

[1] See László Somfai's notes accompanying the recording on Hungaroton SLPX 11603.

Together with the Stefi Geyer Violin Concerto, this was the only major work of Bartók's that remained unpublished during his lifetime, and perhaps for similar reasons. Even the authorship of the poems remained unknown until the 1960s, when it emerged that the outer four are by Klára and the middle one by Wanda. They are unsurprising adolescent pieces, Wanda's being an over-enthusiastic essay on 'the night of wild desire' and Klára's, more skilful, having again erotic love as their theme, with the exception of the last, which expresses juvenile feelings of alienation. What is surprising, perhaps, is that Bartók should have found such material interesting, with the vastly more sophisticated expressive worlds of his First Quartet, *Bluebeard's Castle* and the op. 12 pieces already behind him. But then he was always susceptible to a pretty teenage girl. And one need not coarsen the matter by supposing that his feelings for Klára and her girlish associates were ever physically expressed or even intended. The important point is that something in his creative nature throve on contact with the fresh and unsullied, whether that was to be found in folksong or in the young women who had already featured prominently in his life: the Arányi, Jurkovics, Ziegler and Gleiman sisters, Stefi Geyer and now Klára Gombossy.

This association between folksong and maidenhood is borne out by the op. 15 songs, whose vocal lines are often distinctly pentatonic, as in this example from the fourth number:

Ex. 29
Five Songs op. 15: no. 4

jöt - tél _____ ak - kor   fe - lém.

The piano part, though, is of course anything but pentatonic, and in fact conflicts with the voice not only in harmony but also in metre, presaging the kind of complementary accompaniment that Bartók was to find useful in his greatest set of solo folksong arrangements, the Twenty Hungarian Folksongs. The need for such complementation is the same in both works. Whatever his feelings for Klára and Wanda, Bartók could not really adopt to himself, a man in his mid-thirties, the sexual imaginings of young girls, any more than he could really speak with the voice of an anonymous peasant. His accompaniments – intended, after all, for himself as performer in the first place – are the expression of a more individual and complex personality who yet allows himself to be swayed by the simple and natural, whether it be a folksong or a melody he had invented himself for a girl's verses.

But of course there is no exact and schematic correlation that links Bartók always with the accompaniment, Klára and Wanda always with the voice. Many touches in the piano suggest folksong simplicity: the arpeggiated chords, especially in the fifth song, that could come from some kind of guitar, or the bare fourths and fifths, though often in clashes between the hands, of the second song. At the same time, there are things in the voice parts that are wholly personal to Bartók. It cannot be an accident, for instance, that the refrain of Wanda's song, setting the words 'This is the night of wild desire', includes prominently a reversal of the Stefi motif, descending in enthusiastic certainty instead of straining upward.

This song is dated 27 August 1916, and its immediate successor in the cycle was probably written around the same time, the other three Klára songs having been composed the previous February, along with the Suite op. 14 for piano. Having little in common with the op. 15 songs, this is a set of four short movements that continue the process already at work in the piano pieces of 1908–11, the process of textural paring and of bringing structure to the surface. Each of the movements has features of ABA symmetry, though in each of them the repetition is much altered: 'I do not like to repeat a musical thought unchanged',[2] Bartók later said, affirming his concurrence with Schoenberg and indeed with the general temper of his time. Naturally this causes problems for a composer so intent on symmetrical balance (Webern was even fonder of symmetry, but Webern felt rather less compunction about repeating). Yet even within this tiny Suite Bartók finds different ways of overcoming the difficulty: he brings back his material in fractured form (first movement), or swings it through different modes (second movement), or changes it in register and harmonisation (third movement), or spaces it out in an apotheosis (fourth movement), using in all these cases, and in the more small-scale kinds of variation here abounding, the techniques that had come out of his work on folk music.

The actual substance of the Suite also draws on the same source. The main theme of the first movement has the Romanian flavour that usually enters Bartók's music when he writes in the 'acoustic' scale, and the third movement, with its rapidly circling ostinatos, Bartók admitted was influenced by the music he heard among the Arabs at Biskra. What the Suite also shows – and this is by no means at loggerheads with its folk-music inclinations – is Bartók's preoccupation with regular divisions that through their regularity would dissolve the forces of the old major-minor tonality. Thus the wild Arab dance is based on a mode of alternating minor and major seconds, taken up later by Messiaen under quite different musical circumstances as his 'second mode of limited transposition'. Much is made too of the tritone, and in particular of the augmented triad. As it was originally planned, the whole Suite was founded on an augmented triad, B flat being the central pitch of the opening Allegretto, the Scherzo and the slow finale, while D has the same function in the Arab-style Allegro molto between Scherzo and finale, and F sharp governs the Andante, placed second. This Andante, however, was dropped, to give the unusual but effective pattern of three fastish dance movements succeeded by a Sostenuto.

Part of the effectiveness is owed to the contrasts among the first

---

[2] Quoted in Bence Szabolcsi: 'Bartók's Principles of Composition', Crow, 19.

three movements, which range not only from Romania to North
Africa but also from artificial modes to, again, the stark augmented
triad in the second movement, the Scherzo. This makes use too of
another regular division of the octave, the whole-tone scale, which
can be regarded as two augmented triads a major second apart, and
which is prominent too in the first movement – an indication that the
contrasts here depend on homogeneity. A certain homogeneity of
structure has already been remarked; there is also the common
feature that each movement exhibits at its end a 'clearing' into a
particular mode after music of more complicated harmony. In the
first movement, the last eleven bars are pure whole-tone music; the
second corkscrews into a three-note fragment of the chromatic scale;
and the third ends resolutely in one form of the 'second mode':

Ex. 30
Suite op. 14: third movement

Following directly upon this music – an 'attacca' is marked – the
finale could not be more different in its softness and suspension. But
the change is not wholesale, or else this fourth movement could not
properly wrap up the work. It does so because it offers an alternative
interpretation of the basic subject matter. Where the earlier movements had removed diatonic forces and replaced them by insistence
on a pivotal note or, still more so, by the rhythmic pressure of

ostinato movement, the finale accepts non-tonal features and with them their stasis. The very opening bar introduces a rhythmic motif that will remain throughout, a weakly swaying motif (unaccented crotchet, accented crotchet, unaccented quaver) totally unlike the robust dance patterns of the earlier movements. It also introduces a chromatic step up and down, giving a tritone – fourth – tritone progression in which the normally disruptive tritone is felt to be the consonance. All in all, the Suite is the first work wholly typical of Bartók in its harmony, its rhythm, its keyboard layout and, not least, its immensely fruitful fusion of 'natural' folksong and 'artificial' construction.

Besides the Suite and the op. 15 songs, Bartók also in the remarkable month of February 1916 began a second set of five songs, following the previous group as op. 16, and turning from juvenile versifying to the condensed utterances of one of the greatest Hungarian poets of Bartók's day, Endre Ady. Just four years older than Bartók, Ady held similar ideals about the creation of a genuinely Hungarian art in line with the most progressive work being done abroad (Yeats might be a comparable figure in our own literature), but it seems that he was not as personally close to the composer as Balázs. Ady's poems of lost love, however, evidently spoke directly to him, just as Balázs's drama of isolation had done five years before, and by April 1916 he had completed the opus. At this stage, of course, the op. 15 group consisted of only three songs: in later making it up to five he made sure that the two sets balanced each other, the one an exercise in identifying with adolescent

Ex. 31
Five Songs op. 16: no. 1

1 Bartók and his sister, Elza, photographed in Bratislava in 1892, the year
of *The Course of the Danube*

2 Bartók in travelling clothes for his first Transylvanian folksong
collecting tour, 1907

3 The composer surrounded in his Budapest flat by furniture he had ordered from Transylvania, 1908

4 A folksong notated by Bartók, with his corrections

5 Stefi Geyer, the recipient in 1907 of Bartók's most intimate letters and
dedicatee of his First Violin Concerto

6 The composer's first wife and his mother, Márta and Paula Bartók,
September 1915

7 A page from the manuscript of Ten Easy Pieces

8 Bartók photographed in 1916, when he was at work on his Second
String Quartet

9 Family celebrations of Bartók's fifty-fifth birthday, with, from left to right, his second wife Ditta, his mother, his second son Péter, himself and his sister

10 A rehearsal of *Contrasts* in 1940 by the original performers, Joseph Szigeti, Bartók and Benny Goodman

11 The composer near the end of his life with György Sándor, who gave the first performance of his Third Piano Concerto

womanhood, the other much more credibly personal in its significance.

Inevitably the musical style is much changed. Where the op. 15 songs are often vocally pentatonic and outgoing, the Ady cycle is chromatic and inward, though there are moments where the general favouring of fourths, tritones, sevenths and ninths in the harmony leads to a sumptuous modality near Messiaen's manner (See Ex. 31). This is from near the start of the first number, and it is typical of the cycle in at least two respects: the blithe freedom of the vocal line from the piano harmony, and the shadowy undercurrent of a slow waltz tempo that reinforces the feeling of hurtful memory. There is in the second song, for instance, a conspicuous three-beat pattern (quaver, dotted quaver, semiquaver) which evokes a dragging waltz, and which is harmonically shaped along the lines of the Suite's finale, with a minor ninth opening out to a minor tenth and then closing in again. Nor, of course, is this the only link that ties opp. 14–16: all three works were originally designed in five movements, and all have a slow finale – not a public expression like the funeral march that had ended op. 12, but a private withdrawal. In op. 15 this withdrawal had taken place to a poem of wintry loneliness succeeding four rapturous songs. In op. 16 the tone of the last op. 15 song is omnipresent, and the finale has to be stark and bleak indeed to make its effect of numbness. So it is, but at the same time the simpler piano style and the 3/4 metre look back to the first song of the group, and so there is a certain five-part symmetry to the work.

This is enhanced by the confessional intensity of the centrepiece, where the poet addresses his bed, sometime scene of dreams and loving, but now 'coffin cold'. The poem is intricately composed of two-phrase lines, each first phrase being a repetition of the preceding second phrase (AB, BC, CD, etc), which Bartók takes as stimulus to a play of motivic variation, rather as he does in the last song in setting the refrain 'I die, alas' to a three-note idea that twice expands and contracts its intervals. As for the other two songs, the second and the fourth, both are more flamboyant, though within the cold region of the whole work. The second is almost a piano solo with vocal phrases spread over it (the singer also takes a relatively low profile in the third and fourth songs), and the fourth too abounds in rippling keyboard figuration – echoes of autumn in the second song, ocean laughter in the fourth – together with tidy motivic work suggesting again the world of the Suite. More generally in these songs it is as if the vivid and expansive style of the op. 15 set had been brought up against the hard reality of the op. 14 Suite, but the work also reverberates further back in Bartók's output, at least as far as *Bluebeard's Castle* when it comes to speak of tears. Such a correspondence is perhaps to be expected. After all, the Balázs opera and the opp.15–16 songs were the only works in which Bartók set words by a named poet, as opposed to the anonymous folksongs and folksong adaptations of his own that he used in all his succeeding vocal works. If the Ady set, in particular, is much less familiar than the opera, that must be largely due to the reluctance of recitalists to trust their Magyar (and the songs, like any songs, are untranslatable). It may also be unfortunate that Bartók has no reputation as a song composer, simply because the loneliness expressed here is the loneliness too of the work in his output.

However, the greatest work of this period was one in a domain that was very much Bartók's own: it was his Second String Quartet op. 17 (1915–17). Since the First, almost a decade before, his style had changed very considerably, but he had written no movements of a sonata character. There had, though, been two big scherzos: in the op. 12 orchestral pieces and in *The Wooden Prince*. And sure enough it is the scherzo in the Second Quartet, as in the First, that has the greatest force and presence. Following what had already become Bartók's common scherzo practice, it contains a variety of secondary ideas that contribute to a feeling of rondo form, but the main material, so placed in relief, is clear cut, vigorous and absolutely unmistakable in its D-centred tonality (note the relation of the opening idea to Ex. 26 from *The Wooden Prince*):

Ex. 32
String Quartet no. 2 op. 17: second movement

This is quite different from the gargoyle scherzo material brought into play in the orchestral set and the ballet, much more like the emphatic gestures of the third movement from the Piano Suite. But, by contrast with the arrangement in the First Quartet, the Second has its scherzo in the middle, bounded on one side by a moderato in sonata form and on the other by a slow finale. In this case, then, the folk accents are not the outcome of a steady process of opening, but instead they power a whirlwind at the work's centre.

The first movement is very vaguely in A, with F sharp minor (the relative minor of A major) as secondary key: this tonal atmosphere, together with the moderate tempo, the abundance of material, the corresponding length of the exposition and the constant motivic alteration, points a kinship with Schoenberg's F sharp minor quartet, his no. 2 of 1907–8. Like that work too, Bartók's Second Quartet would seem to have some autobiographical significance. The very fact of having a slow finale is enough to suggest that, since the natural course of music is to end fast: the exceptions, like Tchaikovsky's Sixth Symphony and Mahler's Third and Ninth, must indicate some special meaning. However, in the case of Bartók's Second Quartet, any private significance is still more obscure than it was in the First. The same Stefi motif has been detected in the secondary material of the first movement's exposition, but it is now simply a seventh chord, $F^\sharp - A - C^\sharp - E^\sharp$, to which no particular weight need be attached. Moreover, the finale is not a funeral march as in op. 12, nor a response to images of desolation as in the two song cycles, but rather a spiritualisation, played largely with mutes and very slow. What is spiritualised, it turns out, is the tense material of the first movement, now drifting slowly in motivic memories, but though this is in line with Bartók's taste for palindromic structures, there is no sense of return. Instead the distance from the first movement to the third is made to seem all the greater for the fact that the latter remembers the former in so disintegrated a fashion. Again the process seems to mirror some obscure psychological reality.

The musical reality is just as strange. The first movement moves through the three customary phases of sonata form, but, as already indicated, the exposition is lengthy, and contains plenty of development of its own (so too does the recapitulation). Indeed the main thrust of the movement, such as it is in so halting a tempo, is achieved largely by motivic answering with change: something to which the quartet as a medium is peculiarly well adapted. The following example comes from the start of the coda, where one theme, passed around an augmented triad (C – A♭ – E) gives rise to another at the conclusion of another augmented-triad cycle (F× – B – D♯):

Ex. 33
String Quartet no. 2 op. 17: first movement

The first idea here, simply a scale pattern up and down a minor third, has been heard at the end of the exposition, in F sharp Dorian, and at the end of the recapitulation, in A, its conclusiveness helped in both cases by its being much more tonally stable than what has gone before: part of the function of the coda is then to upset the balance again. The second idea, emerging on the first violin at the end of the quotation, is one variant of the perpetually varying main theme, which in its first form consists of two rising fourths, a falling semi-tone and a falling fourth, another semitone fall and a rise of a minor third. This provides the most usual intervals of the whole movement, and it is the dominance of fourths and semitones that is responsible not only for the harmonic uncertainty but also for the flavour of Hungarian folk music.

That flavour becomes of course a much sharper tang in the central scherzo, though here, as in the corresponding movement from the Piano Suite, the music of Algeria may also lie in the background. In any event, the movement is not only formally in-genious in its rondo-scherzo combination but exactingly quick and colourful for its executants. Bartók savours in particular the frenzy of a pizzicato note stuck into fast-bowed music (see Ex. 32 above), though the strangest sound in the whole quartet is the final prestissimo of this movement, taking a pace of ten notes per second, where the basic material is consumed in a shimmering haze.

After the decisive D of this movement, the final Lento moves around and towards the half A minor of the opening, ending bitterly on a low A–C chord plucked by viola and cello. Melodically, too, the minor third has much to say here, though so also do the semitones and perfect fourths from elsewhere in the first movement, all these echoes being either fragmentary or else, in the case of one Magyar-style tune that can be regarded as the 'second subject', absorbed into a new continuity. The detection here of sonata form is beset by more difficulties than was the case in the first movement, partly because the material is so aerial and adrift, partly because there is not the usefully tonal subject to give some semblance of harmonic propriety. But however one describes its form, it is a fitting and totally original conclusion in its survey of a landscape discovered in the first movement and now bereft of both the Scherzo's energy and that first movement's emotional poignancy. Whatever its meaning in his private life, it left Bartók musically a changed man.

Of course, any great work changes its creator, but Bartók's Second Quartet sounds like an unusually profound exercise in self-analysis. It staunched finally the stream of late Romantic expressiveness that had filtered down from the early works as far as the first movement of this piece. It was at last a big composition created with a musical style based throughout on folk music (though without any direct quotation, which Bartók always avoided in his original music). And it confirmed that Bartók's most personal utterances were to come not in vocal music, like the recent songs – not even in music for his own instrument, like the recent Suite – but in works where four parts could take to pieces and reconstruct the elements of his musical language: in string quartets.

The work had its first performance from the Waldbauer Quartet on 3 March 1918, and though the war was still continuing, Bartók's life appeared to be recovering the secure course it had known at the première of the First Quartet eight years previously. *Bluebeard's Castle* was at last staged in May, and in the summer Bartók was able again to collect Transylvanian and Slovak folksongs, though these were to be almost his last expeditions. His music might still be little understood generally, but he had made his mark among the progressive intelligentsia of Hungary: in February 1917 an issue of the magazine *Ma* was devoted to him, and adorned on its cover with a reproduction of the manuscript of the piano postlude from the first of the op. 15 songs (slightly different from the final version, not least in its flat spelling). However, the achievement by which Bartók appears to have set most store was his acceptance by Universal Edition, partly because 'no other Hungarian musician has been given such an opportunity by a foreign publisher'[3], partly because his works would now, after a gap of six years, be available in print. The first to benefit were all for the piano; the Suite, the Romanian arrangements of 1915 and the Allegro barbaro.

As for new compositions, the only work Bartók completed in 1918 was the set of three piano Studies op. 18. These are slightly longer movements than those of the Suite, and distinctly weightier, richer in harmony and sonority. Where a lean two-part texture had been the norm in the earlier work, the second study has a central section of clashing high diatonic chords, close once more to Messiaen and said to have influenced him[4], while around this the fabric is one of double octaves proceeding above or below sweeping arpeggios. The outer movements, both fast, are similarly demanding in the breadth of the keyboard that has to be kept in play. The first is a grim toccata mostly in the middle and bass registers, with the two hands locked together in pounding steps of a ninth or a tenth, and the last is again an exercise in perpetual motion, this time confined to the left hand, the right splashing on chords that conflict with the left-hand harmony. Here, especially, Bartók is further from a sense of key or mode than in any other work of his, and as if aware of this he begins the piece with the 'sphinx' of a six-note group that is used almost as a series: this was, of course, the very time when Schoenberg was working towards his definition of twelve-note serialism. Bartók's practice in this third Study is not by any means serial, but there is an element of calculation in the constant reference back to the opening pattern, bespeaking a concern about the construction of music in such a non-tonal environment, a concern shared by Schoenberg at the same time. The following quotation shows, for example, the initial idea and the start of the final section:

[3] Quoted in Ujfalussy, 151.
[4] See Paul Jacobs's notes accompanying his recording on Nonesuch H 71334.

Ex. 34

Three Studies op. 18: no. 3

The Studies in general have the obsessiveness and flamboyance expected of technical exercises for the virtuoso, but they are also studies in another sense for the much larger work on which Bartók embarked in the same year of 1918: *The Miraculous Mandarin*. As in the case of *The Wooden Prince* five years before, he discovered his scenario in the pages of the magazine *Nyugat*, which in 1917 published the text of a 'grotesque pantomime' by Menyhért Lengyel.[5] And though *The Miraculous Mandarin* is often referred to as Bartók's second ballet, the term 'pantomime' is exact and significant. It is a narrative taking place in mime and dance, not a spectable with big dance numbers like *The Wooden Prince* (though, as has been noted, there is a special significance to the pantomime episodes in that earlier score, particularly the central encounter between the Prince and the Fairy). As a pantomime *The Miraculous Mandarin* presented Bartók with severe problems of musical structure, problems never faced on such a scale by Stravinsky, whose danced works are all decisively ballets. One may imagine that Bartók would have foreseen the possibility of concert performance of his score, but a pantomime

[5] English translation in Crow, 111–16.

without dancers might easily sound like an opera without singers. If only for that reason, therefore, it was necessary to give the piece a certain musical structure, and Bartók began by subtly altering the Lengyel libretto to give it symmetry. In his version, two passages of violent, driving movement are each followed by actions in triplicate. First, the introduction, setting the scene in a garret over a busy city street, gives way to three scenes of seduction in which a girl is forced by her three accompanying ruffians to lure men up from the street so that they can be robbed. Then, when the gang find they have trapped something more than they had bargained for in their third victim, the mandarin, a pounding chase is succeeded by three attempts at the visitor's murder, where Lengyel had had four. Bartók's only other substantive change is to suppress the girl's name, Mimi: perhaps he did not wish an unhelpful confusion with the operatic heroine, but then characters in a pantomime do not need names.

The musical shape of *The Miraculous Mandarin* is enhanced by connections between the introduction and the chase. Both build up steadily in ostinato patterns to a climatic cut-off, and both are rooted in an ugly harmony of tritone plus fourth (introduction) or fifth (chase). But the needs of musical balance are not taken much further. In particular, Bartók does not allow purely formal criteria to hamper the possible effectiveness of his music in underlining the drama. Thus the three seductions are all closely linked musically because it helps the drama that they should be: each is based on a sinuous clarinet melody, rising in tonality from A to C and then to E, and becoming each time more elaborately embellished and developed, so that the lure becomes ever more flamboyant and urgent. There is, however, no such connection among the three encounters that follow between the girl and her victims, nor later among the three murder attempts and their aftermaths. Instead, Bartók seems here to concentrate wholly on finding pointed musical illustration, and *The Miraculous Mandarin* rivals even the tone poems of his admired Strauss in the faithfulness with which it recounts its narrative.

Perhaps the most striking are those moments where the orchestra appears to embody a corporeal sensation, as where, when the mandarin 'begins to tremble in feverish excitement' in looking at the girl, there are ripping glissandos and wobbling tremolos in horns and woodwind. Another example comes right at the end, where irregularly echoing string chords mark the mandarin's faltering breathing, and his final expiration is contained in a loud, malignant glissando in the double basses. But the score is no less true when its representation of events is effected through symbol or expressive character. The girl here is fully as detailed a character as Judith in *Bluebeard's Castle*, and there is great poignancy in her scenes with each of her clients – first a shabby roué, then a shy young man, and finally the mandarin – even though she is plainly an idealised portrait: the classic prostitute who seeks only affection. Here, for example, is the bashful beginning of her dance for the young man, played by a solo bassoon, and its passionate continuation, given out by all the violins in octaves:

Ex. 35
The Miraculous Mandarin op. 19

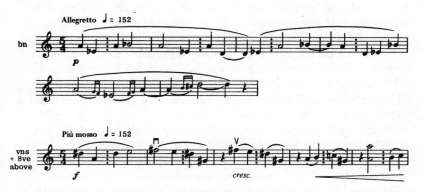

Quite apart from the differences in orchestration and dynamic level, the first keeps coming back to its doubtful opening tritone and remains uncertain about the division of the bar, whereas the second, taking its courage in its hands and raising the whole line by a tritone, lifts itself away from secretive hiding (the boldness is almost tangible when the melody strikes to F sharp in the second bar instead of falling back to D sharp), and once it has made its break it settles on a decisive 3:2 partition of the beats.

This is just one small example of how Bartók uses melodic contour to transcribe feeling, and how the transcription can be enriched when a tune is developed: what he had learned of this in Liszt and Strauss is quite as important here as it is in *Bluebeard's Castle*. In the longer scenes involving the mandarin, of course, there is opportunity for the technique to be used still more powerfully. But although the mandarin's emotions may be forcefully, even bodily injected into the score, and although this is ostensibly his story rather than the girl's, he remains an obscure figure, as Bartók no doubt intends. Perhaps, after one exercise in self-revelation in *Bluebeard's Castle*, Bartók wanted his identification with the mandarin to be less palpable, though the mandarin's periods of stillness and violent outbursts accord with what we know of the composer's behaviour, and the mandarin, like the Hungarian composer, is a man caught between East and West. His appearance in the street is noted by a melody in stereotypical Chinese pentatony, but one harmonised with the tritone-fifth chord whose inversion had suggested modern city life in the introduction.

For Bartók, the essence of the mandarin would seem to be that he is a natural being, which is another reason why he should be enigmatic, for he cannot communicate, whether with the affection of the girl or the brutality of the thugs; he can only act. Significantly, his arrival in the garret, after his pentatonic approach, is marked by the simplest event in the score: a bare minor third, B – D, blared out by all the brass. After the girl has recovered from her alarm and repulsion, she begins a waltz, which like her dance for the young man, but over a much wider span, grows from modest beginnings into an excited, highly charged number. His sudden arousal, however, is as unwelcome as it is unexpected, and the chase ensues.

Bartók provided a concert ending at this point, so creating a balanced form of three seduction scenes contained within a frame of hectic activity, but to stop at this point misses some of the score's greatest riches in the musical mimicry of the murder attempts. The chase is interrupted when the thugs rush out: as usual, their 6/8 metre identifies them with the senseless hurry of the street even more than had the mandarin's harmony. Their first thought is to stifle him under the bedclothes, but he survives to gaze out from them longingly at the girl. They then try stabbing him with a rusty old sword, but again he lives on and gazes at the girl. Finally they try hanging him from the lamp hook, but all that happens is that his body begins to glow 'with a greenish-blue light', whereupon the girl realises what must be done. She has her accomplices cut him down; she embraces him, and he dies.

Obviously in this latter part of the work the pantomime element in the music is strong, which is presumably why Bartók was ready to cut it for concert performance, but the scenes of the mandarin's miraculous survivals are extraordinary musical achievements. The two sections in which he looks at the girl, after the smothering and the stabbing, are linked by a 'longing' motif slithering down a minor third (the first occurrence, in the cellos as quoted below, uses a quarter-tone to divide the minor third into two equal parts: possibly Bartók owed the innovation to Alois Hába, who had written his first quarter-tone piece in 1917). However, these two sections are quite different in atmosphere. While the second has a quite conventional background of rippling celesta and violin tremolandos, the first sports one of Bartók's most remarkable effects in the fine grading of timbres around a characteristic cimbalom-style wobble in the piano:

Ex. 36
The Miraculous Mandarin op. 19

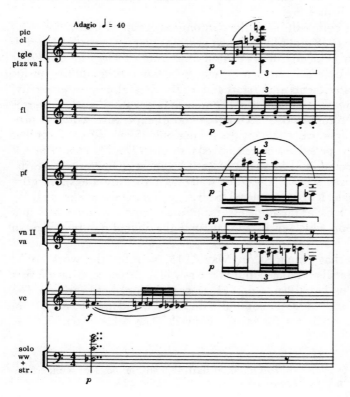

Nowhere else is Bartók quite so fastidious, though certainly *The Miraculous Mandarin* owes some of its sparkled richness to the conjoining of percussive and sustained sounds: this is a feature, too, of the clarinet seductions earlier on. However, the score's most disconcerting colour turns out to be that of the human voice, introduced in chorus, singing 'O' in bare octaves with the horns at the point where the mandarin's body begins to glow. In 1911 Bartók had been powerfully impressed by a performance of Delius's *Mass of Life*, and though his enthusiasm can be explained partly by his personal acquaintance with Delius, whom he had met the year before, and partly by his admiration for the Nietzsche text, he also noticed the wordless choruses. As he wrote to Delius: 'We had never heard anything like that before. I think you are the first to have attempted such a thing. I believe this field offers many possibilities – quite remarkable effects could be obtained.'[6] And in *The Miraculous Mandarin* they are.

The composition of the pantomime occupied Bartók between October 1918 and May the next year: the war was over, and Bartók was very evidently in possession of a score of *The Rite of Spring* (though only a piano score), which he came near quoting in his motor movements at the start and for the chase. But more generally, *The Miraculous Mandarin* is an entirely personal work, in terms both of compositional techniques and of expressive world. It provided a tight, trenchant excuse for diatonic-chromatic conflicts that had been opened in a more leisured fashion in *The Wooden Prince*. It had opportunities for some of Bartók's most characteristic motifs: the barbaric scherzo, the erotic waltz (as in the Ady songs), the grim slow finale. It also completed the trilogy of the stage works in taking another look at the hopelessness of male-female relationships in a civilisation which curbs and corrupts the animal nature of human beings.

All that remained, in May 1919, was for the work to be orchestrated and staged, but that was still some way off. Bartók first scored his Four Pieces op. 12 as preparation, but work on *The Miraculous Mandarin* continued until 1924, and in its passage from piano to orchestra the music changed.[7] The delay has sometimes

[6] Demény (1971), 110–11.
[7] See Aurél Nirschy: 'Varianten zu Bartóks Pantomime: Der wunderbare Mandarin', *Studia musicologica*, ii (1962), 189–223.

been interpreted as due to official objections to the subject matter, but the correspondence suggests an eagerness to stage the pantomime on the part of Gyula Wlassics, chief director of the Budapest Opera.[8] The problem would seem to have been rather that Bartók's style was again in ferment at the beginning of the 1920s, and that *The Miraculous Mandarin* was bound to take account of this as it was scored; it may even have helped precipitate the development. Nevertheless, the work certainly did create a scandal when it was new. The first production, which eventually took place in Cologne in 1926 on a double bill with *Bluebeard's Castle*, had to be taken off the stage after a single performance, and though a Prague production in 1927 was done with success, the planned Budapest staging of 1931 was cancelled after the dress rehearsal. Bartók's most powerful dramatic work was not, therefore, seen in his own country until 1946, the year following his death.

[8] Demény (1971), 163–7.

7

Postwar crisis

The orchestration of *The Miraculous Mandarin* took place in an atmosphere of crisis that was not only musical but also political and personal. At the end of the war Hungary had been declared a Soviet Republic on the Russian model, but the communist government lasted only until 1 August 1919, after which Admiral Miklós Horthy took control as nominal regent. Bartók's political opinions, at this or any other time, remain obscure. Probably he gave little thought to politics. But he was very definitely exercised by government interference in his own sphere of music, and wrote to his mother to voice his disgust at the expulsion of Dohnányi in the autumn of 1919 from the directorship of the academy, which he had recently assumed.[1] He himself was on leave at this time, ostensibly for reasons of health, though he seems to have been seriously looking for a position elsewhere: the same letter to his mother considers the possibilities of moving to Germany or Vienna (where he found the performing and teaching of music operated at a higher level than in Budapest), or else to Transylvania, now part of Romania (where presumably he would have continued his folksong work).

In the event he remained in Budapest and braved the hostile conditions. During the summer of 1920 he and his family were obliged to leave the house in Rákoskeresztúr where they had lived since 1912, and to take two rooms in the Budapest house of József Lukács, father of the philosopher. By May 1922, however, they were able to take their own flat in Budapest, for their financial situation was being eased by Bartók's spreading reputation as a composer and his resumed activity as a performer on the international circuit. As far as the former was concerned, his renown was for the moment that of a prominent member of the avant-garde. In March 1921, to honour his fortieth birthday, the Universal Edition journal *Musik-*

[1] See Demény (1971), 144.

96

blätter des Anbruch devoted a special number to him, including a brief autobiography and a selection of appreciations (Egon Wellesz wrote on the quartets). Then in May 1922 there was the first foreign production of *Bluebeard's Castle* and *The Wooden Prince*, in Frankfurt, followed in November that year by a performance of the First Quartet at the new Donaueschingen Festival, by Paul Hindemith and his colleagues in the Amar Quartet. Meanwhile as a performer Bartók had gone abroad for the first time since the war in February–March 1920 to Berlin; then in March–April 1922 there were recitals in London, Aberystwyth and Paris, in the last of which places Bartók was able to meet Stravinsky, Ravel and Szymanowski, 'as well as a few young (notorious) Frenchmen'.[2] In May 1923 he returned to London and also visited Huddersfield.

All this needed new repertory. His first new work after the *Mandarin* was the set of Eight Improvisations on Hungarian Peasant Songs op. 20 (1920), after which came the two sonatas for violin and piano (1921 and 1922), of which the first was designated op. 21 in a letter[3] but eventually became the work to mark his abandonment of opus numbers. Perhaps this was stimulated by a discovery made in op. 20. Hitherto Bartók had carefully distinguished in his output between original works, to which he gave opus numbers (the only exceptions were the suppressed Stefi Geyer concerto and the Allegro barbaro), and folksong arrangements, to which he did not. The fact that the Eight Improvisations have an opus number is obviously an acknowledgement that they are different in kind even from the Fifteen Hungarian Peasant Songs of 1914–17, as indeed they are; but equally Bartók must have been aware that this was not such an unusual case in his music, that the blending of personal and national traits had become too intimate for any realistic distinction to be made.

The Improvisations depend, however, on making a clash of that blending. They bring folksong into contact with the piano style and the harmony of the Suite and the Studies, and though one can often detect in them Bartók's characteristic arrangement form of three varied strophes plus coda (shown especially clearly in the first), the tunes are also raided for rhythmic motifs and harmonic intervals that

[2] Demény (1971), 160.
[3] Ibid.

97

can be freely developed around them. This may generate a contrast of two quite dissimilar worlds, as at the opening of the seventh piece, where a folksong in C Aeolian/Phrygian is answered by widespread chords that open the minor third of its first line out to a minor tenth:

Ex. 37
Eight Improvisations op. 20: no. 7

Also of interest here is the mirroring of the 'original' music around what is on the piano an imaginary note: the F half-sharp below middle C. Symmetrical harmonies of this kind, achieved by inter-locking musical ideas with their inversions, will again contribute to the stillness of certain passages in the violin sonatas. Here the aim is to reconcile their lingering with the decisive movement of the tune, and in achieving that Bartók makes a last return to the Debussyan landscape of 'Dawn' from the Ten Easy Pieces: this Improvisation he aptly chose as his contribution to the musical symposium in memory of Debussy published in *La revue musicale*.

Within the context of op. 20, however, the Debussy memorial is unusual, a slow movement between three scherzos and a quick finale. And the predominance of fast music lends a different character to the encounter of folksong and abstracted reference, one that may imply a quizzing of the peasant material or even a mockery of it. Examples include the hammering at a banal rhythmic figure that the song repeats in its every line (second piece), or the drunken harmonisation on its fourth appearance of a Phrygian-pentatonic tune with expanding-contracting intervals over a drone fifth (fifth piece):

Ex. 38
Eight Improvisations op. 20: no. 5

There is a note of sarcasm here that sounds too at one point in the autobiography Bartók wrote for the *Musikblätter des Anbruch* at this same time. After declaring that 'the situation today permits no thought of the possibility of pursuing ethnomusicological work', he concludes: 'Moreover, there is nowhere in the world a real interest in this branch of musical science – possibly it does not have the significance some of its fanatics have ascribed to it!'[4]

For Bartók, of course, doubting the value of folk music was tantamount to doubting the value of himself, and his creative confusion at this point is amply documented in the violin sonatas. No

---

[4] 'Selbstbiographie', *Musikblätter des Anbruch*, iii (1921), 87–90.

other large-scale work by him – and the First Sonata is one of his longest works, playing for thirty-five minutes – has harmonic progressions so complex, themes so indefinite, forms so difficult to perceive. Indeed, the sonatas are less 'Bartókian' than, say, the Second Quartet or *The Miraculous Mandarin*, and for reasons stemming from this they have often been criticised – as if, for example, the sonata structure of the First Sonata's opening movement were a failed attempt at a design better achieved in the Fourth Quartet, when one can more generously and usefully see it as a late return to the Reger line of restless, asymmetrical sonata writing. More generally, too, Bartók's uncertainty of direction communicates itself through great expressive richness and much beauty of line and texture, not dimmed by the fact that the sonatas turned out to be a cul-de-sac at a bewildering crossroads.

Their nature has much to do with their genre. Bartók had not written for solo violin since the Geyer concerto, and the instrument retains here its airborne world of feeling and caprice; also remembered, just possibly, is Stefi's motif, for the initial piano texture of the First Sonata is a chiming of seventh chords in G with added sixth chords in C sharp. However, this is very much by the way, and the sonatas were not a personal offering along the lines of the concerto: Bartók wrote them for Jelly d'Arányi, now living in England with her sister and sometimes sharing recitals with him. If there is an autobiographical strand in these sonatas, then it might well concern not d'Arányi but Márta Bartók, for while Bartók's performing career was beginning to flourish, his marriage was disintegrating. A joint husband-wife letter to the expatriate psychologist Géza Révész of May 1923 contains no hint of domestic turmoil,[5] but by August the marriage was over and Bartók had married another young student of his at the academy, Ditta Pásztory (1903–82), who, like Márta before her, gave birth to a son about a year after her marriage: the wedding was on 28 August 1923, and Péter Bartók, destined to become the composer's 'American' son while his half-brother Béla remained with Márta in Europe, was born on 31 July 1924. Bartók had commemorated the spent passion of a finished relationship before, in the Stefi Geyer concerto and in the op. 15 songs; it may be that the violin sonatas owe some of their emotional turmoil to a similar source.

[5] Demény (1971), 162–3.

The stimulus was, however, also more purely musical. It came from the excited, flamboyant state Bartók's style had reached in *The Miraculous Mandarin*, to which the sonatas are in some sense pendants, both picking up echoes from the greater work on Bartók's desk at the time: the finale of the First, for example, sets out like the Mandarin's chase from a 2/4 pounding on a fixed tritone-fifth chord. There were also external influences. Because of his withdrawal from public musical activity and then the war, Bartók had been isolated from contact with his composer contemporaries outside Hungary for some years, but now the barriers were down, and the vanguard Stravinsky current in the *Mandarin* was followed by more unsettling forces in the sonatas. Those who regret the obscurity in these works have tended to blame an unassimilated dose of Schoenberg, and no doubt Bartók did learn much from the piano sonorities of the latter's op. 11 as also from his proto-serial conscientiousness in keeping all twelve notes in play. But Bartók's harmonic manner is his own. His chords typically flicker much more readily with tonalities than Schoenberg's while avoiding the strong triadic pulls of Berg's; often, like examples already mentioned in the *Mandarin*, they contain one strongly consonant and one strongly dissonant interval:

Ex. 39

Violin Sonata no. 1: first movement

This is from the opening of one of the more strongly urged sections from the First Sonata's first movement. The piano is making chromatic jumps first upwards and then downwards, with an accented iambic rhythm to add impetus in an atmosphere of dissipated harmonic forces (the alternative is stasis, and the whole sonata can be seen as an exercise in avoiding or else indulging the harmony's tendency to stand still). In each iamb the first chord is an expression of the six-note set laid out initially as a minor sixth over a tritone, then another minor sixth over a tritone a semitone below. This arrangement changes when the steps are downward, but the second chord is always a minor sixth over a fourth (hence a span of a dissonant minor ninth) with octave doublings. The prominence throughout of the minor sixth in the harmony preserves some consistency, but the second chord feels more at rest than the first simply because it has fewer notes. However, these same chords, and the sets they represent, are also capable of harmonic processes of longer range: the entire first movement, for instance, moves through different forms of the six-note set, which gives rise not only to chords but to thematic motifs, such as the one in the violin called forth by the piano in the quotation above.

The formal, harmonic and melodic complexity of the First Sonata are all of a piece with its enlarged tonality. Bartók himself is said to have regarded the work as being in C sharp minor, and though this statement causes the same problems as his key ascriptions for the Bagatelles, the problems become rather less if one understands Bartók's C sharp minor as focussed not on the usual triad but on the above-mentioned six-note set in a form consisting of the minor triad with added major third, tritone and sixth (C♯ – E – E♯ – G – G♯ – A♯): these are the notes, for example, rippling in the piano at the end of the first movement, though there spelled with flats. At one point, too, there is a reference not to the key of C sharp minor but to the repertory, when the opening violin solo of the slow movement quotes in bars 10–11 the theme that starts Beethoven's op. 131 quartet:

Ex. 40
Violin Sonata no. 1: second movement

The presence of this quotation adds to the sense here of self-communion, which is further enhanced by the way the Beethoven thought is adumbrated in bars 8–9 and then progressively distorted as the music continues its climb. Such an impression of a composer thinking his way is not usual in a Bartók adagio: Bartók is normally more fully present in his quick movements, whereas the slow ones are often genre pieces, like the funeral march of the op. 12 pieces, or else there is no real slow movement at all, as in the op. 14 suite. But in the slow movement of the First Violin Sonata there is a feeling of identification, which may have been intensified by the composer's relationships with young women violinists as also by his experience of peasant fiddling, to which he had given much attention in his Romanian research.

Little folk influence, however, is to be detected in the handling of the instruments, other than in the cimbalom-like flurries that had been part of Bartók's piano style since the 1903 violin sonata.

Instead the gloriously varied textures of the First Sonata, particularly, reflect again the different influences pressing in upon Bartók as he rediscovered contemporary music, and in terms of sonority the most useful models were obviously those in the same genre, especially Debussy's Violin Sonata (1916–17) and Szymanowski's *Myths* (1915), which perhaps stimulated the generosity of ornament and the fine use of harmonics in this sonata. Where Bartók departs from all predecessors, though, is in making the violin so independent of the piano. At the very start, for instance, the piano's C sharp-coloured cloud is answered by the violin with a sustained C. The line to which this gives rise excludes only two notes: C sharp and its dominant G sharp. Meanwhile the piano also excludes only two notes: C and E flat, those at first most prominent in the violin part. So it continues, and though the finale at least joins the two instruments in vigour, the final cadence expresses only tangential concord, with C sharp major and minor in the piano supporting E major in the violin (the minor third connection of tonalities is another important feature of the sonata's harmony):

Ex. 41
Violin Sonata no. 1: third movement

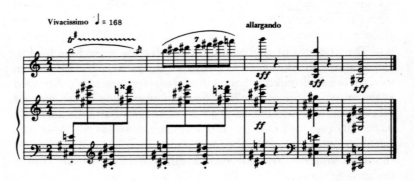

Comparison with the ending of the Second Sonata says much about the difference between the two works:

Ex. 42
Violin Sonata no. 2: second movement

Here the rich chords of the First Sonata are replaced by barer essentials, and the harmony is correspondingly clearer, the form more straightforward. Also, although the violin and the piano keep their own identities, their paths belong more evidently to the same network, as here, where the piano's slow descent in fifths is mirrored by the winging ascent of the violin in F sharp major-minor, to which it keeps until its final surprise landing on E in anticipated agreement with the piano – though this cannot be such a surprise when the register is so high as to attenuate sense of pitch. In further contrast with the First Sonata, the Second ends on a simple major triad, if one spread over more than five octaves: this must be the oddest statement of C major in the repertory, and though C major was indeed the key that Bartók felt this sonata to be in, any more confident assertion is not to be expected. To be sure, the C of the Second Sonata is more apparent than the C sharp of the First, but it is heavily compromised, particularly by the presence of the tritone F sharp as substitute dominant (the main theme even avoids G in order to press the claims of F sharp).

For all the differences between the sonatas, however, they are agreed on one thing: the necessity of ending with a rondo of stamping dances of the kind already encountered in the Second Quartet (the finale of the First Sonata is especially close to this), in the Scherzo of the Four Pieces op. 12 and in the grotesque puppet's dance in *The Wooden Prince*. Only the approach is different. The First Sonata has the conventional three-movement pattern, Allegro appassionato – Adagio – Allegro, whereas the Second has just two continuous movements: a Molto moderato in concise but rhapsodic sonata form, ending with a striking recall of the glowing body music from *The Miraculous Mandarin*, and then leading into the finale, which twice pointedly remembers the first movement. The effect, then, is that of a single introduction-and-allegro form, and a more arrowed move towards the finale than in the First Sonata, where the three movements, diverse though they be, are all of equal weight.

The obvious follow-up was a structure in which everything is contained within one dancing movement, and this Bartók achieved in his next work, the Dance Suite for orchestra (1923). Where the violin sonatas had represented him as a musician on the international stage, the Dance Suite was a national composition, commissioned with Dohnányi's *Festival Overture* and Kodály's *Psalmus hungaricus* for a concert to celebrate the fiftieth anniversary of the unification of Buda and Pest to form the Hungarian capital. The choice of those three composers to be so honoured can scarcely have been accidental when all of them had suffered reverses on Hubay's assumption of control at the academy, and when Bartók, in particular, had recently been under public attack on two grounds. In May 1920 he had been accused in the press of being unpatriotic because his writings drew attention to the presence of a Romanian musical culture existing in Transylvania, which was claimed as part of Hungary. Then in January 1922 the first performance of the Four Pieces had brought disparagement and dismay from the critics, including even those who had championed Bartók in the past: given that *The Miraculous Mandarin* had not yet been scored or the First Violin Sonata performed, op. 12 was considerably the most difficult Bartók work yet to be heard.

Under the circumstances, one might have expected that Bartók in the Dance Suite would want to prove himself, as Hungarian and as musician. On the first count, though, he certainly felt no need. The work is a suite not only of dances but also of nations, like op. 14, visiting several of those he himself had studied in the field: the contents are indicated below, with his own ascriptions of models:[6]

---

[6] Ibid., 202.

I   Moderato, A chromatic (partly Arab)
      Ritornello   Tranquillo, G Aeolian (Hungarian)
II   Allegro molto, B flat Dorian (Hungarian)
      Ritornello   Tranquillo, G Aeolian (Hungarian)
III Allegro vivace, B pentatonic (Hungarian-Romanian-Arab)
IV Molto tranquillo, A flat Dorian (Arab)
      Ritornello   Tranquillo, G Phrygian (Hungarian)
V   Comodo, E chromatic (primitive)
      Finale   Allegro, C/G (various)

The Dance Suite is thus at once a celebration of the particularities of human cultures and a festival in which different races are joined together. Moreover, its tonalities are very much clearer than those of the violin sonatas. There is never any doubt as to the central pitch, and in most sections a single mode dominates throughout: the outstanding exception is the finale, which is designed to reconcile some of the differences that have been exposed, quoting much earlier material.

In its handling of the orchestra, too, the Dance Suite makes a move into clarity. It was completed on holiday at Radvány in northern Hungary in August 1923, the month of Bartók's second marriage, and a time when *The Miraculous Mandarin* was still being finished: as in the violin sonatas, there are traces of the pantomime (of the introductory music, for example, at the start of the finale, with the same trombone klaxon effects). However, the orchestra of the Dance Suite is much more an ensemble of soloists and rude blocks, one well gauged to make a decisive effect, not intricately deployed for finesses such as the *Mandarin* boasts. Direct, therefore, in both scoring and harmony as well as in its rondo form (rondo as understood by Musorgsky in his *Pictures at an Exhibition*, the ritornello serving as narrative frame and preparation), the Dance Suite is the first of the big, popular orchestral works of Bartók's maturity. It is also, like the two earlier suites for orchestra, a work of symphonic measure, containing the essence of introduction (I), first movement (II), scherzo (III), slow movement (IV), second scherzo (V) and finale. This was, after all, the first orchestral work Bartók had written for immediate concert performance since those suites and the *Two Pictures*, all works more than a decade old. With it he emerged definitively from a period of creative inwardness to create an ebullient, outward-looking fantasy.

Some caution is needed, though, in interpreting Bartók's change of style at this point. Certainly the Dance Suite is in every way easier to grasp than the violin sonatas, but then it belongs to a very different genre, and we have little information about how Bartók would have approached other media in the early 1920s because he composed so few works: the Dance Suite was followed at a distance by the song cycle *Village Scenes* (December 1924), and then there was nothing until the summer of 1926. Partly this silence may be explained by the pressure of work to be done on *The Miraculous Mandarin*; partly, if the published version of a newspaper interview can be believed, Bartók was put off his stride by the continuing criticism of him for being 'un-Hungarian'.[7] This may well be so. Certainly it would have been characteristic of him to have reacted doggedly by marrying different musical cultures as he had in the Dance Suite, or giving his attention to minorities as he did in *Village Scenes*, a set of five songs based on Mixolydian (nos. 1–4) and Lydian Slovak material but going a little beyond arrangement, if not quite as far as the Eight Improvisations had gone. The first two, both slow, are each in two stanzas with a brief coda; the remaining three, in a fast-slow-fast pattern, all contain pairs of songs (or in the case of the last a piano dance and a song) arranged in alternating symmetry after the pattern of 'Evening in the Country' from the Ten Easy Pieces. This last triptych was effectively arranged for female chorus and chamber orchestra to make a work for the League of Composers in New York, the first of Bartók's compositions to have its first performance in a country where his reputation was steadily growing.

Meanwhile in Europe he was also continuing to build his career as a pianist, which may be another reason why he composed less freely. There were return visits to London and Paris in December 1923, concerts in Czechoslovakia, Transylvania and north Italy in the spring of 1924, a highly successful tour of Romania in October that year (no doubt fuelling the jingoist attacks back home), and journeys through Italy (March 1925), Holland (October 1925) and Italy again (March 1926), not to speak of odd appearances throughout central Europe. As Bartók explained in a letter to Edward Dent, inviting him to be on the jury for the Zurich festival of the International Society of Contemporary Music in February 1924 (he did indeed take part), he could only accept on condition that he be

[7] See Ujfalussy, 212.

allowed to withdraw if concert engagements turned up, because it was 'imperative for me to give concerts or do anything else which brings in money'.[8] Soon, though, he was to find this necessary activity not keeping him from composition but rather stimulating a whole new creative phase.

[8] Demény (1971), 165–6.

8
The pianist

As a composer-pianist Bartók had to write himself a repertory. Of course, his programmes were not limited to his own music: when concentrating on the new Hungarian school he liked to include pieces by Kodály; he also played Beethoven sonatas and music from the seventeenth and eighteenth centuries, and as an accompanist to violinists – a role he fulfilled often, working not only with Jelly d'Aranyi but also with other Hungarian virtuosos, notably Joseph Szigeti and Zoltán Székely – he would be as likely to perform the sonatas of Beethoven and Debussy as his own. When at home he also took some responsibility in introducing new works from abroad, including Stravinsky's *Piano Rag Music*. Nevertheless, and despite the fact that his performing opportunities were limited by his teaching obligations,[1] he could not be always depending on the stock of piano music he had composed between 1908 and 1918, since when there had been only the Improvisations and a reduction of the Dance Suite. Nor was it very satisfactory that his only concerto, discounting the op. 2 Scherzo which he never played, was the twenty-year-old Rhapsody. He perhaps became convinced of that during the winter of 1925–6, when he played the Rhapsody in Bucharest, Amsterdam (under Monteux) and Berlin (under Walter), and when he mentioned in an interview that a concerto must be his next work.

Within a year he had not only kept that promise but composed two important solo works, the Sonata (June 1926) and the suite *Out of Doors* (June–August); the First Piano Concerto followed between August and November. There were also, in this remarkable year of the piano, a set of Nine Little Pieces and three pieces (eventually nos. 81, 137 and 146) to form the beginnings of a much larger compilation, *Mikrokosmos*, to which Bartók would be adding for the next dozen years, though mostly during the period 1932–8, until he had

[1] See Demény (1971), 178.

110

produced a collection of 153 pieces in six volumes. Here part of the initial stimulus was not his own need as a performer but the wish to write pieces for his young son Péter, to whom the first two volumes of *Mikrokosmos* were dedicated. However, though the first pieces of the first book are such as a small child could hope to master after only a few lessons, as the series continues so the difficulties increase, and the last book ends with virtuoso stuff dedicated to the English pianist Harriet Cohen. *Mikrokosmos* was the container for nearly all the piano music Bartók wrote during his years of greatest activity as a performer: the only things it could not accommodate were the Three Rondos on Folktunes, simple transcriptions in the manner of *Village Scenes* (the first had been written in 1916; the other two followed in 1927), and the *Petite suite* arranged in 1936 from five of the Forty-four Duos for violins. After a first performance of seventeen pieces in London on 9 February 1937, Bartók regularly included items from the expanding collection in his recitals, and in 1940 he made recordings for Columbia of most of the sixth book and much of the fifth and fourth.

This was the third of only four occasions on which he was able to make commercial recordings of his solo piano music.[2] In 1929 for HMV he recorded the Suite op. 14 and half a dozen pieces of 1908–11 (the very first appearance of Bartók's music on records had come in 1925: the Second Quartet played by the Amar, with Hindemith on viola). Then around 1936 he recorded a selection of later short pieces for the Hungarian label Patria, and the 1940 Columbia sessions were followed in or around the next year by recordings, again of shorter items, for Continental Records, a small American company run by a fellow Hungarian. There were also recordings of a few folksong arrangements, of the trio *Contrasts* and of the Sonata for two pianos and percussion, but Bartók left no record of how he played his Sonata, *Out of Doors* or his works with orchestra (there are scraps only of amateur recordings of the Rhapsody op. 1 and the Second Concerto). He may even have avoided his more awkward music, perhaps feeling it unsuitable for a mass medium: the 'Chromatic Invention' is the only piece from the last book of *Mikrokosmos* he did not record.

---

[2] All the surviving recordings of Bartók's playing are assembled in two sets issued by Hungaroton, LPX 12326–33 and LPX 12334–38.

Even so, and though one may regret the paucity of the documentation, there is enough to present problems. Bartók himself pointed out the two sides of the issue in an article of 1937, when he wrote: 'It is a well known fact that our notation records the composer's idea on music paper more or less inadequately; hence the existence of contrivances with which one can record precisely the composer's every idea and intention is indeed of great importance. On the other hand, the composer himself, when he is the performer of his own composition, does not always perform his work in exactly the same way. Why? Because he lives; because perpetual variability is a trait of a living creature's character.'[3] The difficulty lies, of course, in deciding what is meant as a precise record of 'every idea and intention' and what is a natural product of 'perpetual variability', though the latter can be valuable as an object of study for performers. There are, for instance, four different Bartók recordings of the 'Evening with the Székely', including a piano roll from the early twenties, each of the four quite individual in the rhythm it takes at the start, and the four together providing a lesson in the kind of rubato such folksong-like themes imply.

Harder to interpret are those cases where Bartók takes decisions that quite flout the text. His embellishment of a simple piece from *For Children* in a radio recording may be accepted as an instance of living variability; quandaries arise when his tempos depart from his own meticulous instructions. In 1930, we are told,[4] he heard a record of a brass band arrangement of his Allegro barbaro and was appalled not by the transcription but by the speed: it turned out that this highly conspicuous piece had been on sale for twelve years with the wrong metronome marking. He thereupon decided to give every movement he wrote not only a metronome marking but a timing, even including the very elementary pieces at the start of *Mikrokosmos*, and spreading in the major scores of the mid-1930s to curtail every section with a note of its proper duration. The trouble is that the timings and the metronome figures do not always agree. There are some cases where the second was obviously derived from the first: 'Bulgarian Rhythm', no. 113 from *Mikrokosmos*, has forty-nine 7/8 bars and a marked duration of one minute; the metronomic speed is

[3] 'Mechanical Music', in *Essays*, 298.
[4] László Somfai's notes accompanying LPX 12326–33.

appropriately, but most unconventionally, $\downarrow\downarrow. = 49$. In other pieces there is a divergence that Bartók's recordings may not always help to resolve. The table below exemplifies the difficulties with reference to *Mikrokosmos*, listing all those pieces which Bartók recorded and which have no tempo gradients or only very marginal ones: a timing can thus be extrapolated from the metronome marking, and compared with the printed timing and with Bartók's own duration.

piece no.	metronome	timing	Bartók
97	1' 33"	1' 40"	1' 50"
100	42"	45"	45"
108	53"	1'	58"
113	1'	1'	1' 04"
118	50"	57"	50"
126	40"	40"	37"
130	46"	45"	45"
131	48"	45"	53"
133	1'	1' 05"	57"
139	52"	58"	57"
147	1' 42"	1' 45"	1' 53"
149	1' 04"	1' 10"	1' 10"
150	1' 20"	1' 20"	1' 12"
152	1' 12"	1' 13"	1' 11"
153	1' 44"	1' 40"	1' 43"

What this comparison shows is that there are many cases where all three sources are in agreement, within the bounds of what is significant (see especially nos. 130, 152 and 153). Where the two printed indications are in disagreement, Bartók may prefer the metronome (nos. 118 and 139) or the timing (no. 149). He may also be appreciably faster than either (nos. 126 and 150) or slower (nos. 97 and 147). As far as the latter is concerned, perhaps his extreme disregard of the score comes in no. 144, a piece too flexible in tempo for a timing to be calculated from the metronome speed, where the marked duration is 3' 25" and his version plays for 4' 11".

Faced with such discrepancies, Bartók performers can only use their own judgement after taking note of all the documentation – scores and recordings – available to them. One may note also that, whatever the commercial opportunities open to him, Bartók could very easily have made private recordings of all his works in 'authentic' performances: he was constantly using gramophone recording machines in his folksong work. The fact that he did not must cast doubt on his trust of recordings as adjuncts to the score, which is not to say that his recordings are not fascinating windows, if dimmed and blurred by age, into his musical personality. And here matters of large-scale tempo become somewhat secondary. Bartók can execute prodigious feats of virtuosity, as in his race through Scarlatti's B flat sonata K.70, and he can be grandly expressive in things like Liszt's *Sursum corda*. But there is always a feeling that the character emerges from the music rather than the player, and this is something that comes out time and again in first-hand accounts of Bartók at the piano.[5] It is perhaps another aspect of this characteristic that his playing sounds so natural, with subtleties of rhythm intimately shaped on the ebb and flow of ideas (there is never anything mechanical in even the most straightforward rhythm), and with harmonic progressions revealed by tiny variations of weight rather than colour (the effect of this in his recording of Beethoven's 'Kreutzer' Sonata with Szigeti is extraordinary). Finally one must judge that the sparseness of Bartók's recorded output is to be regretted not on documentary grounds but more because it deprives one of more contact with a pianist of a rare kind.

Even so, it is a pity he did not record any of the great works of 1926 in which his style took another leap. Once again the change has to be understood in the light of the genres in which he was working, for he wrote nothing that was not for the piano in that year, and he was evidently possessed by at least two highly pianistic images: first that of the percussive piano, driving through motor rhythms on noisy chords, and secondly that of imitative counterpoint flowing between the two hands. Neither of these was very new. The first had been heard in the Allegro barbaro fifteen years before, and there are examples of strict counterpoint in many other pieces of the same period. However, the music of 1926 takes both much further, and for the first time brings them together, so that, for example, the first movement of the Sonata is more acutely violent than the Allegro barbaro because it has reason, in the shape of contrapuntal artifice and sonata form, attempting to take hold of the barbarity.

Bartók's understanding of each may also have been deepened by

[5] See for example Lajos Hernádi: 'Bartók – Pianist and Teacher', Crow, 152–8.

influences from outside. On the one hand he was impressed by the pounding pulsations of *The Rite of Spring*, which in October 1924 he had applauded as 'the most grandiose musical opus of the past thirty years'[6] (one wonders why this was the period he chose: perhaps he was still remembering *Also sprach Zarathustra*, composed in 1895–6). As far as the Piano Sonata is concerned, however, another, nearer Stravinsky score was still more influential: *Les noces* (1914–23). This, with its orchestra of pianos and percussion, provided models of sonority, pulsing rhythm and even harmony: the clangorous clash of E minor and C sharp in the first movement of the sonata (bars 55ff) is particularly close to the Stravinsky work. By comparison with this, the influence of Henry Cowell's cluster playing, which Bartok had admired in 1923,[7] would seem very secondary, though it is noteworthy, and characteristic, that Bartók should in the next year have asked Cowell if he had any objection to his technique being taken over. In fact his use of clusters was quite modest, though enough to make an effect of noise, as in this example from the finale of the Sonata:

Ex. 43
Piano Sonata: third movement

The other strand of influence, the polyphonic, is evident less in the Sonata than in the First Piano Concerto and, most purely, in the first four of the Nine Little Pieces, which have the title 'Dialogues' and are two-part contrapuntal inventions. Bartók himself admitted as much

[6] Interview quoted in Ujfalussy, 216.
[7] Letter from Cowell quoted in Halsey Stevens: *The Life and Music of Béla Bartók* (New York, second edition 1964), 67.

when he wrote to the musicologist Edwin von der Nüll that he had 'been occupied with pre-Bach music and I think that traces of these studies are revealed in the Piano Concerto and the Nine Little Piano Pieces'.[8] The 'studies' were concerned with editions he made around this time of keyboard works by Italian masters of the seventeenth and eighteenth centuries: Marcello, Michelangelo Rossi, della Ciaia, Frescobaldi and Zipoli. He drew on this repertory for his recitals, and he also drew on Baroque imitative counterpoint in such passages as this, from the slow movement of the concerto:

Ex. 44
Piano Concerto no. 1: second movement

Here everything springs from a motif consisting of a minor plus a major second, a motif that also tightly binds the first movement of the Sonata. Though the violin sonatas were only a few years old, this Piano Sonata is a sonata of quite a different kind: formally, harmonically and thematically (the three planes are of course connected). In particular, the long and flexible themes of the violin sonatas are replaced by minimal, very distinct ideas, which may be no more than rhythmicised motifs, or may alternatively extend the motif in the manner of a folksong: there are instances of both among the main ideas of the first movement, all based on that three-note pattern covering a minor third:

[8] Edwin von der Nüll: *Béla Bartók* (Halle, 1930), 108.

Ex. 45
Piano Sonata: first movement

All of these plainly state a tonic, and under only slightly different circumstances they might have found themselves in a Baroque toccata, but in Bartók's Sonata tonalities are abrasively contradicted, either by chords containing seconds, sevenths or ninths, or else by twinning with a rival key. The interval of such bitonality has clear structural importance in the first movement of the Sonata, where the principal idea (Ex. 45a) is confronted across a fourth (E against B, G against D, C against G), while Ex. 45c and 45d are associated with disagreements across a minor second and a minor sixth respectively. The development section is distinguished by a shift to bitonality across a tritone, after which the recapitulation brings back the original scheme.

The bitonal divergences of this movement, and even more so its semitonal negations of key, are all of a piece with its incessant pulse: scarcely a quaver beat is missed as the music hammers its way onward. Each of the other movements, too, is similarly pulse-bound. The central 'Sostenuto e pesante' is no lyrical escape but instead a piece in which perpetual even motion is simply decelerated, becoming stiff and monumental, and the finale, in which a B mixolydian folksong-like theme is subjected to alternately more and less extreme variation to give an impression of rondo form, this finale again races on a constant quaver pulse. Motor rhythms of this kind were common in the music that came out of *The Rite*, and Bartók's insistent ostinatos and percussive chording bring his Sonata close to the machine music being written at this time by Honegger (*Pacific 231*, 1923), Prokofiev (Symphony no. 2, 1924–5) and certain Soviet composers. The Sonata is, however, calculated in a manner typical only of Bartók. The pulse speeds of the three movements are related in the proportions 3:1:4, and there is some evidence that the internal proportioning of the movements was planned.

This is a matter of some controversy. The Hungarian scholar Ernő Lendvai has adduced from Bartók's later instrumental scores various systems of composition, including the preference for intervals with Fibonacci numbers of semitones (each number in the Fibonacci series is the sum of the last two, thus: 1–2–3–5–8–13–etc) and the division of movements into parts according to the Golden Section.[9] There is unfortunately no evidence for this in any of Bartók's writings or sketches, but then he always liked to cover his tracks and destroyed most of his sketches.[10] Also, the fit in some cases is just too neat to be ignored. In the first movement of the Piano Sonata, for example, the recapitulation begins after 656 quavers in a movement of 1062 quavers, which coincides to the nearest quaver with the Golden Section: in other words, the second part of the movement is related in length to the first as the first is related to the whole. This is, of course, to ignore the faster tempo introduced near the end of the movement, but in music of this pulsating kind one can justifiably reckon number of rhythmic units as a measure of musical quantity.

If this were the only example of such a design, then it could be ignored as a coincidence, but in fact exactly the same proportioning, with the recapitulation starting at the point of Golden Section, occurs too in the first movements of the Sonata for pianos and percussion, *Contrasts* and the Divertimento for string orchestra, to give only a few examples that are exactly parallel. There would also have been a good aesthetic reason for Bartók to plan his movements so, since the start of the recapitulation is the decisive point in a sonata movement, and since the Golden Section had been recognised from

---

[9] Ernő Lendvai: *Béla Bartók: an Analysis of his Music* (London, 1971).
[10] See László Somfai: 'The Budapest Bartók Archives', *Fontes artis musicae* (1982), 59–65.

antiquity as a harmonious division. Moreover, such a technique would have been entirely consistent with his appeal to abstract standards of order, beginning in the works of 1926 and increasing to a climax of ingenuity in those of the next decade. The condensation of ideas around a single motif in the first movement of the Sonata is another instance of this; so too is the gearing of the three movements' speeds, even if this was probably stimulated by *Les Noces*.

The outer movements of the First Piano Concerto, composed straight after the Sonata, show the same 3:4 ratio of speeds as well as many other points of style in common. Again the first movement is harnessed to a quaver pulse in 2/4 units, and again it is in sonata form, though with a slower introduction. There is even an association of key, since Bartók described the Sonata as being in E major[11] and the concerto in E minor, though once again these attributions have to be considered in the light of a new interpretation of tonality. In the first movement of the Sonata, for instance, E as a pole is normally fused with B a fourth below, and the main secondary poles are those a minor third on either side, G and C sharp: once more the notes of a diminished-seventh chord have central structural importance, as will happen again in many later works. In the concerto, as befits a big public work, tonalities are clearer, though E minor is only the focus for a variety of modes, and indeed modal scales with little alteration provide much of the material of the outer movements, by contrast with the Sonata, where enigmatic scale fragments are at issue. The differences between the two works are inevitably crystallised in their final cadences. In the Sonata, the first movement ends with a treble E crushed against a noisy chord in the low bass, the finale with octave Es offset by Ds and Fs. The corresponding movements of the concerto end with a chord of E plus its fifth (B) and its fifth's fifth (F sharp), and then with just an E–B chord.

Nevertheless, the piano is the same percussive instrument in the First Concerto that it is in the Sonata. The outer movements are similarly heavy with ostinatos, with reiterations, with complex chords that make a noise effect and with scales thickly doubled in thirds in the bass. The central Andante makes the new kinship of the instrument explicit, for the piano is at first accompanied only by

[11] See H.C. Becker: 'Béla Bartók and his Credo', *Musical America* (17 December 1927).

timpani, drums and cymbals in a mood of quiet nocturnal signalling: a motif of three repeated quavers is the main stimulus to the dialogues. The middle section brings a change with a weave of woodwind polyphony over the piano and percussion, and then there is a return to the manner of the opening, joined finally by trombone glissandos to erupt the music into its finale. Absent altogether from the slow movement, the strings are used in the others predominantly as a chordal mass, with melodic lines being taken mainly by the wind.

This division of labour is maintained in the Second Piano Concerto, composed between October 1930 and October 1931, where the first movement is for piano, percussion and wind only (the obvious model is Stravinsky's stringless Piano Concerto of 1923–4). Bartók had introduced his First Concerto at the opening concert on July 1 of the 1927 ISCM Festival in Frankfurt, when the conductor was Furtwängler (two weeks later in Baden-Baden he played his Sonata in a concert that also included Berg's Lyric Suite). In October 1927 he played the concerto in London, Prague and Warsaw; in November there was a performance in Vienna with Webern conducting; in February 1928 there were a few performances at the end of his first, two-month-long tour of the United States; and in the spring he played the work in Budapest, Cologne and Berlin.[12] It is understandable that after a few years of such exposure Bartók felt the need to write another concerto, which he introduced again in Frankfurt, on 23 January 1933, this time with Hans Rosbaud conducting. Once more performances quickly followed in major European cities, though not in Budapest, where Bartók had again withdrawn from playing his own music: he did not give the concerto there until 1938.

The Second Concerto is much clearer in style than the first, and its G major tonality, the tonality of Ravel's exactly contemporary and similarly extrovert concerto, is now much less sullied by chromatic adjacencies and bitonality: it is bravely declared by the opening trumpet tune, which cheekily speeds up the theme from the finale of Stravinsky's *Firebird*. The counterpoint is a counterpoint more of lines than blocks, and even strays into the world of J.S. Bach at one point (first movement: bars 155ff), while textures and formal

---

[12] For fuller details see Ujfalussy, 241.

outlines are more crisply illuminated: each of the outer movements has a notated cadenza, that in the finale punctuated by bass drum and timpani. In the slow movement, too, the piano is once again accompanied by percussion, but the atmospheric assemblage of the First Concerto is replaced by a clean duet for piano with trilled pedal notes in the timpani. This alternates with an extraordinary chorale in piled-up fifths on the strongs, all the more marvellously strange because it introduces instruments new to the work:

Ex. 46
Piano Concerto no. 2: second movement

There is thus a total contrast of veiled harmony with percussive polyphony, but the movement contains also a contrast of speed, for the Adagio in verses for strings and piano-timpani duo opens to receive a scherzo for full orchestra. And the symmetry goes further, for the finale remembers themes and textures from the first movement.

In all these respects of symmetry and clarity the Second Concerto is typical of Bartók's music of the 1930s. The remaining works of 1926, *Out of Doors* and the Nine Little Pieces, show a quite different face. *Out of Doors* is a suite of character pieces of the sort Bartók had written before the war, but taking account of much more recent developments in his style: the first of the five pieces, 'With Drums and Pipes', is a near relative of the first movements of the Sonata and the First Concerto, having the same martellato quavers in 2/4 metre, and the finale, 'The Chase', not only alludes to *The Miraculous Mandarin* but is the extreme instance of Bartók's obsession with ostinatos during this period (its mechanism has to be rudely disrupted or it might continue forever).

Since the percussiveness of the first movement is more that of the concert hall than the field and 'The Chase' has absolutely nothing of bucolic hunting horns about it, the suite's title has to be justified by the inner movements. The first two of them add to established keyboard repertories: the wistful 6/8 boating song in the 'Barcarolla' and the bagpipe dance, favoured by various eighteenth-century composers and more recently by Schoenberg in his Piano Suite (1923), in 'Musettes'. In each case, though, the style is very much Bartók's own, established particularly by the grey fourths of the 'Barcarolla' and by the ostinatos, noise chords and ornamental twiddles of 'Musettes', where the plural title is perhaps meant to indicate that the piece is more a cross-cutting of different bagpipe impressions than a dance.

The fourth piece of *Out of Doors* is to an even greater extent music of texture: it is 'The Night's Music', dedicated like the Sonata to Ditta, and instancing for the first time a kind of itchy, wide-awake nocturne to be found in several later scores, especially where the piano is joined by percussion instruments (as in all three concertos, the Sonata for pianos and percussion and the Music for Strings, Percussion and Celesta). Here the background, in atmospheric and purely acoustic terms, is provided by an E sharp – A natural cluster in the middle of the piano, softly repeated throughout the piece. Almost constantly undamped, therefore, these strings will be activated by lower notes, as here by the C sharp and D in the bass (the G sharp and A in the cluster are their third harmonics), while figurations in the upper treble pick out higher resonances:

Ex. 47
Out of Doors: 'The Night's Music'

This response to the piano as a resonating instrument is a feature of the whole piece: the main tune that arrives, as if from the distance, is doubled at a distance of three octaves, with the effect of reinforcing the eighth harmonic, and the night character of the music is owed not only to the stylised evocations of toads and crickets that one may hear in it but also to the concentration on resonance effects, to which in life the ear is more attentive during the stillness and dark of the night. Bartók may have found some cues for this in Schoenberg's piano music of 1909–12 and also in certain of Debussy's preludes ('Feux d'artifice', for example, similarly concludes with fragments of tune heard over diffuse texture). However, his awareness of the piano's acoustic character was the awareness of the performer: it is obvious on his records from his clear, luminous voicing of polyphony and his careful weighting of chords. It is the same awareness, too, that enabled him, in music very different from the night's, to create noise effects simply and economically in the Sonata (as in Ex. 43), knowing that the resonances of the piano would confuse harmony that might be heard as such if the same chords were played by wind instruments. None of these piano works of 1926 could be transcribed for orchestra: the soloist in the First Concerto could not have the same rugged force if he did not know that he was operating in a world closed to the rest, except for the percussion whom he dominates easily by having pitch at his command.

The Nine Little Pieces are a scrapbook of this period. They are arranged in three volumes, of which the first contains the 'Four Dialogues' that twine by imitation and motivic variation. The second book is a miniature suite, again with four pieces. First and last are two more wholly individual essays in eighteenth-century dance forms, a 'Menuetto' of curious character, quietly grumbling, and a 'Tambourine' in which rude peasant festivities are as alive in

Bartók's mind as the example of Rameau. Between these come an 'Air', a folksong set in a sparkling foil of A major, and 'Marcia delle bestie', living up to its name with stamping ostinatos. Just one piece is left for the last book, and it is indeed much longer than any of the rest: a 'Preludio, all'ungarese' in two thematically related sections, slow and fast, which might have opened *Out of Doors* if that work had become a Magyar partita, as still it sometimes promises.

That such a diverse group as the Nine Little Pieces should have been published together seems somewhat accidental, especially when all could have been accommodated within *Mikrokosmos*. This vast collection offers a pianist a thorough training not only in keyboard technique but in general musicianship. Naturally most of the pieces are for piano solo, but there are also songs (nos. 65, 74, 95 and 127) and duet pieces designed to extend the young pianist's range of experience. Moreover, the titles draw attention more often to matters of musical substance than to technical points: even in the first volume one finds 'Imitation and Inversion', 'Canon at the Octave', 'In Dorian Mode', and so on. The beginner is thus introduced to the very basics of Bartók's musical language, to bitonality (nos. 12, 42, 66), to changes of metre (nos. 12, 41, 55) and of accentuation (nos. 32–3), to ostinato and variation as techniques for building musical forms, to canon and other contrapuntal ingenuities, and everywhere to different modes. In his notes to the first volume, evidently addressed to the child pianist, Bartók is rather charmingly at pains to assure his young readers that though the modes have a venerable history in Western music, 'they are still flourishing in the folk music of Eastern Europe (Hungary, Rumania, Yugoslavia, etc.) and Asia and are not at all antiquated'. Sometimes he prefaces a piece with a notation of its mode, as for instance in the case of 'Melody with Accompaniment' from the second book, where the mode is the 'acoustic scale' on G.

For a composer reluctant to expatiate on his musical philosophy, Bartók's notes to the first volume of *Mikrokosmos* are extraordinarily revealing in more than modal matters, as if he sensed an unaccustomed security with this audience. He underlines, for instance, the expressive power of music, 'contrary', as he drily remarks, 'to the opinion of post-war years': here he was clearly thinking of Stravinsky's remarks about music's inability to express anything,[13]

---

[13] Igor Stravinsky: *An Autobiography* (London, 1975), 53.

remarks that appear to have set him apart from the composer whose *Rite* and *Les noces* he so manifestly admired. True to his word, he often in *Mikrokosmos* chooses titles that indicate expressive or illustrative aim: 'Dragons' Dance', 'Merriment' and 'Stumblings' are examples from the third book. It is altogether appropriate, therefore, that the two patrons of the collection should be J.S. Bach and Schumann, masters in the keyboard miniature of musical structure and musical suggestion, and each given an explicit homage in the same third book (nos. 79–80).

The range of reference is, however, much wider than this. There are, of course, folksong arrangements, though only the few that Bartók needed to introduce songs into his collection: he had, after all, provided an abundance of such material for young pianists in *For Children*. There are also pieces which acknowledge some basis in folk music, whether modal in the case of 'In Yugoslav Mode' from the second book (the mode is Mixolydian E) or rhythmic in that of the final Six Dances in Bulgarian Rhythm and two items from the fourth book ('Bulgarian rhythm' was Bartók's term for irregular compound metres like the 4+3+2/8 of the first dance: no other relationship to Bulgarian music is implied). 'From the Island of Bali', from book four, ventures further afield, and does so with an evident knowledge of Balinese music from transcriptions or recordings: possibly Bartók encountered the work of Colin McPhee when he was in New York in 1927–8 or later. Geographical virtuosity is matched too by historical awareness, with another eighteenth-century dance piece, a more properly classical 'Bourrée', balanced in the fourth book by exercises in resonance ('Harmonics' and 'Melody in the Mist') that are elementary introductions respectively to Schoenberg's technique of silently undamping strings and to the world of 'The Night's Music'. Ragtime and jazz even emerge in the unlikeliest places, in the 'New Hungarian Folk Song' (book five) and in the Six Dances in Bulgarian Rhythm.

More generally it is inevitably Bartók's musical personality that dominates *Mikrokosmos*, and the other paradigms – Bach, Schumann, gamelan music, jazz and the rest – are those he himself found useful. Since the collection dates in large part from well after 1926, its links with the great works of that year are not strong, though there is some brighter echo of the Sonata in the 2/4 perpetual motion of 'Chords Together and Opposed' in the fifth book. However, many pieces in their simplicity show up basic, almost permanent elements of style that may well be obscured in more complex compositions. For example, Bartók's liking for unusual scales, bringing with them unusual harmonic functions, is demonstrated baldly in such a piece as 'Thumb under' from book four, which is in straightforward octaves or double octaves throughout:

Ex. 48
Mikrokosmos: no. 98 'Thumb Under'

This is clearly in G, but the scale is an invented one: it is most easily described as Dorian with an augmented fourth. Moreover, though the piece continues by repeating the above music up a fifth, there is no sense in which D acts as dominant in this melody: that function is assumed either by B flat or C sharp, two notes from the diminished seventh chord on G.

Other very characteristic features of Bartók's pitch structures, abounding particularly in his music of the 1930s, are intervallic compression and expansion, and mirror inversion (the latter has already been considered in connection with the Eight Improvisations). 'Line and Point', coming near the end of the second book, is an exemplary case of the former technique, since it exists in two forms, one based on Dorian or Aeolian pentachords (e.g. E – F sharp – G – A – B) and one based on compressions of those pentachords into fragments of the chromatic scale (E – F – F sharp – G – A flat). The same piece also exhibits reflective symmetry, as does, in a notably interesting way, the last piece of book four, 'Two-part Study'. This is a dialogue comparable with those from the Nine Little Pieces, with the two voices heard first mirroring one another around middle D sharp:

Ex. 49

Mikrokosmos: no. 121 'Two-part Study'

The inversion here is not intervallic but scalic, and the two hands, as so often in *Mikrokosmos*, are operating in different scales: the right hand is in Mixolydian E with the addition of A sharp; the left is in the 'acoustic scale' on D, also with the addition of A sharp. The point of this becomes clear if the two scales are played or written out in contrary motion:

Ex. 50

As will be observed, the resulting intervals are all minor seconds, major seconds and minor thirds (or their octave transpositions), since the second and seventh degrees of the E scale, with the corresponding notes of the D scale except for the cadential C, are omitted. There is, therefore, a tight harmonic consistency in the combination of the image and reflection projected in the music: an inversion-produced consistency to be found often in Bartók's music of this period as also in Webern's.

Mikrokosmos is full of conceits of this kind that contain, indeed in microcosm, the essence of methods used over much wider spans and with more complex material in such contemporary works as the Fifth Quartet, the Sonata for two pianos and percussion, and the Music for Strings, Percussion and Celesta. Progressing from unassuming little scales to the heights of the Bulgarian Parnassus, it is a guide, therefore, not only for pianists but for anybody who would comprehend Bartók's musical world.

9

Simplicity and complexity

The extremes of *Mikrokosmos* are represented also in the music Bartók wrote in the late 1920s and early 1930s, during the few years straight after the remarkable piano year of 1926. On the one hand there was the single-movement Third Quartet, his largest instrumental structure and arguably his most complex. On the other there was a return, as already mentioned, to folksong arrangement, and even to the composition of light music in folk style (the Rhapsodies for violin and piano).

It is tempting to see the Third Quartet, which is dated September 1927, as having been stimulated by Bartók's experience of Berg's Lyric Suite just two months before: for one thing, it has a greater variety of playing techniques (sul ponticello, sulla tastiera, col legno, glissando) than he had used in a quartet so far. However, the connection is more convincing in the case of the Fourth Quartet, in terms both of range of colour and character of movement, for this Fourth Quartet shares with the Lyric Suite a concentration on a particular kind of texture and expression in each movement, whereas the essence of the Third Quartet is instability. Moreover, the violin sonatas provide a stepping stone from the Second Quartet to the Third in a progression of increasingly esoteric colourfulness, and they were written long before the Lyric Suite – though not, of course, before Bartók would have had the opportunity to acquaint himself with earlier quartet compositions by Schoenberg, Berg and Webern. It is within Bartók's own world, too, and not within Berg's that one must look for the Third Quartet's stylistic antecedents, and they are fairly clearly to be found in the Piano Sonata and the First Concerto of the previous year.

Three kinds of link stand out. First there is the conversion of the string quartet into a medium hardly less percussive than the piano, which Bartók achieves not only by special effects – col legno, martellato attacks on the tailpiece – but also, and more generally, by an insistence on repeated multiple-stopped chords in strident dissonance:

Ex. 51
String Quartet no. 3

The stamp of *The Rite of Spring* is still clearly to be felt here, but the conflict in the harmony of fifth and tritone is as Bartókian as *The Miraculous Mandarin* and is central to this quartet.

The other connections with the works of 1926 are in motivic fabric and contrapuntal texture. Like the Piano Sonata, the Third Quartet is based on fragmentary ideas subjected to almost incessant variation, but over a larger span and therefore to greater extremes of change. It is the same with the counterpoint. Since the string quartet is so naturally a polyphonic medium, this new work is drawn into a polyphonic expression of its material much more readily than was the case with the Piano Sonata or the First Concerto, but still the cast of contrapuntal thinking is recognisably the same. In particular there is the same interest in quick canonic imitation and in the confrontation of an idea with its inversion, though imitations and inversions may both be subtly varied, partly because of Bartók's stated dislike of exact repetition, partly because of his penchant for changing the scale, as in the example mentioned above from *Mikrokosmos*.

One essential difference from the sonata and the concerto is formal. Both those works of 1926 had been in the most traditional of patterns, with two quick movements surrounding a slow one. The Third Quartet, by contrast, takes its cue from the Second Violin Sonata in prefacing a characteristic 2/4 allegro with a substantial movement that works as slow introduction. The balance, however, is significantly shifted. The slow movement, 'Prima parte', is not in anything that could be called sonata form even at this date: it is, rather, a joined sequence of meditations on several small motivic cells, of which the most important is formed of a rising fourth and a falling minor third. However, the ensuing allegro, 'Seconda parte', does have sonata structure buried within it, with a development that finds issue in a passage of fugato, followed by a clear thematic recapitulation that moves on into a coda in which the biting semitonal conflicts persist. Altogether this fantasy-sonata form is vastly more open-ended than the sonata-finale form of the Second Violin Sonata, and of course the work cannot end there: it continues with a 'Ricapitulazione della prima parte', which is not so much a 'recapitulation' as a revisiting of certain ideas from the introduction in a new context. Indeed, its lack of recapitulative character is rather strikingly demonstrated by the absence from it of the fourth–minor third motif so pervasive in the opening section: it is a return to the same stage, but with the principal character departed. After this one might logically expect a 'Ricapitulazione della seconda parte', were it not that the 'Seconda parte' has already had its recapitulation in the proper place: what follows and completes the work is therefore a 'Coda', related to the 'Seconda parte' in terms of theme, harmony and tempo, but again, despite its name, leaving the quartet to rest on an upbeat. Where the First Quartet had ended on a chord of two piled-up fifths, the Third concludes with three (C sharp – G sharp – D sharp – A sharp), bringing no sense of achieved finality but rather a feeling that the music has been cut off almost against its will, with unfinished business remaining to be considered, as it had remained at the end of the 'Seconda parte'.

Astringent and restless harmony is not, however, a feature only of the last bars but is central to the character of the work, which is perhaps the least ingratiating thing Bartók wrote in terms of sonority. Sometimes it has been supposed that its harmonic awkwardness results from a concentration on line, almost as if the chords were accidental. This could only be tested, perhaps, by having one of the four parts played, say, a semitone sharp, but it seems unlikely as an explanation. For one thing, the harmonic acerbity is most marked in those passages that are homophonic, like the ending, or like Ex. 51. Here Bartók positively exults in dissonance – there can be nothing accidental about images so strongly presented – whereas when the quartet is most polyphonic its harmonic peculiarities strike the ear less forcibly because the play of variation is so demanding of attention. Secondly, there is good internal evidence that Bartók was, after the Piano Sonata and the First Concerto, exploring the very different possibilities of clusters in the quartet medium: the work opens, indeed, with the three lower instruments playing a chord of C sharp – D – D sharp – E spread over two octaves and a major second. Finally, the work depends almost continuously on frictions between rival tonal centres, as has been demonstrated in the first movement of the Sonata. At the start of the 'Seconda parte', for example, the second violin maintains a D – D flat trill for thirty-nine bars, while the cello introduces the first version of the main theme in D Dorian and the viola has a little chromatic run landing on E flat. The E flat – D conflict then resurfaces regularly throughout this part of the quartet: again Ex. 51 is to the point.

The slow-fast-slow-fast form of the Third Quartet can be related, as mentioned, to the slow-fast of the Second Violin Sonata and thereby to other binary models, not least the lassú-friss of Hungarian gipsy music. However, another influence seems more pertinent: that of Beethoven. The integration of slow and fast music within a single movement was something that Beethoven strove for and achieved in quartets and sonatas from op. 18 no. 6 onwards. Bartók's Third Quartet, applying that principle to a whole work, is a further indication that Beethoven had become the predecessor against whom he was judging himself, however much he might be continuing to learn from older and newer sources.

Bartók entered his Third Quartet in a competition for new chamber music organised by the Musical Fund Society of Philadelphia, one of the oldest musical institutions in the United States. He was in America between December 1927 and February 1928 making his first tour, and then towards the end of 1928 he heard that the Philadelphia prize was to be divided between him and Alfredo Casella. This must have been welcome news given the state of his finances (his half share was three thousand dollars), but it must have seemed a little like ancient history, for by this time he had already completed his Fourth Quartet, dated July–September 1928. And though it came within a year of the completion of the Third, this Fourth Quartet is utterly different.

Whereas the essence of the Third Quartet's form is uncertainty, with jumps backwards and forward between different kinds of music, the Fourth Quartet is partitioned with the utmost clarity into five movements, arranged in a mirror symmetry that makes the superficially analogous patterns of the First Suite or the First Piano Concerto look lax and coincidental. The finale has many motivic

131

connections with the first movement, and gathers such a number of correspondences that at the end it actually runs into the tracks taken by its predecessor and concludes with the same music. Moving inwards, the second and fourth movements are both scherzos, again related in terms of motif and also in speciality of colour: the former is a 'Prestissimo, con sordino', the latter an 'Allegretto pizzicato'. Moreover, while the outer movements both end firmly on C, these even-numbered scherzos reach a major third above (second movement) and below (fourth movement), so that the quartet as a whole outlines an augmented triad. The central 'Non troppo lento' lies outside this scheme, and indeed outside the urgent polyphonic working of the rest of the quartet, consisting as it does of solo murmurings that grow into melody against static harmonic support from the other three instruments:

Ex. 52
String Quartet no. 4: third movement

Like the string music of the Second Piano Concerto's slow movement, this still centre of the quartet is based harmonically on piles of fifths, and in particular on the sequence D—A—E—B—F sharp—C sharp—G sharp (which provides the notes of the A major scale). In the quotation above, taken from the start of the movement, the pile is compressed into the narrowest possible compass; one may note, too, that the chord sustained by the upper instruments is symmetrical about the D sharp and D with which the cello begins, as if the solo instrument slots into a hole made for it. As the movement continues, so the placing and constitution of the underlying chord changes, but the tower of seven fifths on D remains close to the surface, and at the end it is this chord that is left sounding, now stretched over a range of more than two octaves and with its notes picked off one by one until only the basic D remains at the top.

The twin scherzos surrounding this movement are both highly distinctive, with colour effects that include not only muting and pizzicato but also a deeper penetration of glissandos than had come in the Third Quartet (second movement) and a new kind of pizzicato in which the string is pulled so hard it snaps against the fingerboard (fourth movement): this is often called a 'Bartók pizzicato' in recognition of its first use here. There are also relationships of speed and timing, the second movement being roughly twice as fast as the fourth and twice as long in terms of rhythmic units, so that the two movements have very similar durations. Still more striking are the analogies of theme and form. Both movements are based on rising and falling scale patterns, but whereas in the second movement the scale is chromatic and its range a fifth, the fourth movement sports with 'acoustic scales' playing over an octave. The two movements are thus related in the same way as are the two versions of 'Line and Point' from *Mikrokosmos*, providing a clear instance of the way that piano compendium shows facets of Bartók's compositional technique that underpin other, more complex works of the period. As for their formal structure, in both cases one can descry a fundamental ABA pattern, with the middle section in each movement based on a three-note chromatic motif, but in both the return of the A material is much disguised by development incorporating aspects of the B music. Each central section is therefore not so much a trio as a secondary part of the movement, to be joined next with the primary material in a fusion of conflict. And that conflict is expressed on several different levels: thematically in the dichotomy between scales and small motifs, harmonically in the chromatic-diatonic distinction which is reversed between the two movements (i.e. the B material is diatonic in the chromatic second movement and chromatic in the diatonic fourth), and timbrally in the introduction of the new techniques – the glissandos and the Bartók pizzicatos – in the middle sections.

If the even-numbered movements thus show an old symmetrical archetype, the scherzo and trio, made newly asymmetrical, this same kind of constant development is a feature too of the outer movements especially the first. To describe this movement as being in sonata form is just but incomplete, as may be suggested by a comparison of the opening with the start of the 'recapitulation':

Ex. 53
String Quartet no. 4: first movement

exposition

recapitulation

The initial three-part counterpoint of the exposition duly returns, metrically displaced but with little other change. However, it is then repeated in a new configuration, which did not happen before, and, still more devastating to any sense of return, it is saddled with a small chromatic motif that only appeared before in the seventh bar, as one of several important thematic units. This is the clue to the dual nature of the movement, which is not only a sonata structure but also a form articulated by the increasing invasion of this six-note idea.

A similar invasion takes place in the finale, whose main theme is related to the six-note idea in the same way that the main theme of the fourth movement is related to that of the second: by an expansion from segments of the chromatic scale to segments of a diatonic ones:

Ex. 54
String Quartet no. 4: fifth movement

The opening context for this theme is one of stamping discords in the manner of the Third Quartet, with C–G fifths boxed in by the addition of D flat and F sharp as chromatic adjacencies. Another characteristic feature of the Fourth Quartet openly displayed in its finale is the answering of themes by their inversions, those inversions being not intervallic in the style of the Viennese school but scalic in the way already demonstrated in *Mikrokosmos*. The six-note motif then reappears in its original form just over halfway through (bars 218–19 in a movement of 392 bars), and steers the movement towards its ending in affirmative imitation of the first allegro.

Although the Fourth Quartet came so quickly after the Third, it must be obvious that it is a very different sort of work. The differences, however, are differences of form rather than style. In its harmony the new quartet is quite as abrasive as its predecessor, and in its quasi-percussive handling of the strings it is no less intransigent. It is also, like the Third Quartet, very much a polyphonic work, except in its middle movement. It is, indeed, even more intensely alive with canons and invertible counterpoint, the greater prominence of these strict devices going hand in hand with the greater formal clarity that so marks off his quartet from no. 3, as if the fierce conflicts of that work, responsible for a somewhat amorphous form, had now been channelled into the tightest imaginable structures. All at once, within a year, Bartók had achieved the intensive symmetries that were to serve him for the next decade.

He must have realised, nevertheless, that these two quartets of 1927–8 were not likely to become immediately popular, so harsh was their style – too harsh, indeed, for even such an appreciator of motivic architecture as Anton Webern.[1] Possibly for that reason, since he needed money, he began at the same time to write easier music. An example is the set of *Hungarian Pictures* (1931), transcribing five of the 1908–11 piano pieces for standard symphony orchestra, about which he wrote to his mother in tones that are almost cynical: 'This is the sort of thing that will be performed because the music is pleasing, it is not very difficult to play, and it is by a "known" composer.'[2] He could not, though, undertake even this task without the utmost care and artistry, to be found also in other popularisations of the period: an orchestral version of the Sonatina as *Transylvanian Dances*, another of the 'Ballad' and all but one of the 'Old Dance Tunes' from the Fifteen Hungarian Peasant Songs, and an orchestrated suite of five numbers from the Twenty Hungarian Folksongs. All these came from 1931–3, and very possibly they were stimulated not only by financial concerns but also by Bartók's renewed contact with folksong arranging in the solo and choral adaptations of 1929–30 – adaptations, which, given the inaccessibility of the language, Bartók can hardly have hoped would themselves be great commercial successes.

It was different with the orchestral suites, and with two works that had come a little earlier, in 1928, the year of the Fourth Quartet. These rhapsodies could serve many functions. Based on folkdances – the first, according to Bartók, on Romanian and Hungarian material, the second adding also Ruthenian[3] – they provided useful lighter items for recitals he was giving with violinists: they were dedicated to two of his regular partners, Szigeti and Székely respectively, of whom Székely had already, two years earlier, arranged the 1915 Romanian Folk Dances for violin and piano. Bartók also made the first rhap-

---

[1] Hans Moldenhauer: *Anton von Webern* (London, 1978), 465.
[2] Demény (1951), ii, 110.
[3] Demény (1971), 202.

sody available for cello and piano, and both for violin and orchestra, again using a standard symphonic ensemble: the First Rhapsody in his version does include a part for cimbalom, Bartók's only music for that so Hungarian instrument, but replacement by a piano is allowed. Violinists also have the freedom to choose just half a rhapsody, for each work comes in two separable parts, headed 'Lassú' and 'Friss', and admitting a return in certain passages to that style of Hungarianism which Bartók had avoided since the period of *Kossuth*. But each rhapsody is a medley of dance tunes bringing together the Hungarian gipsy and the Romanian peasant: the latter's presence is vivid at, for instance, one point in the Second Rhapsody where Bartók writes in the 'acoustic scale' on D using a key signature for the soloist of F sharp and G sharp (similar modal signatures crop up now and again in *Mikrokosmos*). In terms of musical style these pieces are obviously relaxed, but not in their virtuoso demands, including multiple stopping, sprinklings of harmonics and quick strumming across the four strings.

Just three years later, in 1931, Bartók catered for a very different clientele in his Forty-four Duos for violins. These came about as a result of a request from Erich Doflein, violin teacher at the music academy in Freiburg, who was collecting instructive violin music and suggested Bartók might like to adapt some pieces from *For Children*. In the event Bartók preferred to write new material, but he kept to the simple style of folksong arrangement exhibited in the children's piano collection, extending it only, as he was also doing in *Mikrokosmos*, by the inclusion of tunes from a wider spread of peoples: 'Hungarian, Slovak, Rumanian, Serbian, Ruthenian and even Arab', in his own words.[4] The Duos are also inevitably conditioned by their medium, which invites canonic treatment practically throughout. No doubt this was in accordance with Bartók's tastes so soon after the Fourth Quartet, but it also serves an educational purpose, requiring the pupil to listen carefully and imitate the teacher's phrasing, even though the task may be complicated by bitonal clashes or by unusual intervals between the canonic voices. In such ways the Duos present musical challenges to compensate for their technical straightforwardness, and though their first aim is to provide teaching material, some few of the later and more difficult

---

[4] Ibid, 220.

numbers have enough spirit and cunning to make them suitable recital repertory.

For all his preoccupation with string music in the quartets, rhapsodies and duos of 1927–31, Bartók's public career at this time continued to be that of a pianist, and of course there was also the Second Piano Concerto, coming just before the Forty-four Duos. In January 1929 he made a tour of the Soviet Union, visiting Kharkov, Odessa, Leningrad and Moscow, and writing back to his mother his impressions of foreign places and customs, just as he had from America in the previous year.[5] There is something naive in his wonder at an avocado eaten in Los Angeles and a 'real skyscraper' seen in Russia, and though it may be that a childlike tone is natural in a letter addressed to mother, it would certainly seem that by this date Bartók was long past confiding his most serious thoughts to prose. No letter from his later years is remotely as revealing as those he had sent two decades before to Stefi Geyer, with whom he was able to renew acquaintance and musical collaboration on a visit to Basle immediately after his Russian journey. It was on this occasion that he got to know Paul Sacher, who was to commission his two works for string orchestra: the Music for Strings, Percussion and Celesta (1936) and the Divertimento (1939).

Within Hungary conditions were not so favourable. There was a plan at last to stage *The Miraculous Mandarin* in the year of his fiftieth birthday, 1931, but again it foundered on the brutal truths of the scenario. The award of the Corvinus Wreath, a Hungarian decoration, was no recompense, and he did not attend the presentation ceremony, though it would be unwise to read too much into this: he clearly had no high opinion of such honours, as revealed in his attitude to receiving in the same year the Chevalier de la Légion d'Honneur.[6] He seems also to have been somewhat dubious about another mark of his international standing, the invitation to sit on the Permanent Committee for Literature and Art, a body associated with the League of Nations.[7] The first meeting he attended was in Geneva in July 1931, when the one matter he seems to have been anxious to discuss was the Italian government's ban on Toscanini for

[5] Ibid, 183–7, 192–4.
[6] Ibid, 220.
[7] See Crow, 167–72.

refusing to conduct the Fascist anthem. However, the Hungarian chargé d'affaires dissuaded him from pressing this. As the only musician on the committee it was beholden on him to come up with some musical topic for consideration, and so he 'drafted something (about gramophone records)', but he well realised that any debates were quite meaningless when the committee had no financial powers, and he probably regarded later meetings – in Frankfurt in 1932, again in Geneva in 1933 and in Budapest in 1936 – as occasions to talk with other outstanding creative men, among whom he seems to have been most impressed by Thomas Mann.[8]

Apart from that, the League of Nations episode is of interest in providing some evidence that Bartók felt he could and should be speaking on themes of international import. Sometimes there is something touchingly parochial in his view: 'If the money spent in one year on armaments all over the world were allocated to folk music research, we could collect the folk music of the entire world.'[9] Evidently he did not think too deeply about international politics, but he was passionate in his defence of the objectives he took to be moral imperatives, notably the fraternity of nations. In January 1931, six months before the Geneva conference, he had written to the Romanian folklorist Octavian Beu: 'My own idea, however – of which I have been fully conscious since I found myself as a composer – is the brotherhood of peoples, brotherhood in spite of all wars and conflicts. I try – to the best of my ability – to serve this idea in my music; therefore I don't reject any influence, be it Slovakian, Rumanian, Arabic or from any other source. The source must only be clean, fresh and healthy!'[10]

In terms of musical style, Bartók had indeed provided models of fraternal relations in the Dance Suite and the violin Rhapsodies, especially; he had also proved himself quite non-chauvinist in the attention he had given to Slovak and Romanian folk music, and in his willingness to adapt scales and other musical features from those sources. He seems to have intended, however, to create a more explicit image of the 'brotherhood of peoples', for after his death was found the unfinished draft of what looks like a cantata text on the

[8] Ibid, 167–78.
[9] 'Why and How to Collect Folk Music', in *Essays*, 24.
[10] Demény (1971), 201.

subject of three countries vying with each other and clearly due to be made to see the sense of cooperation.[11] The likelihood is that this presumptive cantata was one of two he intended to add to his single work of this kind – indeed, his single major vocal work of any kind apart from *Bluebeard's Castle* and the Ady songs: the *Cantata profana* for tenor and baritone soloists, double choir and orchestra which he composed in the summer of 1930, between the Four Hungarian Folksongs for unaccompanied choir and the Second Piano Concerto.

The text of the *Cantata profana,* like the incomplete draft of its sister work, is by Bartók himself, a Magyar version of one of the Romanian colindas he so much admired: 'texts truly preserved from ancient pagan times!'[12] he called them on one occasion. This one tells of a man and his nine sons, to whom he had taught no art but hunting. Once, while engaged in this pursuit, they had gone deeper and deeper into the forest until they passed over a haunted bridge and on the other side were changed into stags. Their father then went off after them, crossed the bridge and found their tracks as stags. On discovering the nine stags themselves, he dropped to his knee and took aim, but the leader of the herd, the erstwhile dearest of his sons, bade him not fire, for otherwise they would be bound to crush and kill him. The father replied by begging them to come home, where refreshment waited and their mother grieved. But the lead stag answered that this was now impossible: their antlers could not pass through the doorway; they were made only to roam the forest and drink from springs.

It is not difficult to see this legend as an allegory of growing up; apparently it can be understood too as the Romanian people's myth of their own emergence as a separate nation. To Bartók, however, perhaps the crucial point was the accordance of dignity and rightness to a natural as opposed to a civilised state: the implicit elevation of the peasant above the townsman, and hence the preference disclosed already in *The Wooden Prince* and *The Miraculous Mandarin*, to say nothing of the composer's whole approach to folk music. Significantly, the most purely lyrical passage in the work is that where the lead stag, interpreted by the tenor soloist, sings of spring water, a passage

[11] Ibid, 349–50.
[12] 'Romanian Folk Music', in *Essays*, 120.

heard at the end of the second of the three movements and then, with embellishment, at the close of the whole work.

The title of the piece signals Bartók's relish of the pagan origins of his story, but the term 'cantata' may suggest too a nod towards Bach, though it is not the latter's church cantatas so much as his Passions that provide formal suggestions, particularly for the framing of solo 'arias' within choral narration in the second movement. Bartók would have been familiar with other applications of Baroque oratorio form to the music of his time, not least in Kodály's *Psalmus hungaricus* (1923) and Stravinsky's *Oedipus rex* (1926–7). However, the *Cantata profana* is a more continuous structure than either of these: there are no discrete numbers, and the three marked movements are joined without any break. The main structural principle is, rather, one that he had made his own in the recent Fourth Quartet: it is that of the palindrome. And indeed, since he later referred to this sort of musical symmetry as 'bridge form',[13] it may be that the magic place of the *Cantata profana* held a peculiar significance.

It is, however, the second movement, containing the dialogue between father and son, that displays the work's symmetry most obviously. There are three 'arias': one for the tenor calling on the father not to shoot, one for the baritone asking his sons to return home, and then another for the tenor singing of the lure of the wild, so forming an ABA pattern. This symmetry is intensified by the surrounding choral commentary, and also by the distinction between the tempo giusto chorus and the rubato solo declamations, these having the marking Agitato. At the end, though, there is a coda in the form of a brief duet outside the palindromic scheme, a duet of parting rather than meeting. The father, who in his 'aria' had tried to bring his sons back to a home in C, is now chromatically confused as he goes (this is his last appearance in the work), while the son, who had voiced his independence in and around F sharp, moves from this note to cadence in D Mixolydian.

D is indeed the tonic of the cantata, which even ends on a D major triad, but Mixolydian and major are by no means the only available modes. The tenor solo that trickles down over the choral texture at the end is in the 'acoustic scale' on D (D – E – F sharp – G

---

[13] Introduction to score of the Music for Strings, Percussion and Celesta.

sharp – A – B – C – D), and equally clearly the overlapping scales in the strings at the start are in a mode which is the exact inversion of this (D – C – B flat – A flat – G – F – E – D), so establishing the endpoints of the symmetrical arch, though of course the two modes are quite different in effect: the one at the start, lacking the fifth degree, lends itself to music of a chromatic kind, whereas the 'acoustic scale' is commonly associated in Bartók with music of the most open diatonic character.[14]

There is another way in which the short last movement, recapitulating the story in choral narration, is both equivalent and antithesis of the first movement, in which the chorus tells of the family, the hunt and the magical transformation. Those three parts of the first movement are musically distinguished, the first being done to moderato music around D, the hunt described in a vigorous fugue in F and the enchantment taking place slowly around A, so that the whole movement outlines a rising D minor triad. Once again, the finale is related by inversion, which in this case produces a rising G major triad, the three brief sections being centred on G, B and D respectively.

As in the Fourth Quartet, the large-scale symmetry is mirrored on the smallest scale by other reflective details: passages which move in contrary motion, places where a melodic idea is immediately succeeded by its inversion, and rippling canonic imitations. The choral medium lends itself particularly well to this last, and the *Cantata profana* is fuller of canons and invertible counterpoint than any other major work by Bartók, often with the double choir providing eight parts, whether to generate complex textures or to double four-part polyphony in fourths or fifths:

[14] See Lendvai, 67ff.

Ex. 55

Cantata profana: first movement

This example comes from the point in the second movement where the chorus is telling of the father taking aim at the stags, and Bartók's apt image of impending catastrophe is a quick canon at the octave and unison with only a crotchet to separate adjacent entries. The tumbling of lines over one another keeps all, or all but one, of the notes of the Phrygian scale on G sounding all the time: a characteristic use of the mode as a vertical unit.

Passages like this make the *Cantata profana* a very challenging work for the choir, and it is challenging too for the soloists, especially for the tenor, whose high register is not spared at all at the impassioned climax of concern and independence addressed to the father in his first 'aria':

143

Ex. 56

Cantata profana: second movement

Bartók was obliged to alter the cruellest bar here for the singer at the Hungarian première in 1936:[15] the easier version substituted for the falling major seconds a rising contour, C double sharp – D sharp – F sharp – A, which opens out the chromatic compactness essential to the intensity of the original and also muddles the canonic relationship with the woodwind line that follows. One can understand why Bartók should have been reluctant to tinker with a score so tightly bound by imitative and harmonic connection, and so powerfully expressive as it stands. But one can understand too why a work so difficult to perform lay unheard for nearly four years before its first performance (by the BBC, keen promoters of Bartók and his music in the later 1920s and 1930s), and why it has remained a rare visitor to the concert platform.

[15] See Demény (1971), 252.

10

Symmetries and contrasts

The period between the composition of the *Cantata profana* and its first performance, from 1930 to 1934, was one of relatively slower creative achievement. In 1930–1 came the Second Piano Concerto and the Forty-four Duos, but after that there was another of those gaps that punctuate Bartók's output. It would be possible to explain this in terms of his commitments as a pianist, playing the Second Concerto all over Europe in 1933–4, and as an unconvinced cultural diplomat on the League of Nations committee, but he had been no less busy in 1927–8 when he had managed to write two string quartets. And in fact his productivity began to increase again when he took on a new and time-consuming task, for in 1934, at his own request, he was relieved of his teaching post at the Academy of Music and given a salaried appointment with the Academy of Sciences to work on classifying at last the corpus of Hungarian folk music that had been growing steadily throughout the span of more than a quarter of a century since his first collecting trips with Kodály. This task he took up in September 1934; the Fifth Quartet, his first work for three years apart from the choral Székely Songs and some orchestrations, he wrote between August 6 and September 6 of the same year.

Like its two major instrumental predecessors, the Fourth Quartet and the Second Piano Concerto, this Fifth Quartet is a five-part palindrome, but though the existence of five distinct movements suggests a strong connection with the Fourth Quartet, it is the concerto that is the nearer relation, formally and harmonically. On the largest scale, the Fifth Quartet and the Second Concerto both centre on a scherzo, enfolded within the slow movement of the concerto and between the parallel slow movements of the quartet. At the more local level, too, these works are alike in that they are much more diatonic than most of Bartók's music of the 1920s. Here again the *Cantata profana* provides a bridge, for it was the first of his non-folksong works to conclude with a major or minor triad since

The Wooden Prince of a decade and a half before, paving the way for the very strong G major quality of the Second Piano Concerto. The Fifth Quartet is not tied to the major-minor system in at all the same manner, but then it belongs in a very different genre: Bartók must have realised that any concerto must be a popular success or it is nothing, whereas quartets can be addressed to a more intimate public. The comparison ought therefore to be between works of the sane kind, and certainly the Fifth Quartet is more different from the Fourth than the Second Piano Concerto is different from the First.

The main harmonic difference is that central pitches – if not always tonics in the old major-minor sense – are much more apparent than is the case in the earlier quartet, and if there are many fewer triads here than in the Second Piano Concerto, that is because the tonality of the Fifth Quartet is one of notes rather than chords. There can, for instance, be no mistaking the fact that the outer movements have their home on B flat, but on B flat the note rather than in B flat the key: both movements end on B flat in octaves, without any triadic suggestion. But of course the major-minor system is not forgotten. Right at its start the quartet seems to insist on its independence by claiming E, its augmented fourth, as its dominant, and this tritone relation is of crucial significance in the outer movements. However, the arrival of E also brings with it the introduction of a dominant E's normal tonic, A, so producing a tritone plus fourth or fifth conglomerate (B flat – E – A) typical of Bartók's harmony since *The Miraculous Mandarin*.

However, the emphasis in this quartet is on individual notes rather than chords, and the harmonic colouring is achieved quite as much by horizontal as by vertical means: in other words, the meaning of a note is indicated not only by what it sounds with but by how it is introduced. So much of the Fifth Quartet is made up of accented notes preceded by motivic patterns that the work might almost be called a quartet of cadences, and some of the possible effects of these cadences may be illustrated with reference to the central scherzo. The following example shows the first, second and last appearance of the main theme, which owes its identity more to the unusual and omnipresent metrical pattern (another instance of 'Bulgarian rhythm') than to melodic contour – in which, indeed, melodic contour constantly shifts to shed a different light on the principal note:

Ex. 57

String Quartet no. 5: third movement

The first quotation may be described as being in C sharp Dorian, and its shaping as an arpeggio in thirds which begins on C sharp makes that note a decisive tonic. The second, most easily assigned to C sharp Phrygian, compresses the motif and is a little more equivocal. The third is in a symmetrical mode of alternating major and minor seconds, and here the symmetry unsettles any firm feeling of tonality so that the final landing on C sharp is insouciant.

If the significance of notes can be subtly changed by such means, the structural backbone of the quartet in terms of its central pitches remains quite clear, and the formal outline is correspondingly sharp by comparison with the Fourth Quartet. The first movement, for example, is built on an ascending whole-tone scale from B flat, though the meaning of that central pitch changes as the movement proceeds. Its first subject is anchored quite decisively to B flat, often despite itself; the second strives desperately to get away from C; and the third, smoother than either of these, is in a D that looks always towards its dominant of A. The development is then framed within the sphere of E, a tritone removed from the original B flat, after which the three subjects are recapitulated, but with their senses reversed. The mellifluous third subject comes back first, in an F sharp arrived at from the subdominant of B; then comes the second digging down towards A flat, and finally the first chained again to B flat. This feeling of reversal is achieved by inverting not only the themes but the harmony, as may be indicated by a comparison of the third subject in its initial and recapitulated forms:

Ex. 58
String Quartet no. 5: first movement

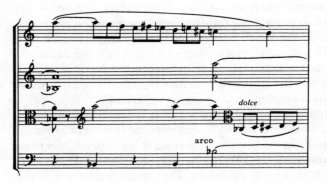

By contrast with the case in the Fourth Quartet (see Ex. 53), the fact of recapitulation is here quite unmistakable, but no less so is the fact of inversion.

Games of inversion are still more intensively pursued in the finale, which is even more packed with canons and small-scale mirrorings than the Fourth Quartet or the *Cantata profana*. It is another example of a big, fast 2/4 movement in Bartók, combining the picturesque detail of a rondo with the continuous sweep of a sonata structure. At the end, as in the Fourth Quartet, it rejoins the path that the first movement had taken in concluding, but it also remembers other movements. Indeed, the symmetry of this quartet is constantly and nicely being undermined by the gathering of memories: perhaps the first striking example comes when the scherzo in its sixteenth bar recalls a prominent motif from the preceding adagio. In the case of the finale, the memories are mostly of the first movement, as the palindrome requires, but there is one wholly extraordinary passage in which an idea from the adagio reappears in thoroughly degraded form, as if it were being played on a barrel organ. This is the first instance of naked parody in Bartók since *Kossuth* thirty years before, and it is all the more disruptive for coming in a work where surface detail seems so much to be conditioned by general principle. Parody is, however, no more than an extreme form of the technique of variation that is central to this quartet, affecting the presentation of thematic material in ways described with reference to the scherzo, and making it possible for themes to have quite different functions in different movements, as has also been indicated.

The relative harmonic and formal clarity of the Fifth Quartet by comparison with the Fourth is allied with a relative absence of special effects. There are many fewer intrusions of the Bartók pizzicato or of col legno, sul ponticello, glissandos and harmonics. However, the Fifth Quartet is very far from being a drab piece. The trio at the centre of the scherzo – and therefore at the centre of the entire work – is an astonishing conception, with a simple folktune heard against drones and a very fast ostinato to which eventually are added its inversion and its double at the major second, strict polyphony here dissolving into a textural effect in a way that looks forward to the music of Ligeti. The two slow movements, an Adagio molto in second place and an Andante in fourth, are also powerfully atmospheric, besides being clearly linked in their motifs, particularly as they start. The adagio could easily pass as another image of 'night music', with its twittering trills in extreme registers, its chorales luminous with fifths in the manner of the Second Concerto's middle movement, and its timbral particularities (this is where the work's only Bartók pizzicatos come). The fourth movement departs from a vaguely similar world, and similar material, to become a nocturne of a more human sort, one of highly expressive ideas that form themselves and dissolve over textures vibrant with repeating figures.

It is symptomatic of the change in Bartók's style around 1930 that the movements of the Fifth Quartet should outline not an augmented triad – as in the Fourth Quartet and the original version of another B flat work, the op. 14 Suite – but a minor one, for the two slow movements centre on D and G respectively; the central scherzo, with its C sharp, then supplies the tritone clash so essential also to the local harmony. In the manner of its construction, however, the Fifth Quartet is the apotheosis of techniques of symmetry to be found throughout Bartók's work, and hence a direct continuation from the works of 1926–8. Nothing shows this more clearly than the finale. Much of the material here, not excluding the movement of disruptive irony near the end, springs from a motif announced at the start in vigorous unisons, a motif which divides a fourth into two adjacent major seconds and a minor second. The following passage shows this motif in contrapuntal elaboration, the two violins in unison canon with a descending version in the major mode, the other two instruments also in unison canon with an ascending Mixolydian form:

Ex. 59
String Quartet no. 5: fifth movement

The same motif also governs the harmony at the next level up, since
the principal notes of the scale fragments execute a downwards
movement from D to C, then B flat, then A.

Such passages give to the Fifth Quartet a feeling of obsessional
neatness which might be enervating were the musical substance not
so powerful in its harmonic frictions and rhythmic drive. As it is, the
impression is one of a highly complex harnessing of highly complex
forces: the one moment when the reins are slackened, allowing the
emergence of the barrel-organ tune, reveals the difficulty of the
undertaking. At the same time, the close structure controls the
expressiveness of the ideas. When motifs are answered so often by
imitations and inversions, or when they are systematically assembled
and dismembered, they become elements of musical architecture as
much as agents of musical expression, and in that respect the Fifth
Quartet is Bartók's ultimate achievement in taking hold of the unruly
ideas that had been occurring to him for thirty years.

He was well aware that this development in his music was
something he shared with his contemporaries, that the great richness
of *Bluebeard's Castle* and *The Miraculous Mandarin* was paralleled
in the early atonal music of Schoenberg and the first Dyagilev ballets
of Stravinsky at very much the same time, and that the tight motivic
integration and formality of his more recent style bore comparison
with Schoenberg's serialism and Stravinsky's neoclassicism – not in
detail, of course, but in motivation and effect. His perception of this

relationship was clear, since he felt no obligation to take sides in the Schoenberg-Stravinsky antagonism and could, as an interested observer at ISCM festivals and collector of new scores,[1] see the contemporary musical world whole. Indeed, one measure of his perspicacity is that his judgements now seem commonplace, even though at the time few others could see through the welter of conflicting trends. As he told an interviewer in 1932: 'In nearly every great modern musical work one may, in fact, perceive an effort towards a clarity of construction, a rigorous severity of composition coupled with a tendency to do without flourishes.'[2] And in his own case he traces this to the influence of peasant tunes, 'the classical examples of the art of expressing any musical idea with the highest perfection, in the shortest form, and using the simplest and most direct means.'[3]

Much of his travelling around this time was occasioned by folk music work as well as concert giving. In the spring of 1932 he attended a conference on Arab music in Cairo; in 1934 he studied recordings of Romanian folk music in Bucharest; and in November 1936 there was his last collecting expedition, to Turkey. Meanwhile in Budapest, where he lived in a rather splendid villa from 1932 to 1940, he worked on the classification of Hungarian folk music, from which there came two choral works that were his only compositions of 1935, the year after the Fifth Quartet. These were the twenty-seven Two- and Three-part Choruses for treble voices and *From Olden Times* for men's choir, both based on folksong texts with original, though naturally folksong-flavoured, music. In style and shape *From Olden Times* recalls the *Cantata profana*, since again it is riven with strict counterpoint and has a three-part form moving from chromatic darkness in the first song, 'Nobody's unhappier than the peasant', to pentatonic light in the third, 'Nobody's happier than the peasant': as these opening lines suggest, the two songs are also textually both similar and antithetical, the former bemoaning the peasant's lot of hard work, oppression and poverty, the latter exulting in his free and natural life, while the centrepiece is a short and lively dance song. The Two- and Three-part Choruses also

[1] See Vera Lampert: 'Zeitgenössisches Musik in Bartók's Notensammlung', *Documenta bartókiana*, v (Budapest, 1977), 142–68.

[2] Magda Vámos: 'A 1932 Interview with Bartók', Crow, 183.

[3] Ibid, 185.

celebrate the joy of peasant existence, not primarily in their texts but in the fresh diatonic purity of their musical language. This was something Bartók had achieved also in his other children's collections, *Mikrokosmos* and the Forty-four Duos, and the twenty-seven choruses are very much comparable with the latter group in their liking for canon. However, the vocal medium can embody such purity more absolutely, especially when children's voices are at issue, and these little songs contain an essence of Bartóks simplicity not found elsewhere.

They even impressed the composer himself. Bartók was not prone to express himself favourably about his own music, but in a letter after an early performance of eighteen of these choruses, in Budapest on 7 May 1937, he commented on the 'great experience' of hearing the 'freshness and gaiety' of the children's voices, reminding him in their naturalness of 'the unspoilt sound of peasant singing'.[4] He does not mention that at the same concert *From Olden Times* also was sung, and introduces the fact that he played a selection from *Mikrokosmos* only to say that these pieces 'were not so important as the children's choruses', though the Hungarian language, from which Bartók's music in the twenty-seven choruses and in *From Olden Times* is inseparable, has inevitably placed these works at a distance from choirs and audiences in other countries.

It was, nevertheless, to the wider world that Bartók was generally looking. The Budapest Opera revived *The Wooden Prince* in 1935 and *Bluebeard's Castle* in 1936, but still *The Miraculous Mandarin* was missing, and still much of his music was viewed with suspicion on account of its modernity and its internationalism: in 1935 he was insultingly offered the Greguss Medal for his First Suite, a work three decades old (of course he declined the award, fiercely). He may have relented his decision not to play his own music in Budapest – the May 1937 concert was a homecoming there – but the main works were being written for foreign performance, as indeed had been the case since the solo piano works of 1926. Of all Bartók's later major compositions, only the Fourth Quartet had its first performance in Budapest, and from 1934 onwards most of his works were commissioned by foreign patrons: Elizabeth Sprague Coolidge, the American amateur of chamber music, in the case of the Fifth

---

[4] Demény (1971), 257.

Quartet; Paul Sacher in the case of the next instrumental work, the Music for Strings, Percussion and Celesta (1936).

The title of his work is slightly misleading, since the celesta is not specially more important than the other tuned percussion instruments Bartók uses: piano, harp, xylophone and timpani. However, singling it out does draw attention to the fact that the work is conceived for string orchestra (in fact for two string orchestras placed on opposite sides of the platform) with the addition of both unpitched and pitched percussion instruments. Bartók's liking for the latter had been evident in many of his earlier orchestral scores, especially *The Miraculous Mandarin*, and since the First Piano Concerto, with its careful instructions to the percussion players, he had shown a care for precisely articulated noise effects. The Music for Strings, Percussion and Celesta brings these interests together with colourful string scoring that comes out of the three recent quartets. It also, and again the title indicates as much, avoids being a symphony quite as cunningly and decisively as had the earlier suites. There are, to be sure, four movements, but the sonata allegro is second not first, and the highly intricate construction in the style of the Fifth Quartet is fundamentally antisymphonic because it is about symmetry rather than steady change.

This symmetrical patterning is strongly marked in the slow first movement, which is based on a chromatic theme heard first on A in the violas of both orchestras:

Ex. 60
Music for Strings, Percussion and Celesta: first movement

Successive canonic entries then take the theme both ways around the circle of fifths: up to E, down to D, up again to B, down again to G, and so on until both upward and downward steps have arrived at E flat, the tritone opposite of the initial A. This is the climax, accentuated by the loudest dynamic level and the most open harmony, with E flat played in repeated octaves by all the violins and violas. Then more quickly, and with the theme often only in inverted fragments, the steps retrace themselves back to A, which is reached with the theme played simultaneously right way up and in inversion at a distance of two octaves under a shower of celesta arpeggios. The movement ends with a microcosm of itself as violins play scales in contrary motion from A out to E flat and back to A again.

Indeed, so beguiling is the structure of this movement that attention may be diverted not only from the expressiveness of the theme but also from its musical niceties, which can be explored the more readily because in its first presentation it is a rare example of monody in Bartók before the late Sonata for solo violin. It can most readily be analysed as being based on part of an asymmetrical scale which alternates minor thirds and pairs of minor seconds:

Ex. 61

This is the form of the scale used tentatively in the first phrase and then fully in the second, which ends on what can be regarded as the 'final' of B flat, the only note to appear in both ascending and descending versions (it is accented and metrically emphasised on the way up in both phrases). The third phrase transposes the scale up a semitone and runs it backwards; the prominence given earlier to C (crotchet duration) as being two steps up from the final in the descending form is now taken by D sharp (accent and first beat), similarly two steps up from the final of B in the new descending form:

Ex. 62

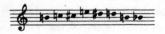

Finally the fourth phrase moves back down a semitone but keeps the scale in its reversed form, so that there is a feeling of symmetrical return to B flat.

Clearly, to analyse the whole of the Music in even this

elementary way would require more pages than can be accommodated here, but such a study might show how the precision of this composition – the sense it conveys of working like a well-oiled machine – is dependent on a choice of materials with exact functions, like the theme's quartering into statement, expansion, retrograde development and retrograde restatement, this last being perfectly conclusive because it preserves the pitch outline of the third phrase while re-introducing the rhythmic hiccough of the earlier two.

The remaining three movements complete a slow-fast-slow-fast pattern that may be compared with that in the Third Quartet, though in terms of its harmonic style the Music for Strings, Percussion and Celesta occupies a middle ground between the very diatonic Second Piano Concerto and the more blistering Fifth Quartet, just as it comes between those works in genre. It also has the same kind of five-part palindrome in its third movement, a nocturne more eerily picturesque than the parallel adagio in the Fifth Quartet: not for nothing is it one of the most popular borrowings for background music to films of a macabre or mysterious nature. The second movement begins by rousingly exploiting the possibilities of antiphonal exchange between the string orchestras, possibilities which had remained dormant in the opening andante. What results is often a quick dialogue that adds another dimension to sonata contrast and that also helps in the speedy development of themes by statement and altered restatement. A more permanent feature of Bartók's sonata structures, to be found as early as the Second Quartet, is the recapitulation in triple metre of material first heard in duple, and tonally too the movement is characteristic in being grounded in C with a prominent tritone relation. The first two movements together thus outline the diminished seventh chord A – C – E flat – F sharp, which is a central feature of the adagio that follows: this is, therefore, another example of Bartók's use of a symmetrical division of the octave to underpin a whole work. The finale duly returns to A, but now unashamedly to A major, sounded in strummed chords at the start right across the first orchestra. In form it is a rondo cum dance medley of the sort to be found in the second parts of the violin rhapsodies.

Opening thus from a crabbed chromatic space into an open diatonic one, the Music for Strings, Percussion and Celesta takes the same path as the Fourth Quartet or the *Cantata profana*. However, its arrival in new territory is even more firmly marked, for near the

end of the movement there is a wholesale repeat of the first movement's theme, played in the 'acoustic scale' on C and warmly
harmonised with triads:

Ex. 63
Music for Strings, Percussion and Celesta: fourth movement

This is something quite different from the variational technique of
the Fourth Quartet: here the theme reappears as a quotation from
the earlier movement, as it does too in the adagio, whose five
subsections are punctuated by its four phrases. The second movement exemplifies Bartók's more usual technique of unification by
similarities of motif (the arch shape of phrases, the prominence of
minor thirds and minor seconds); its successors give the resulting
unity an explicit signpost, which may perhaps be taken as Bartók's
warning to himself of the dangers of restrictedness and merely
mechanical perfection in music so closely structured. In fact the
danger is avoided. However finely constructed the music may be, it
sounds natural, and again the opening theme may be taken as a test
case. Something of its structuring has already been indicated, but the
impression is of a natural musical stanza, expressing a musical idea
with the perfection, brevity and simplicity Bartók admired in
folksong.

On 21 January 1937 he attended the first performance of the
Music for Strings, Percussion and Celesta in Basle, during a busy
period of travel that included concerts and recitals in London, Paris
and Brussels. He was not to be able to undertake such a tour again. In
the summer he and Kodály came under attack from a Nazi sym-
pathiser in the press, when once more the main charge was
insufficiency of nationalism. In October 1937 Bartók made his
position clear by refusing Hungarian radio permission to beam his
music to German and Italian stations; earlier that year he had
decided against a holiday in the Dolomites because of his detestation

of the fascists. Instead the Bartóks spent their summer vacation in Carinthia, where the composer probably began sketching a new work that had also been commissioned from Basle, this time to mark the tenth anniversary of the local ISCM group. They had asked for a chamber work, but what was in Bartók's mind was not one of the usual combinations. As he wrote at the time of the first performance: 'For some years now I have been planning to compose a work for piano and percussion. Slowly, however, I have become convinced that one piano does not sufficiently balance the frequently very sharp sounds of the percussion.'[5] Hence the Sonata for two pianos and percussion, and hence too the centring of the music in the keyboards, with the two percussion players providing for the most part accentuation, background, punctuation and rhythmic crossfire rather than primary thematic material: the one outstanding exception comes in the finale, where the rondo theme belongs to the xylophone.

In its musical constitution as in its instrumental formation, therefore, the Sonata is closely comparable with *Les noces*. Both works call for xylophone and timpani, capable of connecting with the high and low registers of the piano. Both, too, have similar requirements among the noise instruments, with Bartók adding a tam tam to Stravinsky's ensemble of drums, cymbals and triangle. The main difference is that he has no use for the bell and crotales that resound at the end of *Les noces*, though he certainly does have use for much that Stravinsky invented in his multiple piano writing: the chords doubled in three or four different registers, the polymodal clashes between pianos or between hands, and above all, as in the similarly indebted Piano Sonata, the percussive style. That helps to make the partnership with percussion instruments natural, as before in the slow movements of the First and Second Concertos, whereas when Bartók uses the piano with melody instruments, in the violin sonatas or *Contrasts*, the disharmony of sound is brought out keenly. The case in the Sonata for pianos and percussion may be indicated by one prominent statement of the first subject in the opening movement, where the theme in the first piano is sharpened by the xylophone and answered by side drums, against the second piano's characteristic background for this work of scales in triads:

[5] 'Béla Bartók über sein neuestes Werk', *Nationalzeitung* (Basle, 13 January 1938), in *Essays*.

Ex. 64

Sonata for Two Pianos and Percussion: first movement

Such writing, largely conditioned by the medium, gives the work a geometric feel, and indeed Lendvai's analysis of this score[6] would indicate that it is filled with all the artifices of his music in the last dozen years. Some of them are obvious, like the typical use of inversion to give a thematic answer (see the example above), or the canons and mirror canons that crowd here as much as in the Fourth Quartet, or the stabilising of the music around the points of a diminished seventh chord: this is the same one as in the Music for Strings, Percussion and Celesta, but with the main direction taken now by C (the finale again interprets that main direction in openly diatonic terms). Other conceits of the Sonata are less apparent to the ear: notably the construction of phrases and whole movements on proportions derived from the Fibonacci series or the Golden Section. However, the arithmetical fit is so good that it is hard to believe it is purely coincidental, even in the absence of any documentary evidence that Bartók pre-planned his music in this way. Fittingly, Lendvai has called the Sonata the 'Makrokosmos' to *Mikrokosmos*, which one may take to acknowledge not only its extension of structural principles from among the six volumes that were not being completed, but also its accommodation within one tight form of much of the solo pieces' variety of texture and movement.

The first movement, Bartók's longest sonata structure, contains its variety within an almost unchanging 9/8 metre, which the three subjects press at different rates and differently divide. The first, quoted above, is marked by three crotchets followed by three quavers at an Allegro molto; the second is rather slower and divides the bar into irregular and changingly arranged units of 4+2+3 (it is, therefore, a highly sophisticated Bulgarian dance); the third sets out from leaping upward sixths and chases off in iambic quaver-crotchet patterns. In the recapitulation, if such it can be called when it is so developed, the second theme comes back first in inversion, followed by the third theme in a substantial fugal passage and then the first in a short coda.

After this the slow movement has a night-music atmosphere reminiscent of the adagio from the Music for Strings, and it is similarly symmetrical in shape. The opening has the first piano moving softly and slowly against unpitched percussion in the

---

[6] Op cit, passim.

manner of the andante from the First Concerto, but when this music comes back it is transferred to the second piano and played below rippling bitonal scales in the first. The central section is much occupied with staccato quintuplets and with a theme in rich parallel harmony marked 'molto espr. la melodia', though the 'melodia' turns out to be little more than a falling and rising chromatic scale. Not so the principal idea of the finale, which is in the 'acoustic scale' on C, therefore retaining the tritones of the first movement but using them not for crashing discord so much as to spice the splendidly normal fifth.

The première of the Sonata was given in Basle on 16 January 1938, with Bartók and his wife at the pianos. Ditta, like Márta before her, had given up any thought of a public career on her marriage to Bartók, and quite possibly she would never have been brought forward had it not been for the needs of the Sonata. However, having established his marital duo Bartók took pains to sustain it. He and Ditta gave public recitals together, and for them he composed more repertory: a set of Seven Pieces from *Mikrokosmos* (1940) and a version of the Second Suite (1941). More immediately, though, there were other tasks and other worries. The Swiss interlude, distinguished by the clean lines, the self-demonstrating forms and the constructive sophistication of both the Music for Strings and the Sonata for pianos and percussion, this interlude was rudely brought to an end, so it would seem by public and private events that sapped the great energy and confidence of the music written for Basle.

Within two months of the first performance of the Sonata came the Austrian Anschluss. A month after that, on 13 April 1938, Bartók was writing to his Basle friend Frau Müller-Widmann to ask if she would take care of his manuscripts; a year later he decided that even Switzerland was not safe enough, and had the material transferred to London. To Müller-Widmann, also, he wrote of his utter loathing for the Nazis and his grief that so many educated Hungarians had become supporters of Hitler. On a more practical level, it was no longer possible for his scores to be published by Universal Edition. Boosey & Hawkes, who had been London agents for Universal, then became his publishers, the first score that came out under their imprint being that of the Sonata for pianos and percussion.

This was followed by a piece commissioned by Benny Goodman,

a great patron of serious composers, who asked Bartók for a two-part work in the style of the violin Rhapsodies that could fit onto the sides of a 78 rpm record. The scoring was to be for clarinet, violin and piano, with the violin included presumably because Goodman had been put up to the idea by Szigeti. In the event Bartók over-stepped the time limit and provided not two movements but three, with a central 'Pihenő' ('Relaxation') to separate the moderato 'Verbunkos' from the final quick 'Sebes'. As a result the finished work partakes of both the popular style of the violin rhapsodies and the more esoteric manner of the quartets: that may be the explanation of the title *Contrasts* quite as much as any conflict of sonority in the use together of a stringed instrument, a woodwind and a key-board. There was, after all, a history of such associations in the clarinet trios of Mozart and Brahms, not to mention two more recent works for exactly the same combination as Bartók's: Stravinsky's suite of arrangements from *The Soldier's Tale* and Berg's version of the adagio from his Chamber Concerto. As one might expect, there are touches of Stravinsky in *Contrasts*, as much of *Renard* as of *The Soldier's Tale*, testifying to the continuing importance that Stravinsky's 'Russian period' held for Bartók: nothing else after Debussy influenced him anything like as much. Nevertheless, the even continuity and the chamber-musical exchanges that master potential contrasts are not at all Stravinskyan.

Nor do they represent all of Bartók. No doubt because of its origins as a lighter work, *Contrasts* is relatively straightforward in form and tonality. Each of the movements is ternary and has struc-tural events happening quite slowly, and although the tritone is prominently used throughout for its gipsy zest, the harmony is fundamentally unruffled. The keys are such as will flatter the clarinet: the first two movements employ the instrument in A and are rooted in A; the finale turns to the B flat clarinet, with the clarinet in A reserved for the middle section, and it duly ends in B flat. Paradoxi-cally it is the central 'Relaxation' that is least relaxed, with its limpid doublings of image and reflection in the melody instruments and its night-music twitterings: like the Sonata for pianos and percussion, this is another development of principles and sonorities from *Mikrokosmos*, though on a smaller scale. Its companions have more the extroversion of concerto movements. The first gives the lead to the clarinet, and combines the proud, march-like verbunkos with a hint of jazz: a homage to Goodman borrowed, as Bartók was the first to remark,[7] from Ravel's Violin Sonata, which he and Szigeti played. At the end there is a clarinet cadenza, with a characteristic gesture of upwards and downwards wobbling scale figures, recalling the seduction ploys of *The Miraculous Mandarin*. In the finale, to balance, the violin is brought forward, or rather the violins, since the movement starts with the player using an instrument tuned in tritones. He then switches to a normally tuned violin for the bulk of the movement, including a cadenza this time in the middle.

Bartók finished *Contrasts* in September 1938, but the first performance in New York four months later included only the outer movements, played as 'Rhapsody' with the subtitle 'Two Dances': the definitive title only emerged the next year, when Goodman, Szigeti and Bartók recorded the work for Columbia in New York during the composer's second American tour. In the interim he completed another violin work which he had begun straight after the Sonata for pianos and percussion in August 1937 but put aside to write *Contrasts*: this was a concerto for Zoltán Székely, finished on the last day of 1938 and first performed in Amsterdam the next spring. Amsterdam, like London and Basle, was one of those cities where Bartók had found more favour than he had in Budapest, but on this occasion he was unable to be present, and was relieved, when eventually he did hear the work in October 1943, to find that 'there was no trouble with regard to the instrumentation'.[8] Presumably, acute though his technique was, he was in the common habit of checking his ideas against a live performance before publication.

The Violin Concerto, which has become known as no. 2 since the posthumous revival of the work written for Stefi Geyer, has sometimes been taken as opening a new period in Bartók's output, and indeed it is, like *Contrasts*, very much richer in triads and generally more openly diatonic than the works of the mid-1930s. Where before Bartók had used a clear harmonic light only in his finales, as in the Fourth Quartet or the Music for Strings, here that light shines throughout, and it would not be too much of a travesty to describe the concerto as being in B major. However, this was not entirely new. Bartók's previous concerto, the second for piano, had

---

[7] See Ferenc Bónis: 'Quotations in Bartók's Music', *Studia musicologica*, v (1963), 355ff.
[8] Demény (1971), 329.

been similarly frank in its tonality, and there are other links too between the works: the cheerful confidence of the orchestral writing, the placing of ripping canons in the brass, or the association of the soloist in the slow movement with a group of like-minded individuals, in this case high woodwind, harp and celesta rather than percussion, the connection being one of pitch range more than sonority. Moreover, the B major of the work is very definitely a Bartókian B major, as may be illustrated with reference to the main theme of the first movement:

Ex. 65
Violin Concerto no. 2: first movement

The presence of minor third and minor sixth, as well as the major degrees, is typical; so too is the precarious emphasis on the flattened seventh, the final turn up through a tritone and the change in the division of each bar in this generous 4/4 (the original marking of 'Tempo di verbunkos' underlines a relationship with the similar swaggering irregular march at the start of *Contrasts*).

What is outwardly serene and secure in this concerto is thus undercut by influences remaining from folk music: rhythmic in the changing interpretation of the metre, intervallic in the Hungarian fourths and harmonic in the colouring of the major mode here with, in particular, Dorian and Mixolydian, Dorian B suggesting a relationship with A major because it uses the same notes. Sometimes the confidence of the movement is more rudely shattered, with a blistering tutti (bars 111–12) or with an excursion into a wilderness where tonal harmony has no rules to cope: that of quarter-tones. Just before the strenuous cadenza Bartók introduces these to surround and question a unison D, and the effect is profoundly unsettling in a work otherwise so supreme in its gestures.

The story goes that Bartók wanted to write a large-scale set of variations in answer to Székely's commission, but that the violinist demurred, wanting a real concerto. This Bartók duly supplied, in three movements lasting for over half an hour altogether. However, he was pleased to point out to Székely that he had fulfilled his own desires as well, since not only is the slow movement a set of variations in free style, but the finale is, at bottom, a wholesale variant of the first movement: again the Second Piano Concerto proves itself a neighbour work. There is thus a deep-running irony between the explicit form, that of a concerto, and the implicit form, that of a set of variations. Possibly one should understand the harmonic structure of the work in the same terms, and see the Dorian flavour, the subtension of a B minor (relative minor of D major) and the spoiling of D in the quarter-tone passage as evidences of ironic reference to the key of the great concertos of Beethoven, Brahms and Tchaikovsky.

However that may be, Bartók was plainly concerning himself also with nearer colleagues, for the second subject of the first movement is a melody using each of the twelve notes once only, except for A, with which it both begins and ends (and which underpins it):

Ex. 66
Violin Concerto no. 2: first movement

One cannot believe that this was accidental on the part of a composer so meticulous and a folklorist so methodical. Equally, it hardly seems likely that Bartók was setting out to show Schoenberg how to write tonal twelve-note music. Rather the explanation is to be found within the context of the concerto. At this point the instabilities latent in the first theme have begun to reveal themselves, and to cause a dispersal of energies into chromatic scales running upwards and downwards. The violin then enters with the twelve-note melody above, not denying the chromaticism but finding within it the means for reassembling features of the first theme: note, for example, the similar pattern in the second and third bars of four quavers followed by a crotchet, the last interval being a falling minor third. As these brief examples may indicate, therefore, the relatively relaxed quality of the Second Violin Concerto is that of sovereign mastery rather than deliberate blandness, a mastery that has learned to accommodate even such unruly assailants as the chromatic scale.

Another commission from Székely was for a new quartet, and there was also a second work to be written for Sacher's chamber orchestra. In July 1939 the Bartóks were back in Switzerland, and the following month the composer stayed on as Sacher's guest, provided with a cottage in which he was to work on the promised piece, 'the invited guest of a patron of the arts' as he described himself in a letter to his elder son.[9] Sacher duly got his music: the same letter notes that the Divertimento for strings was written in fifteen days. Bartók also made a start on his Sixth Quartet, which he completed back in Budapest in November.

The Divertimento is unashamedly light music, though in large and small it shares many features with the Second Violin Concerto: for instance, its F major is similarly, if less complexly, disturbed by modality (the main theme of the finale is blithely Mixolydian), and the slow movement is in and around the submediant. There are also visitations from other works. The slow, effortful chromatic march upwards in the central adagio comes almost bodily from *The Miraculous Mandarin*, and there are games of canon and inversion that recall the Fifth Quartet and the Music for Strings, though the Divertimento is based much more on tunes than on malleable motifs, which limits the extent to which such games can be pursued. Gaiety, however, is no more universal here than is serenity in the Second

Ex. 67
Divertimento: third movement

[9] Ibid, 278.

Violin Concerto. At one moment in the finale, for instance, a brief fugato begins to congeal into a slow cadence from inside which a solo cello takes an independent path (see Ex. 67). Admittedly this is an isolated and extreme case, but it is symptomatic of the tension lying beneath this clean-cut work: the tension, quite possibly, of producing entertainment music to order.

Once again, it was the circumstances of the commission that dictated a lighter manner, though other musicians than Bartók were experiencing the same move towards a greater diatonic clarity in the immediate pre-war years: Stravinsky, Prokofiev and Hindemith all provide parallels. One may wonder, indeed, whether Bartók was beginning to interest himself in the more recent Stravinsky, perhaps in the new 'Dumbarton Oaks' Concerto (1937–8), with which the Divertimento shares a certain, though in Bartók's case slighter, feel of the concerto grosso (Stravinsky's second small-scale concerto, in D, was to be another work for the Basle strings). Yet it hardly seems necessary to invoke influence to explain a common movement so plainly widespread, and one that was even to impinge on Bartók in the genre he had made most his own, the string quartet.

Coming after the five-part palindromes of the Fourth and Fifth Quartets, the Sixth brings a return to four-movement form, though not of a traditional kind. Apparently Bartók's original plan was for four separate movements, but during the course of composition this changed to a novel scheme in which each movement is introduced by a slow introduction, headed 'Mesto' ('sad'). A marking so indicative of expression rather than speed is rare in Bartók, and though there is a venerable antecedent for this particular one in the quartet literature – in Beethoven's first 'Razumovsky' quartet – its use here signals a new personal involvement. Perhaps the first indications of this had come in the Second Violin Concerto, especially at that point in the slow movement when the soloist's first contribution is suddenly answered by the orchestra sweeping down in lush harmony.

More generally, Bartók's stylistic development in the late 1930s is associated with a greater inwardness of expression, since for him major-minor tonality would seem to have been the language of personal feeling, which chromatic and modal alterations made more objective (it was the other way about for Schoenberg). However, there is little preparation in the Violin Concerto, *Contrasts* or the Divertimento for the intensity of the Sixth Quartet, which one might suppose to have been due partly to the customary intimacy of the medium, partly to the rapid deterioration in Bartók's personal situation as in the wider world. While the quartet was in progress the Second World War began, and though Hungary was not yet directly involved, Bartók saw his dream of a 'brotherhood of peoples' briskly dispatched. At the same time his mother's health was failing: she died in December 1939, the month after the quartet was finished, and despite the fact she had reached the age of eighty-two, Bartók felt keen grief at her death and also guilt for having spent three and a half weeks at Saanen when he could have been with her.[10]

The two avenues of personal expression in the Sixth Quartet are passion and parody, to such an extent that one might wonder if Bartók had encountered Mahler. The pattern of movement resembles that in Mahler's Ninth Symphony, with an opening sonata form followed by two satires and a slow movement, and the first movement begins like the first movement of Mahler's Tenth with an isolated and highly chromatic viola line, the first presentation of the Mesto theme:

Ex. 68
String Quartet no. 6

[10] Ibid, 281–2.

But there is a less disputable and more interesting prototype for this at the start of the Music for Strings, Percussion and Celesta, another work in which the same theme turns up in four different movements. The differences between the two point up how far Bartók had travelled in the space of only three years, for where the Music for Strings displays sublime confidence in handling its theme, the Sixth Quartet remains desperately uncertain. The one work ends with the melody rounded out triumphantly in sunny diatonicism, the other with a restatement of the first two phrases almost unchanged: indeed, the only alteration to the pitch contour makes the line still more chromatic, the final D being raised to E flat.

One might interpret the four movements of the quartet as different ways to handle the unsettling musical and emotional substance of the Mesto music, which enjoys a progressively more richly textured and longer exposure before each movement until it takes over the whole of the last. In the opening Vivace the answer to it is a sonata structure based on two main ideas, one a cadence in curling triplets like the principal subject of the Fifth Quartet's scherzo (but now eschewing Bulgarian exoticism for standard 6/8), the other a tune in a variety of C minor: they are perhaps to be read as expansions of the Mesto theme's first two phrases, for they are able to come back, much decelerated, within the finale.

Meanwhile the two middle movements, Marcia and Burletta, have lurched from their Mesto introductions into different forms of distortion. The march theme, a rising major triad followed by a fall to the fourth degree, comes from the start of the Mesto's fourth phrase, via an intermediate expansion played solo by the second violin, which similarly opens the way towards the clownish cadences of the Burletta. But where motivic development of his kind seems primarily an exhibition of creative virtuosity in such works as the Fifth Quartet or the Music for Strings, in the Sixth Quartet it is disturbingly ironic. Comparison with the nearer *Contrasts* is even more revealing. For example, a sequence of abortive appoggiaturas is part of the continuous dash in the trio's finale, but in the quartet's Burletta, loudened and harmonically coarsened, it becomes a gesture of brutal insistence:

Ex. 69

It is the same with the Marcia, where the clarinet melody from the first movement of *Contrasts* is cut off after its first four notes, so that a swaggering verbunkos is changed into a mean march:

Ex. 70

    Both the Marcia and the Burletta are in plain scherzo-plus-trio form, as if their irony had robbed them of any potential for structural elaboration. Both, too, preserve their sarcastic quality all through, the Burletta using dry discords and marginal playing techniques in a manner suggestive of Stravinsky's quartet pieces (Bartók has forgotten his own pizzicato from among the marginal techniques). Most alarming of all, though, is the march's trio, where the cello at the top of its register appears to reproduce the Mesto theme in a grotesquely cheapened form (it is the cello that has led the introduction in this movement), accompanied by violin tremolandos and banjo strumming on the viola:

Ex. 71

String Quartet no. 6: second movement

This is an even more hideous parody than the barrel-organ music of the Fifth Quartet, and, as in that case, specially noisome for coming in so prestigious a genre. Writing to Frau Müller-Widmann on 2 April 1940 Bartók referred to the world situation and went on: 'You can imagine how very embittered I am. There can be no point in writing letters full of lamentations – even though I do not approve of the '*keep smiling*' attitude. On the other hand, it seems hypocritical to write letters and not complain at all. What a dilemma –!'[11] In the Sixth Quartet, though, he had solved that dilemma, and used the language he knew best to express all at once his bitterness, his lamentations and the hypocrisy of optimism.

This letter to Frau Müller-Widmann was written from Naples, where the next day Bartók embarked for his second visit to the United States. Eleven years before he had gone in confidence to win new audiences for modern Hungarian music; now he must have felt more a refugee. Stravinsky, Schoenberg, Hindemith, Britten and others of his colleagues were already in America, and he had been hinting of his wish to emigrate. When he returned, after five and a

[11] Ibid, 282.

half weeks of recitals and lectures, it was with the intention of going back in October. On both sides of the Atlantic the preparations were made. On October 8 the Bartóks gave a farewell concert in Budapest, he playing a Bach concerto and selections from *Mikrokosmos*, she a Mozart concerto (her first solo appearance) and with him the Mozart double concerto. Then they made their journey across a Europe at war to Lisbon, where on October 20 they boarded a ship that would take them from Europe, in his case for the last time. From Geneva he wrote to Frau Müller-Widmann: 'This voyage is, actually, like plunging into the unknown from what is known but unbearable. If only on account of my none too satisfactory state of health; I mean my periarthritis, still incompletely cured. God only knows how and for how long I'll be able to work over there.'[12]

[12] Ibid, 284.

11

America

At first things seem to have gone well for Bartók the émigré. He and Ditta were living in a New York hotel until they found a flat in Forest Hills, Long Island, early in December, and their luggage failed to arrive until the following February, but there were concerts in New York and Cleveland before Christmas, and early the next year a nationwide tour. In January the Sixth Quartet was given its first performance, by the Kolisch Quartet, who had introduced the Fifth Quartet and to whom Bartók dedicated the new work: Székely, the original commissioner, was still in Europe, out of reach. Most important of all, there was the promise of employment. On November 25 he was granted an honorary doctorate by Columbia University, and in March 1941 he began work there on the collection of Yugoslav epic song. This gave him much pleasure, and perhaps contributed to his withdrawal from composition yet again, for after making an orchestral version of the Sonata for pianos and percussion in December 1940 he completed nothing for three years.

The Concerto for two pianos, percussion and orchestra, as the new version of the Sonata was called, has often been disparaged as a regrettable adulteration of a masterpiece in response to a publisher's request. However, Bartók himself may well have been keen to regularise the work: his output is, for a twentieth-century composer, quite extraordinarily normal in its genres, and he is known to have considered making an orchestral version of his only other chamber work for unusual forces, *Contrasts*.[1] More to the point, the Double Concerto has enough new interest to stand as a worthy alternative to its Sonata original. There is very little fresh material, but instead a doubling, underlining and more rarely replacement of the piano parts that usually adds something attractive or significant and does not merely inflate. Among the main intriguing new features are a

---

[1] Letter to Szigeti quoted in Ujfalussy, 344.

celesta doubling the first piano occasionally in the first movement, pedal notes that send steady beams of coloured light through the black-and-white structures of the original, a transfer of the second movement's chordal cadence onto wind instruments, and bizarre string glissandos under the acceleration towards an early climax in the finale (bars 115ff). The rich colouring of this last movement brings out a surprising closeness to the fair scenes of *Petrushka*, and there are many moments throughout where the musical meaning is shifted subtly or sharply: an example of the latter comes when the passage quoted in Ex. 64 is reached and the first piano's motivic declarations are taken over first by strings and high woodwind, then, for the inversion, by reed sextet.

Though Bartók must have intended the Concerto for himself and Ditta, they had no opportunity to play it until 21 January 1943, under Fritz Reiner in New York: that was the occasion of Bartók's last appearance as a pianist. Meanwhile he and Ditta had played the new version of the Second Suite he made in 1941. In the spring of that year they left Forest Hills because of the noise and moved to a flat in the Bronx, which was more convenient for Bartók to get to Columbia. But that became no advantage at the end of 1942, when his research appointment was curtailed and the future suddenly looked more hazardous, all the more so because his health had been declining for some months. In February 1943 he was booked to give six lectures at Harvard, but halfway through the series he was exhausted and had to undergo medical tests, which resulted in a diagnosis of polycithemia. A contingent of Hungarians provided support. Reiner had himself made possible the concerto appearance in January; Ernő Bloogh, an ex-pupil, persuaded the American performing rights society ASCAP to finance treatment for the composer; Don Gabor provided generous fake royalties for recordings made on his Continental label; and Szigeti and Reiner moved Kusevitzky to offer a commission, though Bartók was left to think the idea originated with the great Russian conductor.

The result of this commission was the Concerto for Orchestra, which he began while staying at a sanatorium at Saranac Lake, New York, during the summer of 1943, though it seems with the inclusion of material written the previous year for a ballet. His openness to such a project dates back at least to 1939, when a 'Ballet symphonique' was mooted in his correspondence with his London publisher;[2] then in 1942 came a request from the Ballet Theatre of New York for a score which appears to have turned into the Concerto for Orchestra.[3] As it stands, though, the Concerto is decidedly not a work for dancing. Rather one's visual attention is fixed on the orchestra from which soloists and ensembles are forever being newly selected: it was this 'guide to the orchestra' aspect of the piece that dictated the choice of title, as in Hindemith's work of 1925, probably the first Concerto for Orchestra, or another predecessor much nearer Bartók, Kodály's Concerto for Orchestra of 1939. And sometimes that aspect governs exactly how the music works, most notably in the second movement, 'Giuoco delle coppie', where pairs of instruments play their musical stanzas at different intervals of doubling: bassoons in minor sixths, oboes in minor thirds, clarinets in minor sevenths, flutes in fifths, trumpets in major seconds.

However, the element of display here was by no means just adventitious, for it had been growing in Bartók's orchestral style during the past decade and more. The greater abundance of triads and fifths in his harmony had contributed to a brightening of texture in the Second Piano Concerto and the Second Violin Concerto, and in these works there is already an element of the concerto grosso that makes the Concerto for Orchestra a natural next development, possibly given further stimulus by the clean-cut virtuosity of American orchestras, which was influencing other immigrant composers, like Rakhmaninov, to a bolder, brasher style of instrumentation. Similarly, the structural straightforwardness of the Concerto for Orchestra had already been prepared by the Sixth Quartet, though in expressive tone the new work is worlds apart: not a private searching but a public celebration.

The difference is apparent at once in the first movements of the two works. Both are sonata allegros with slow introductions, but where the quartet opens with its problematic Mesto music, the Concerto for Orchestra begins with an assembling of its instrumental and harmonic materials in full view of its audience. This is characteristic of the work's openness, the way compositional

---

[2] See László Somfai: 'Nichtvertonte, Libretti im Nachlass und anderen Bühnenpläne Bartóks', *Documenta* bartókiana, iv (1965), 44.
[3] Ibid, 45–6.

gambits are brought candidly to the surface. First the cellos and basses in octaves play a pentatonic theme whose intervals are all fourths and major seconds:

Ex. 72

Concerto for Orchestra: first movement

This grows in three successive stages, but still with fourths and major seconds its only intervals, and then at the end of the introduction an accompaniment figure, a scale rising through a tritone, is gradually speeded up to provide the opening for the sonata allegro's first subject, this again emphasising fourths and major seconds:

Ex. 73

Concerto for Orchestra: first movement

Further derivatives of the same pattern include the theme that eventually gives the movement its decisive close:

Ex. 74

Concerto for Orchestra: first movement

Thus the first movement is anchored firmly in F, which in Bartók's diatonic system has the simplicity of C major in the normal one, since the 'acoustic scale' on F has fewest accidentals (just one: E flat): hence the appropriateness of F for those two spirited and joyful works the Divertimento and the Concerto for Orchestra. Equally typical of Bartók's harmony is the use of B as substitute dominant for the second subject, which turns the thrusting dotted rhythm of the main theme into lilting undulation, and also the whole-tone steps that underlie the structure. But by contrast with the case in such works as the violin sonatas, where the same techniques can be found, the chordal repertory is now dominated thoroughly by major and minor triads. The second subject, for instance, is first played by a solo oboe, then repeated in octaves by clarinets, and then given in triads by flutes and oboe.

Apart from anything else, this makes the ensuing 'Giuoco delle coppie' seem a little less insolent, though of course there can be no question of triads when the clarinets are playing in sevenths and the trumpets in seconds. None the less, even here the triad is the determining feature. Part of the joke is that these are improper harmonies, a fact which the orchestration for instruments of vivid tone accentuates, just as the natural fifths are aptly married with the pure sound of flutes. And the sevenths and seconds have finally to find resolution, the clarinets being embraced within a seventh chord and the trumpets coming at last to settle their differences and agree on a unison D, the tonic of this movement.

Chromaticism in the central 'Elegia' is a more serious affair, even if the expression of grief here is impersonal because it is so vast, and also because there is a frank display of thematic transformation which keeps the music from presenting itself as an immediate emotional outpouring: one turn of the development brings the return of an idea from the introduction to the first movement. There is also a connection with the 'Intermezzo interrotto' that comes next, since the closing high B in the piccolo, a recurrent image in the 'Elegia', is seized upon two octaves down by unison strings as the fourth movement starts. This movement then also becomes an exhibition of theme-bending, with Bartók first developing his ideas into a sumptuous melody in G with changing metres, then reducing them to a banal descending-scale theme quoted from Shostakovich's Seventh Symphony of 1941. Reiner had made him listen to this work on a radio broadcast: 'When it was over he never said whether he liked it or not. He was a taciturn man.'[4] He did indeed rarely give vent to any

[4] Bónis: *Life in Pictures*, 260.

177

derogatory views on the music of his contemporaries, but here he breaks his silence musically to scorn the Shostakovich theme with laughter in high woodwind and violins, blow raspberries at it with trombone glissandos, guy it in barrel-organ style and turn it upside down, after which interruption the intermezzo is resumed. The movement ends, as it had begun, in B, and so clears the ground for the exultant finale in F, the last and biggest of Bartók's 2/4 finales, wielding a variety of dances and consummate canonic episodes into an energetic conclusion.

Bartók finished the Concerto for Orchestra within two months of starting it: the score is dated '1943, aug. 15 – okt. 8'. It was duly delivered to Kusevitzky, and given its first performance by him and the Boston Symphony Orchestra on 1 December 1944. For that occasion Bartók wrote a programme note, beginning by pointing out that: 'The general mood of the work represents, apart from the jesting second movement, a gradual transition from the sternness of the first movement and the lugubrious death-song of the third, to the life-assertion of the last one.'[5] That word 'gradual' contains an important clue, for unlike Bartók's essays in five-part form from around 1930 – the Fourth and Fifth Quartets and the Second Piano Concerto – the Concerto for Orchestra is only peripherally palindromic. There are motivic links between the 'Giuoco delle coppie' and the 'Intermezzo interrotto', and both of them are allegrettos, but in tone they are utterly different. They are certainly not interchangeable in the way one might imagine the scherzos of the Fourth Quartet to be. The intermezzo's tie to its predecessor has already been mentioned; equally noticeable is the way the 'Elegia' begins with a return to the sonority, the speed and the pitches of the first movement's beginning, as if it were starting up again after the interruption of the 'Giuoco', which is framed off from its surroundings by side-drum tappings. It serves therefore as an interruption to the larger unity coherent on thematic linkages, that unity being not an intermezzo this time but veritably, were it not for the exhibitionism that justifies Bartók's title, a symphony.

In November 1943, the month after the completion of the Concerto for Orchestra, Yehudi Menuhin played both the Second Violin Concerto and the First Violin Sonata in New York. Bartók

---

[5] 'Explanation to Concerto for Orchestra', *Essays*, 431.

was impressed, and gladly accepted Menuhin's commission for a solo sonata, which he wrote while wintering in North Carolina on funds provided by ASCAP. Before he left he learned that his appointment at Columbia had been renewed, but not that this had been possible only because money had been raised on his behalf by his friends: once again the facts of charity had to be concealed from the intensely proud composer. There was also the offer of a visiting lectureship at the University of Washington in Seattle, which Bartók had been deferring since May 1941, but which he now thought he might take up in January 1945.[6] Prospects were thus brighter at the end of the hard year of 1943 as Bartók set off for his four-month stay in Asheville, North Carolina.

The Sonata for solo violin written there is Bartók's most awkward work: awkward to hear as it is to play, and certainly giving the lie to any suggestion that in his American year he was aiming for a lighter style. That impression arises merely from the fact that four of his American works are concertos; the exception, this Sonata, makes no effort to condescend. It is modelled on the only serious model available in this medium, that of the sonatas and partitas of Bach, but with a more modern notion of the sonata influencing the proceedings just as much. Thus the first movement is headed 'Tempo di ciaccona' and begins as if it is going to be formally a chaconne, but it is only the stately rhythm of the Baroque type that is retained in the opening bars, and that returns twice to punctuate a three-part structure which may be construed as embodying the exposition, development and recapitulation of first-movement sonata form. However, there is nothing here at all like the clear definition of theme and function to be found in the Sixth Quartet and the Concerto for Orchestra. Rather Bartók recaptures the more complex style of his earlier violin sonatas, with piano, and embroiders almost continuously with motifs that bristle with fourths and seconds.

Just as the 'Tempo di ciaccona' is not a chaconne, so the succeeding 'Fuga' is not really a fugue, though it begins like one, with entries as convention requires at the fifth, the octave and the twelfth. Unlike Bach's fugues for solo violin, though, this one breaks down soon after it has acquired its fourth voice, which is not surprising given the extreme degrees of strain to which the music is being put:

[6] See Demény (1971), 328.

Ex. 75
Sonata for Solo Violin: second movement

Once more a strict form lapses into a fantasy on its motifs, though sometimes these adhere again to form larger units, notably at a point near the middle where the fugue theme is treated in two-part canon by inversion. The movement also never loses its difficulty, expressed in chromaticism, plentiful hurdles of multiple stopping (by no means confined to the 'Fuga') and an extraordinary passage towards the end where the fugue subject tries to get out from within a D – A fifth on open strings but stays trapped.

After this comes a slow movement, 'Melodia', on a theme derived from the 'Tempo di ciaccona'. It is in ternary form, with the final section elaborating the first almost beyond recognition, and it also includes a nice use of harmonics, contrasting at one moment the sounds of natural and artificial harmonics of the same pitch. Indeed, the Sonata is altogether a conspectus of Bartókian special effects and their similarly Bartókian precise usage. The finale begins with another instance. Bartók had used quarter-tones as a means of confusing pitch in the Second Violin Concerto and the Sixth Quartet, and he does so again here to make ultra-chromatic the opening slither up from and down to the violin's lowest note. Unfortunately, however, the published score prefers a semitone version:

Ex. 76

Sonata for Solo Violin: fourth movement

original version

published version

The further development of the movement is in alternation between music of this kind and a dance in Phrygian G. Shadowy in the background here is Bach's G minor Sonata, on which Bartók also provides a gloss in having his second movement a fugue and his third a slow movement in B flat.

After finishing the Sonata Bartók returned to New York in April, then spent the summer of 1944 at Saranac Lake, working on the texts of Wallachian folksongs in fulfilment of his commission from Columbia University. His health was still in a poor state, and the première of the Concerto for Orchestra in December was the last occasion he was seen in public. Menuhin invited the Bartóks to spend the summer with him in California, but both of them were too ill to travel so far, and so a third summer was spent at Saranac Lake. There Bartók began to compose again after a gap of more than a year. He had plenty of projects to work on: his publisher had commissioned a seventh quartet, William Primrose had asked for a viola concerto, and Nat Shilkret wanted a contribution to his multi-composer setting of Genesis. However, he seems to have given most time to a private plan, that of providing Ditta with a concerto which she could play after his death and so have for a while a little financial security: he had no reason to suppose that royalties would ever be enough to keep her in a comfortable widowhood. He and Ditta left Saranac Lake at the end of August and returned to New York, where he worked at the Third Piano Concerto until on September 22 he had to be taken from his flat at 309 West 57th Street, his cramped home since the previous year. He was transferred to West Side Hospital, and died there on 26 September 1945.

Bartók

The Third Piano Concerto, virtually complete as Bartók left it, is like the First in E, but wholly different in its treatment of that tonality. It is even more smoothly triadic than the Concerto for Orchestra, and even more regular in form. The first movement has a main theme in E major that modulates to the correct dominant of B major before it reaches a second subject in G; there is a development that moves now quite brazenly up a whole-tone ladder of tonalities, and a recapitulation that is scarcely more than a decorated version of the exposition, returning all the material to E. The finale completes the diminished-seventh chord on E, since it is a rondo with two big fugal episodes in C sharp and B flat, but as with the handling of G in the first movement, any orthodoxy is softened by surrounding normality or else made to seem an excursion from the main business of the movement. Before each of the fugal passages the rondo seemingly evaporates, with solo timpani beating monotone diminuendo.

If the outer movements appear to breathe an air of blithe confidence, the centrepiece is more puzzling. Like the middle movement of the Second Piano Concerto, it is tripartite, with first a dialogue between piano and strings (one thinks also of Beethoven's G major Concerto), then a faster 'trio' which here is a unique blend of scherzo and night music, with finally a variation of the first section. There is, however, no precedent whatever in Bartók for the marking Adagio religioso, nor one for the hymnic concords of the piano and strings in the first part:

Ex. 77
Piano Concerto no. 3: second movement

No other evidence suggests that Bartók ever wavered for a moment from the atheism he had expressed to Stefi Geyer, and it may be that all he intended here was an acknowledgment of the influence of the 'Heiliger Dankgesang' from Beethoven's A minor Quartet (the result of that influence is something curiously close to Copland's serene diatonicism in *Appalachian Spring*, written just before the Bartók in 1943–4). However, the intention remains uncertain. The music seems too honest to be ironic, yet too bland to be real, though less bland in the last part of the movement when the piano chorale is beautifully taken over by the woodwind, leaving the soloist free to decorate.

The simplicity at the heart of the Third Piano Concerto – so attractive, but so hard to accept from a composer of Bartók's intelligence and experience – may have been occasioned to some extent by the fact that he was writing the piece for Ditta. That he should compose a new piano concerto had been mooted in 1939, early in his association with Boosey & Hawkes; there had also been commissions in that commission-heavy winter of 1944–5 for both solo and double piano concertos. But in all probability Bartók planned the score from the first with Ditta in mind, not thinking for his own fingers as he had in all his previous concert music for the piano. There had, too, been an unusually long gap, six years, since his last piano composition, making it difficult to decide how the Third Concerto should be considered in relation to his developing thoughts about the instrument. At the same time, the lack of other works from this period must leave it an open question whether the Third Piano Concerto embodies some musical transcendence Bartók achieved at the end of his life. A movement, even a page from the projected Seventh Quartet might speak volumes here.

The Viola Concerto is not quite so eloquent. For one thing, Bartók was dealing with special problems raised by the medium; for another, he completed the work only in rough draft. When he died his ex-pupil Tibor Serly was entrusted with the task of completing the two last concertos. In the case of the Third Piano Concerto, all that remained to be done was to orchestrate the final seventeen bars, but the Viola Concerto was a great deal further from completion: its state might be compared with that of Mahler's Tenth Symphony. Bartók had sketched out the entire work from beginning to end around a solo part that Serly was able to use practically intact. But the orchestral substance was left in a thin state, particularly in the last two of the three movements, and there were few indications for instrumentation.[7] It also seems more than possible that Bartók would have developed some of his ideas more extensively. Even in the first movement there are places where the texture thins in a rather extraordinary way, and where it is hard to know whether a sense of loss is the expressive intention or just the result of incomplete composition:

Ex. 78
Viola Concerto: first movement

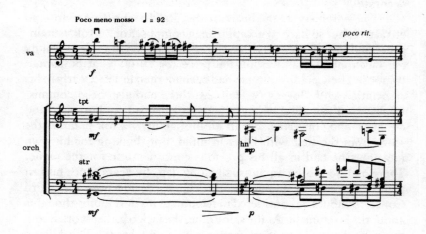

---

[7] See János Kovács's notes accompanying the recording on Hungaroton SLPX 11421.

There is also a strangeness of balance in the form. The first movement is a moderately paced sonata movement with three distinct themes which are duly recapitulated in their original order, the second and third of them coming down a fifth to settle in the A tonality of the first. There is a similarity with the correctness of the Third Piano Concerto's first movement, though the harmony is not so triadic: the style is nearer the Second Violin Concerto. The feeling of sketchiness in the two last movements, however, distances the Viola Concerto from either predecessor. For the slow movement Serly used again the marking Adagio religioso, since in structure the movement resembles the corresponding one in the Third Piano Concerto, having simple slow music around a quick atmospheric middle section, but this middle section consists of only ten bars and the repeat of the slow music is drastically abbreviated. The finale, too, seems much shorter than it ought to be. It is one of Bartók's characteristic 2/4 dance finales, but it is over within 267 bars, compared with 419 in the Sonata for pianos and percussion or 606 in the Concerto for Orchestra (625 if the alternative ending is used). Bartók's last work has to be considered, therefore, as a work whose great beauty is only partially achieved.

12

The future

When Bartók died he was sixty-four, at which age Schoenberg still had a dozen years of composing ahead of him, and Stravinsky had yet to write *The Rake's Progress* and all his late serial works. One may well wonder what Bartók might have accomplished, apart from the completion of the Viola Concerto, if he had survived the war by more than a few weeks. Given his love of Hungary and his remaining there even when politically and artistically he was at odds with most of Budapest, it seems inconceivable that he would have remained a permanent exile. There is little doubt, too, that a composer so capable of irony would have found means to satisfy both the Stalinist masters of postwar Hungary and himself. He would certainly have been pleased to find more official support for folksong research, and perhaps gratified by the turn in public opinion of his own music, for sadly he died before the Concerto for Orchestra became one of the most popular orchestral pieces in the repertory, before his string quartets gained universal recognition as the greatest works of their kind since Beethoven, before his concertos began to be played and recorded by countless outstanding performers as a matter of course. His American tours may have had their successes, but there was certainly not the enthusiasm for him that there was for Rakhmaninov, and the general image of him seems to have been that of an aggressive modernist, the composer of the Allegro barbaro.

If he would have been pleased to find this rapidly changing after the war, he might also have gained satisfaction, and surprise, from the influence his music exerted on younger composers. That influence had already been felt before 1945 by such otherwise very different composers as Olivier Messiaen and Benjamin Britten, but after the war his music became an essential part of the culture on which any young composer would be bound to draw. Karlheinz Stockhausen wrote a dissertation on the Sonata for pianos and percussion,[1] and no doubt learned much that took shape in his own *Kontakte* for piano, percussion and electronic sounds. Pierre Boulez has been no less stimulated by the quite different but similarly Bartókian combination of sustaining and percussive instruments, as in the Music for Strings, Percussion and Celesta and *The Miraculous Mandarin* or his own *Eclat/multiples* and *Répons*. The quartets meanwhile have had their American progeny, notably in the writings and compositions of Milton Babbitt[2] and George Perle,[3] while Peter Maxwell Davies has remarked on their important lesson to him of metrical irregularity.[4] Most particularly, though, as Bartók might have hoped and even expected, his music has been a source of ideas and encouragement to composers of the next two or three generations in Hungary, among them György Kurtág and György Ligeti, the latter in so many ways Bartók's heir: as imaginer of bright, precise orchestral textures, as one interested in pattern and scale as musical rudiments, as an ironist.

So diverse in its effects on subsequent composers, Bartók's music has been interpreted with similar diversity by analysts and critics. Indeed, it may well be that no other twentieth-century composer, not even Webern or Schoenberg, has been subjected to such manifold scrutiny: partly because of the emergence of a highly talented school of Hungarian musicologists for whom the greatest Hungarian musician has held a special fascination, partly because such works as the Music for Strings very much invite analytical attention, and perhaps partly because of an intuitive sense of Bartók's significance. Comparisons with Beethoven, positively demanded by the Third Piano Concerto and implicitly by the quartets, do not in his case seem absurd or even pretentious. No other twentieth-century composer, with the possible exception of Ravel, has such a representative body of work in regular performance worldwide.

---

[1] In the library of the Staatliche Hochschule für Musik, Cologne; a radio talk from the same year, 1951, is reprinted in Stockhausen's *Texte*, ii (Cologne, 1964), 136–9.

[2] See his 'The String Quartets of Bartók', *Musical Quarterly*, xxxv (1949), 377ff, and his own string quartets.

[3] See his 'The String Quartets of Béla Bartók', in *A Musical Offering: Essays in Honor of Martin Bernstein* (New York, 1977), and his own string quartets.

[4] In 'Desert Island Discs', BBC Radio 4, 25 June 1983.

It remains, nevertheless, easier to state Bartók's achievement than to explain it. Yet the important clues would seem to be contained in his own statement, quoted in the fourth chapter above, where he speaks of a liberation from major-minor tonality through his studies of the modes in folksong, and parallel with this the liberation from regular metre he gained from rhythmic analysis of what the peasants sang and played. This guided him throughout most of the forty years he lived after his first acquaintance with folk music, but did so at different times in different ways. First there was a period when the modes and metrical irregularities enriched a basically measured, major-minor language, a period stretching up to the violin sonatas. Then there was a phase when Bartók's sights were fixed more firmly on what was new in his style, and when his music became an assembly of tiny modal-rhythmic patterns. Finally there was the synthesis, when the motifs were brought back again into long lines, and when, in an exactly similar way, the musical surface closed once more over the self-consciousness that had exposed itself in constructive artifice. Only in the parodies of the Fifth and Sixth Quartets and the Concerto for Orchestra does that self-consciousness break through again; otherwise the music has all the naturalness of folksong, as may be illustrated, but scarcely demonstrated, by the big tune from the fourth movement of the Concerto for Orchestra:

Ex. 79
Concerto for Orchestra: fourth movement

It is easy to observe here the prominence of three-note motifs out-lining a major and a minor second, but these are now thoroughly subsumed within the four lines of the melody, which embraces with similar ease the alternation of 3/4 and 5/8 followed by its disturb-ance and the settling in metrical equivocation: a process mirrored on the pitch plane by the ruffling of the pure G mode of the start

(Mixolydian with flattened sixth) and the final redefinition of G but in no certain mode. Very little in music of this period is so openly tonal, but this tonality is of a quite original kind, developed through a close study of the most basic elements of music in folksong. It seems unlikely that so rich a source of musical invention has yet been exhausted.

Appendix A
Calendar

Year	Age	Life	Contemporary musicians and events
1881		Béla Bartók born on 25 March in Nagyszentmiklós	Death of Mussorgsky (42) 28 March; Brahms 48, Debussy 19, Dohnányi 5, Dvořák 40, Elgar 24, Janáček 27, Liszt 78, Mahler 21, Rakhmaninov 8, Reger 8, Schoenberg 7, Strauss 17, Tchaikovsky 41, Wagner 68.
1882	1		Births of Kodály, 16 Dec., Stravinsky, 17 June and Szymanowski, 6 Oct.
1883	2		Births of Varèse, 22 Dec. and Webern, 3 Dec.; death of Wagner (69) 13 Feb.
1884	3		Death of Smetana (60) 12 May.
1885	4	Birth of his sister Elza on 11 June	Birth of Berg, 7 Feb. First performance of Brahms's Fourth Symphony.
1886	5	Begins piano lessons with his mother.	Death of Liszt (74) 10 May.
1887	6	Foundation of the Nagyszentmiklós Music League under the chairmanship of his father.	Death of Borodin (53) 27 Feb.
1888	7	Death of his father on 4 Aug.; his mother starts to support the family by teaching.	
1889	8	The family moves to Nagyszőllős.	
1890	9	First compositions: dances and other small pieces for the piano.	Births of Martin, 15 Sept. and Martinů, 8 Dec.; death of Franck (68) 8 Nov.
1891	10	Enters the Gymnasium at Nagyvárad, staying there with his aunt. Meanwhile the output of juvenilia continues apace.	Birth of Prokofiev, 23 April.

Year	Age	Life	Contemporary musicians and events
1892	11	Returns to Nagyszőllős and there gives his first recital, 1 May, including his own pot-pourri *The Course of the Danube*. In the autumn the family moves to Bratislava, where he starts lessons with László Erkel.	Births of Honegger, 10 March and Milhaud, 4 Sept.
1893	12	Education continues in Bratislava.	Death of Tchaikovsky (53) 6 Nov.
1894	13	The family moves to Beszterce in Transylvania for eight months and then back to Bratislava, where he resumes his studies at the Gymnasium and with Erkel. Compositions include a G minor piano sonata initiating a new series of opus numbers.	First performance of Debussy's *Prélude à 'L'aprés-midi d'un faune'*.
1895	14	Compositions include more piano works and a violin sonata.	Birth of Hindemith, 16 Nov.
1896	15	Plays at concert marking the Hungarian millennium. Writes two string quartets. Death of Erkel (3 Dec.) and transfer to Anton Hyrtl.	Birth of Sessions, 28 Dec.; death of Bruckner (72) 11 Oct. First performance of Strauss's *Also sprach Zarathustra*.
1897	16	Composes a piano quintet and other works.	Birth of Cowell, 11 March; death of Brahms (63) 3 April.
1898	17	Writes more chamber music and three lieder, his first vocal essays. On 8 Dec. travels to Vienna and is accepted at the conservatory.	Golden jubilee of Kossuth's revolt.
1899	18	Decides to study in Budapest after leaving school in the summer. Ill for several months; no significant compositions. Begins studies at the Academy of Music with István Thomán for the piano and Hans Koessler for composition.	Birth of Poulenc, 7 Jan.
1900	19	Enthusiasm for Wagner and Liszt. Koessler's displeasure depresses his creative energies, but a first love affair is memorialised in piano pieces. In the autumn onset of lung disease; convalescence with mother in Merano.	Births of Copland, 14 Nov. and Weill, 2 March.

Year	Age	Life	Contemporary musicians and events
1901	20	Returns to the academy in March and there performs Liszt's B minor sonata in the autumn. No important works.	Death of Verdi (87) 27 Jan.
1902	21	Becomes adherent of Richard Strauss's after hearing *Also sprach Zarathustra* and enlarges circle of musical acquaintanceship in Budapest. Composes Symphony in E flat.	Birth of Walton, 29 March. First performance of Debussy's *Pelléas et Mélisande*.
1903	22	Plays his own transcription of *Ein Heldenleben* in Vienna (26 Jan.) and completes academy course in the summer. Writes violin sonata and *Kossuth*, the latter confirming his dedication to Hungarian nationalism.	Death of Wolf (42) 22 Feb.
1904	23	*Kossuth* played in Budapest (13 Jan.) and Manchester (18 Feb.). He spends the summer in Gerlicepuszta, where he discovers authentic Hungarian folksong. Composes Rhapsody op.1 and Scherzo op.2.	Birth of Dallapiccola, 3 Feb.
1905	24	Visits Paris for the Rubinstein Competition, starts collaboration on folksong with Kodály, and writes Suite op.3.	Birth of Tippett, 2 Jan. First performance of Debussy's *La mer* and Strauss's *Salome*.
1906	25	Tour of Spain and Portugal with the boy violinist Ferenc Vecsey. Publication of twenty folksong arrangements by him and Kodály.	Birth of Shostakovich, 25 Sep.
1907	26	Succeeds Thomán in January as professor of piano at the academy in Budapest. Spends the summer in Transylvania collecting ancient folk music and completing the Second Suite op.4. Discovers Debussy through Kodály.	First performance of Schoenberg's First Quartet.
1908	27	Friendship with Stefi Geyer and composition of the First Violin Concerto. First mature piano pieces written and published.	Births of Carter, 11 Dec. and Messiaen, 10 Dec. First performance of Schoenberg's Second Quartet.

Year	Age	Life	Contemporary musicians and events
1909	28	Folksong collecting in Romania during the summer; marriage to Márta Ziegler.	First performance of Strauss's *Elektra*.
1910	29	First Quartet introduced at all-Bartók concert on 19 March. Birth of his elder son Béla on 22 Aug.	First performance of Stravinsky's *Firebird*.
1911	30	Completes *Bluebeard's Castle* and helps found the New Hungarian Music Association.	Death of Mahler (50) 18 May. First performance of Stravinsky's *Petrushka*.
1912	31	Withdraws from public musical activity in Hungary; writes the Four Pieces op.12.	Birth of Cage, 5 Sept. First performance of Schoenberg's *Pierrot lunaire*.
1913	32	Visits North Africa to collect folk music. First ethnomusicological collection published in Romania.	Birth of Britten, 22 Nov. First performance of Stravinsky's *Rite of Spring*.
1914	33	Inactivity in the face of the world situation.	Outbreak of the First World War.
1915	34	Returns to collecting folksongs in Slovakia, where he meets Klára Gombossy.	Death of Skryabin (43) 27 April.
1916	35	Composes Suite op.14 and songs opp.15–16.	Birth of Babbitt, 10 May. First performance of Debussy's Sonata for flute, viola and harp.
1917	36	Successful première in Budapest of *The Wooden Prince* on 12 May. Completes Second Quartet.	October Revolution in Russia.
1918	37	Concert in Vienna of soldier's songs including arrangements by Bartók. First performance of *Duke Bluebeard's Castle* in Budapest on 24 May. Signs contract with Universal Edition.	Armistice. Death of Debussy (55) 25 March (Bartók's birthday). First performance of Stravinsky's *Soldier's Tale*.
1919	38	Completes piano score of *The Miraculous Mandarin* and begins to consider emigration. Recital in Budapest including first performances of Suite and Studies.	Short-lived communist government in Budapest replaced by right-wing régime.
1920	39	Attacked in the press for want of patriotism. Composes Improvisations op.20.	First performance of Stravinsky's *Pulcinella*.
1921	40	Finishes monograph on Hungarian folksong and writes First Violin Sonata. Birthday celebrated by special issue of *Musikblätter des Anbruch*.	Death of Saint-Saëns (86) 16 Dec. First performance of Janáček's *Katya Kabanova*.

Year	Age	Life	Contemporary musicians and events
1922	41	Begins to re-establish international reputation with recitals in Britain, France and Germany.	Birth of Xenakis, 1 May.
1923	42	Concert on 19 Nov. including first performance of the Dance Suite. Divorce and marriage to Ditta Pásztory.	Birth of Ligeti, 28 May. First performance of Stravinsky's *Les noces*.
1924	43	Birth of his younger son Péter on 31 July.	Deaths of Busoni (58) 27 July, Fauré (79) 4 Nov. and Puccini (65) 29 Nov.
1925	44	Performance of the Dance Suite at the ISCM festival in Prague.	Births of Berio, 24 Oct. and Boulez, 25 March (Bartók's birthday). First performance of Berg's *Wozzeck*.
1926	45	Première of *The Miraculous Mandarin* in Cologne on 27 Nov. Composition of important piano works: Sonata, First Concerto, *Out of Doors*.	Births of Henze, 1 July and Kurtág, 19 Feb. First performance of Kodály's *Háry János*.
1927	46	Completes Third Quartet and begins first American tour in December.	First performance of Stravinsky's *Oedipus rex* and Schoenberg's Third Quartet.
1928	47	Completes Fourth Quartet and begins Russian tour in December.	Birth of Stockhausen, 22 Aug.; death of Janáček (74) 12 Aug.
1929	48	Visits Switzerland and meets Paul Sacher.	First performance of Webern's Symphony.
1930	49	Composes the *Cantata profana* and again retires from active musical life in Budapest.	First performance of Stravinsky's Symphony of Psalms.
1931	50	First attends session of League of Nations committee in Geneva. Completes Second Piano Concerto.	First performance of Honegger's First Symphony.
1932	51	Attends folk music conference in Cairo.	
1933	52	Gives première of Second Concerto in Frankfurt on 23 Jan., his last appearance in Germany.	Hitler becomes German Chancellor. First performance of Strauss's *Arabella*.
1934	53	Retires from teaching to take up full-time work on folk music. Composes Fifth Quartet.	Birth of Davies, 8 Sept.; deaths of Delius (72) 10 June, Elgar (76) 23 Feb. and Holst (59) 25 May.
1935	54	Revival of *The Wooden Prince* in Budapest.	Death of Berg (50) 24 Dec. First performance of Stravinsky's Concerto for two pianos.

Year	Age	Life	Contemporary musicians and events
1936	55	Performs and writes on Liszt for fiftieth anniversary celebrations. Makes last collecting tour in Turkey and composes Music for Strings.	First performance of Prokofiev's *Peter and the Wolf*.
1937	56	Concert of new choral and piano pieces in Budapest. Bans broadcasts to Germany and Italy; composes Sonata for pianos and percussion.	Deaths of Ravel (62) 28 Dec., Roussel (68) 23 Aug. and Szymanowski (54) 29 March. First performance of Schoenberg's Fourth Quartet.
1938	57	Completes Second Violin Concerto and composes *Contrasts*. Transfers to Boosey & Hawkes.	Austrian Anschluss. First performance of Hindemith's *Mathis der Maler*.
1939	58	Writes Divertimento and Sixth Quartet. Death of his mother.	Outbreak of Second World War.
1940	59	Tours USA in the spring and settles in New York in October.	First performance of Stravinsky's Symphony in C.
1941	60	Begins work at Columbia University. Health worsens.	America enters the war.
1942	61	Further deterioration in health.	Death of Rakhmaninov (69) 28 March.
1943	62	Last concert appearance giving the American première with Ditta of the Concerto for two pianos. Composes the Concerto for Orchestra.	First performance of Messiaen's *Visions de l'Amen*.
1944	63	Writes the Sonata for solo violin and is last seen in public at the première of the Concerto for Orchestra.	First performance of Schoenberg's Piano Concerto.
1945	64	Composes his Third Piano Concerto and works on his Viola Concerto. Dies in West Side Hospital, New York, 26 Sept.	Death of Webern (61) 15 Sept. Babbitt 29, Berio 20, Boulez 20, Britten 32, Cage 33, Copland 45, Cowell 48, Dallapiccola 41, Davies 11, Dohnányi 68, Falla 69, Henze 19, Hindemith 50, Honegger 53, Ives 71, Kodály 63, Kurtág 19, Ligeti 22, Martin 55, Martinů 55, Messiaen 37, Milhaud 53, Poulenc 56, Prokofiev 54, Schoenberg 71, Sessions 49, Shostakovich 39, Sibelius 70, Stockhausen 17, Strauss 71, Stravinsky 63, Varèse 60, Vaughan Williams 73.

Appendix B
List of works

Included here are all the works Bartók completed in or after 1902. For details of his large body of juvenilia see Denijs Dille: *Thematisches Verzeichnis der Jugendwerke Béla Bartóks 1890–1904* (Budapest, 1974). Publishers of scores in print are indicated thus: Boosey & Hawkes (BH), Editio Musica Budapest (EMB), Universal Edition (UE). In cases of joint publication, the printing commonly available in the West is indicated. Titles are given first in English, the original, where appropriate, following in brackets.

1 Stage works

Duke Bluebeard's Castle (A Kékeszakállú herceg vára), op. 11
    Opera in one act with words by Béla Balázs
    Composed in 1911, revised in 1912 and 1918 (UE)
    First performance: Olga Haselbeck, Oszkar Kálmán, conducted by Egisto Tango, Budapest Opera, 24 May 1918
The Wooden Prince (A fából faragott királyfi), op. 13
    Ballet in one act to a scenario by Béla Balázs
    Composed in 1914–16, orchestrated in 1916–17 (UE)
    First performance: conducted by Egisto Tango, Budapest Opera, 12 May 1917
The Miraculous Mandarin (A csodálatos mandarin), op. 19
    Pantomime in one act to a scenario by Menyhért Lengyel
    Composed in 1918–19, orchestrated in 1923, revised in 1924 and 1926–31 (UE)
    First performance: conducted by Jeno Szenkár, Cologne Stadttheater, 27 November 1926

2.1 Orchestral works with voice or voices

Village Scenes (Falun – Tri dedinské scény) for female chorus and chamber orchestra, arranged from 1924 song set, 1926 (UE)
    First performance: conducted by Serge Kusevitzky, New York, 1 February 1927
Cantata profana for tenor, baritone, chorus and orchestra to words by Bartók after a Romanian carol, 1930 (UE)
    First performance: Trefor Jones, Frank Phillips, Wireless Chorus, BBC Symphony Orchestra/Aylmer Buesst, London, 25 May 1934

197

Bartók

√ Five Hungarian Folksongs (Magyar népdalok) for voice and orchestra, arranged from 1929 song set, 1933
   First performance: Maria Basilides (contralto), Budapest Philharmonic Society/Ernő Dohnányi, 23 October 1933

2.2 Orchestral works with instrumental soloists

Rhapsody for piano and orchestra, op. 1, version of solo piece, ?1904 (EMB)
   First performance: Bartók, Academy of Music Orchestra/Jenő Hubay, Budapest, 15 November 1909
Scherzo for piano and orchestra, op. 2, 1904 (EMB)
   First performance: Erszébet Tusa, Hungarian Radio Orchestra/György Lehel, 28 September 1961
Violin Concerto no. 1, 1907–8 (BH)
   First performance: Hans-Heinz Schneeberger, Basle Chamber Orchestra/Paul Sacher, Basle, 30 May 1958
Two Portraits (Két portré), op. 5, the first being the first movement of the above, the second, with no soloist, an orchestral version of the last of the Fourteen Bagatelles, scored in 1911 (BH)
   First performance: Budapest, 12 February 1911 (first movement); conducted by István Strasser, Budapest, 20 April 1916 (complete)
Piano Concerto no. 1, 1926 (UE)
   First performance: Bartók, conducted by Wilhelm Furtwängler, Frankfurt am Main, 1 July 1927
Rhapsody no. 1 for violin and orchestra, version of chamber piece, 1928 (UE)
   First performance: Joseph Szigeti, conducted by Hermann Scherchen, Königsberg, 1 November 1929
Rhapsody no. 2 for violin and orchestra, version of chamber piece, 1928 (UE), revised 1944 (BH)
   First performance: Zoltán Székely, conducted by Ernő Dohnányi, Budapest, 26 November 1929
Piano Concerto no. 2, 1930–1 (UE)
   First performance: Bartók, Frankfurt Radio Symphony Orchestra/Hans Rosbaud, Frankfurt am Main, 23 January 1933
√ Violin Concerto no. 2, 1937–8 (BH)
   First performance: Zoltán Székely, Concertgebouw Orchestra/Willem Mengelberg, Amsterdam, 23 March 1939
Concerto for two pianos, percussion and orchestra, version of Sonata for two pianos and percussion, 1940 (BH)
   First performance: Louis Kentner, Ilona Kabos, London Philharmonic Orchestra/Sir Adrian Boult, London, 14 November 1942
√ Piano Concerto no. 3, 1945 (BH)
   First performance: György Sándor, Philadelphia Orchestra/Eugene Ormandy, Philadelphia, 8 February 1946

Viola Concerto, 1945, completed by Tibor Serly (BH)
First performance: William Primrose, Minneapolis Symphony Orchestra /Antal Dorati, Minneapolis, 2 December 1949

2.3 Orchestral works without soloists

Symphony in E flat, piano score 1902, scherzo orchestrated 1903
First performance: Budapest Opera Orchestra/István Kerner, Budapest, 29 February 1904 (scherzo only)
Kossuth, symphonic poem, 1903 (EMB)
First performance: Budapest Philharmonic Society/István Kerner, Budapest, 13 January 1904
Suite no. 1, op. 3, 1905, revised *c.*1920 (EMB)
First performance: conducted by Ferdinand Loewe, Vienna, 29 November 1905 (movements 1 and 3–5 only); conducted by Jenő Hubay, Budapest, 1 March 1909 (complete)
Suite no. 2, op. 4, small orchestra, 1905–7, revised 1920 (UE) and 1943 (BH)
First performance: conducted by Bartók, Berlin, 2 January 1909 (second movement only); Budapest Philharmonic Society/István Kerner, Budapest, 22 November 1909 (complete)
Two Pictures (Két kép), op. 10, 1910 (BH)
First performance: Budapest Philharmonic Society/István Kerner, Budapest, 25 February 1913
Romanian Dance (Román tánc), arranged from piano piece op. 8a no. 1, 1911 (EMB)
First performance: conducted by László Kún, Budapest, 12 February 1911
Four Pieces, op. 12, 1912, orchestrated 1921 (UE)
First performance: Budapest Philharmonic Society/Ernő Dohnányi, Budapest, 9 January 1922
Suite from *The Wooden Prince*, op. 13, drawn ?1921–4
First performance: Budapest Philharmonic Society/Ernő Dohnányi, Budapest, 23 November 1931
Romanian Folkdances (Román népi táncok), arranged from 1915 piano set, 1917 (UE)
First performance: conducted by E. Lichtenberg, Budapest, 11 February 1918
Suite from *The Miraculous Mandarin*, op. 19, drawn 1919 and 1927 (UE)
First performance: Budapest Philharmonic Society/Ernő Dohnányi, Budapest, 15 October 1928
Dance Suite (Táncszvit), 1923 (UE)
First performance: Budapest Philharmonic Society/Ernő Dohnányi, Budapest, 19 November 1923
Transylvanian Dances (Erdélyi táncok), arranged from Piano Sonatina, 1931 (EMB)
First performance: conducted by M. Freccia, Budapest, 24 January, 1932

Bartók

Hungarian Pictures (Magyar képek), arranged from five piano pieces of
    1908–11, 1931 (EMB)
    First performance: Budapest, 24 January 1932 (nos. 1–3 and 5);
    conducted by Heinrich Laber, Budapest, 26 November 1934 (complete)
Hungarian Peasant Songs (Magyar parasztdalok), arranged from nine of
    Fifteen Hungarian Peasant Songs for piano, 1933 (UE)
    First performance: conducted by Gyula Baranyi, Szombathely, 18
    March 1934
Music for Strings, Percussion and Celesta, 1936 (UE)
    First performance: Basle Chamber Orchestra/Paul Sacher, Basle, 21
    January 1937
Divertimento for strings, 1939 (BH)
    First performance: Basle Chamber Orchestra/Paul Sacher, Basle, 11
    June 1940
Concerto for Orchestra, ?1942–3, revised 1945 (BH)
    First performance: Boston Symphony Orchestra/Serge Kusevitzky,
    Boston, 1 December 1944

3.1 Quintet, quartets and trio

Piano Quintet, 1903–4, revised ?1920 (EMB)
    First performance: Bartók, Prill Quartet, Vienna, 21 November 1904
String Quartet no. 1, op. 7, 1908 (BH)
    First performance: Waldbauer-Kerpely Quartet, Budapest, 19 March
    1910
String Quartet no. 2, op. 17, 1915–17 (UE)
    First performance: Waldbauer-Kerpely Quartet, Budapest, 3 March
    1918
String Quartet no. 3, 1927 (UE)
    First performance: Waldbauer-Kerpely Quartet, London, 19 February
    1929
String Quartet no. 4, 1928 (UE)
    First performance: Waldbauer-Kerpely Quartet, Budapest, 20 March
    1929
String Quartet no. 5, 1934 (UE)
    First performance: Kolisch Quartet, Washington, DC, 8 April 1935
Sonata for two pianos and percussion, 1937 (BH)
    First performance: Bartóks, Fritz Schiesser, Philipp Rühlig, Basle, 16
    January 1938
Contrasts for violin, clarinet and piano, 1938 (BH)
    First performance: Joseph Szigeti, Benny Goodman, Endre Petri, New
    York, 9 January 1939 (outer movements only); Szigeti, Goodman,
    Bartók, New York, April 1940 (complete)
String Quartet no. 6, 1939 (BH)
    First performance: Kolisch Quartet, New York, 20 January 1941

3.2 Duos and solo

Duo for violins, 1902
Andante in A for violin and piano, 1902 (EMB)
Sonata in E minor for violin and piano, 1903 (EMB)
    First performance: Sándor Kőszegi, Bartók, Budapest, 8 June 1903
    (third movement); Jenő Hubay, Bartók, Budapest, 25 January 1904
    (complete)
From Gyergyó (Gyergyóból) for recorder and piano, 1907 (EMB)
Sonata no. 1 for violin and piano, 1921 (UE)
    First performance: Jelly d'Arányi, Bartók, London, 24 March 1922
Sonata no. 2 for violin and piano, 1922 (UE)
    First performance: Jelly d'Arányi, Bartók, London, 7 May 1923
Rhapsody no. 1 for violin and piano, 1928 (UE)
    First performance: Joseph Szigeti, Bartók, Budapest, 22 November
    1929
Rhapsody for cello and piano, arrangement of the above, 1928 (UE)
Rhapsody no. 2 for violin and piano, 1928 (UE), revised 1945 (BH)
    First performance: Zoltán Székely, Géza Frid, Amsterdam, 19
    November 1928
Forty-four Duos for violins, 1931 (UE)
    First performance: Imre Waldbauer, György Hannover, Budapest, 20
    January 1932 (extracts)
Sonata for solo violin, 1944 (BH)
    First performance: Yehudi Menuhin, New York, 26 November 1944

4 Piano works

Four Pieces, 1903 (EMB): Study for the left hand, Fantasy no. 1, Fantasy no.
    2, Scherzo
    First performances: Bartók, Nagyszentmiklós, 13 April 1903 (Study);
    Bartók, Budapest, 27 March 1903 (Fantasy I); Bartók, Budapest, 25
    November 1903 (Scherzo)
Marche funèbre from *Kossuth*, 1903
Rhapsody, op. 1, 1904 (EMB)
    First performance: Bartók, Bratislava, 4 November 1906
Petits morceaux, arranged from the second of the 1904–5 folksongs and the
    first of the Pósa songs, ?1905–7 (EMB)
Three Hungarian Folksongs from the Csík District (Három Csík megyei
    népdal), arrangement of *From Gyergyó*, 1907 (EMB)
Fourteen Bagatelles, op. 6, 1908 (EMB): Molto sostenuto, Allegro giocoso,
    Andante, Grave, Vivo, Lento, Allegretto molto capriccioso, Andante
    sostenuto, Allegretto grazioso, Allegro, Allegretto molto rubato,
    Rubato, (Elle est morte . . .), Valse (Ma mie qui danse . . .)
    First performance: Bartók, Berlin, 29 June 1908
Ten Easy Pieces, 1908 (EMB): (Dedication), Peasant's Song, Torment,

Slovak Peasants' Dance, Sostenuto, An Evening with the Székely, Hungarian Folksong, Dawn, Hungarian Folksong, Finger Exercise, Bear Dance

Two Elegies (Két elégia), op. 8b, 1908–9 (EMB)
　First performance: Bartók, Budapest, 21 April 1919

For Children (Gyermekeknek), eighty-five pieces in four volumes, 1908–9 (EMB), revised as seventy-nine pieces in two, 1945 (BH)

Two Romanian Dances (Két román tánc), op. 8a, 1909–10 (EMB)
　First performance: Bartók, Paris, 12 March 1910

Sketches (Vázlatok), op. 9b, 1908–10 (EMB): Portrait of a Young Girl, See-saw, Lento, Non troppo lento, Romanian Folksong, In Romanian Style, Poco lento

Four Dirges (Négy siratóének), op. 9a, 1909–10 (EMB)
　First performance: Ernő Dohnányi, Budapest, 17 October 1917 (extracts)

Three Burlesques (Három burleszk), op. 8c, 1908–11 (EMB): Quarrel, A Bit Tipsy, Molto vivo capriccioso
　First performance: Ernő Dohnányi, Budapest, 17 October 1917 (nos. 1–2)

Allegro barbaro, 1911 (UE)

Two Pictures, op. 10, arrangement of orchestral work, c.1911 (EMB)

The First Term at the Piano (Kezdők zongoramuzsikája), eighteen pieces, 1913 (EMB)

Sonatina, 1915 (EMB)

Romanian Folkdances (Román népi táncok), set of seven, 1915 (UE)

Romanian Christmas Carols (Román kolinda-dallamok), two sets of ten each, 1915 (UE)

The Wooden Prince, op. 13, piano score (UE)

Suite, op. 14, 1916 (UE)
　First performance: Bartók, Budapest, 21 April 1919

Three Hungarian Folktunes, c.1914–18, revised ?1942 (BH)

Fifteen Hungarian Peasant Songs (Tizenöt magyar parasztdal), 1914–18 (BH)

Three Studies, op. 18, 1918 (UE)
　First performance: Bartók, Budapest, 21 April 1919

The Miraculous Mandarin, op. 19, four-hand piano score (UE)

Eight Improvisations on Hungarian Peasant Songs, op. 20, 1920 (UE)
　First performance: Bartók, Budapest, 27 February 1921

Dance Suite, arrangement of orchestral work, 1925 (UE)

Sonata, 1926 (UE)
　First performance: Bartók, Budapest, 8 December 1926

Out of Doors (Szabadban), 1926 (UE): With Drums and Pipes, Barcarolla, Musettes, The Night's Music, The Chase
　First performance: Bartók, Budapest, 8 December 1926 (nos. 1 and 4)

Nine Little Pieces, 1926 (UE): Four Dialogues, Menuetto, Air, Marcia delle bestie, Tambourine, Preludio – All'ungherese

First performance: Bartók, Budapest, 8 December 1926 (all but one)
Three Rondos on Folktunes (Három rondo népi dallamokkal), no. 1, 1916,
    nos. 2–3 1927 (UE)
Petite suite, arrangement of five of the Forty-four Duos, 1936 (UE)
Mikrokosmos, 1926, 1932–9 (BH):
    Book 1: thirty-six pieces and four exercises
    Book 2: thirty pieces and fourteen exercises
    Book 3: thirty pieces and thirteen exercises
    Book 4: Notturno, Thumb Under, Crossed Hands, In the Style of a
    Folksong, Diminished Fifth, Harmonics, Minor and Major, Through
    the Keys, Playsong, Children's Song, Melody in the Mist, Wrestling,
    From the Island of Bali, Clashing Sounds, Intermezzo, Variations on a
    Folktune, Bulgarian Rhythm 1, Theme and Inversion, Bulgarian
    Rhythm 2, Melody, Bourrée, Triplets in 9/8 Time, Dance in 3/4 Time,
    Fifth Chords, Two-Part Study
    Book 5: Chords Together and Opposed, Staccato and Legato, Staccato,
    Boating, Change of Time, New Hungarian Folksong, Peasant Dance,
    Alternating Thirds, Village Joke, Fourths, Major Seconds Broken and
    Together, Syncopation, Studies in Double Notes, Perpetuum mobile,
    Whole-tone Scale, Unison, Bagpipe, Merry Andrew
    Book 6: Free Variations, Subject and Reflection, From the Diary of a
    Fly, Divided Arpeggios, Minor Seconds Major Sevenths, Chromatic
    Invention, Ostinato, March, Six Dances in Bulgarian Rhythm
Seven Pieces from *Mikrokosmos* arranged for two pianos, 1940 (BH):
    Bulgarian Rhythm, Chord Study, Perpetuum mobile, Canon and Inver-
    sion, New Hungarian Folksong, Chromatic Invention, Ostinato
Suite for two pianos, arrangement of orchestral Suite no. 2, 1941 (BH)
Concerto for Orchestra, piano score, 1944, unpublished

5.1 Works for mixed chorus

Four Slovak Folksongs (Négy tót népdal, Štyri slovenské piesne) for four
    voices and piano, ?1916 (EMB)
    Probable first performance: conducted by Emil Lichtenberg, Budapest,
    5 January 1917
Hungarian Folksongs (Magyar népdalok), four songs, 1930 (UE)
    First performance: Kecskemét Municipal Choir/Zoltán Vásárhelyi, 11
    May 1936

5.2 Works for women's chorus

Two Romanian Folksongs for four voices, completed by Benjamin Suchoff,
    ?1915 (BH)
Two- and Three-part Choruses, nos. 22–7, to words from folksongs, 1935
    (EMB)

5.3 Works for men's chorus

Evening (Est) for eight voices to words by Kálmán Harsányi, 1903 (EMB)

Four Old Hungarian Folksongs (Négy régi magyar népdal) for four voices, 1910, revised 1912 (UE)

First performance: Szeged Chorus/Péter König, Szeged, 13 May 1911

Slovak Folksongs (Tót népdalok, Slovácké ludové piesne) for four voices, five songs, 1917 (UE)

First performance: Wiener Männergesangverein, Vienna, 12 January 1918

Székely Songs (Székely dalok) for six voices, six songs, 1932 (EMB)

From Olden Times (Elmúlt időkből) for three voices, three songs to folksong words adapted by Bartók, 1935 (Magyar Kórus)

5.4 Works for children's chorus

Bell Sound (Harangszó) for two voices to words by Béla Sztankó, ?after 1905 (in school textbook)

Two- and Three-part Choruses, nos. 1–21, to words from folksongs, 1935 (EMB)

Five numbers arranged with school orchestra (EMB), two others with small orchestra (BH)

6.1 Art songs

Four Songs to words by Lajos Pósa, 1902 (Bard)

Evening (Est) to words by Kálmán Harsányi, ?1903 (EMB)

Five Songs, op. 15, to words by Klára Gombossy and Wanda Gleiman, 1916 (UE)

Five Songs, op. 16, to words by Endre Ady, 1916 (UE)

First performance: Ilona Durigó, Bartók, Budapest, 21 April 1919

6.2 Folksong arrangements for solo voice and piano

'Piros alma leesett a sarba' (The red apple has fallen in the mud), 1904 (in magazine *Magyar Lant*)

Hungarian Folksongs (Magyar népdalok), four songs, 1904–5 (no. 1 EMB)

To the Little 'Slovak' (A kicsi 'tót'-nak), five children's songs, 1905 (no. 3 in Demény's Hungarian edition of the letters)

Hungarian Folksongs (Magyar népdalok), ten songs, another ten arranged by Kodály, 1906, revised 1938 (EMB)

Hungarian Folksongs (Magyar népdalok), ten songs, 1906 (four EMB)

Two Hungarian Folksongs, ?1906 (no. 1 EMB)

Four Slovakian Folksongs, c.1907 (no. 2 lost, the others EMB)

Nine Romanian Folksongs, 1915, completed by Benjamin Suchoff (BH)

'Kruti Tono vretena' (Tony turns his spindle round), Slovak song, ?1916 (EMB)

Eight Hungarian Folksongs (Nyolc magyar népdal), nos. 1–5 1907, nos. 6–8
  c.1917 (BH)
    First performance: Desző Róna, Bartók, Budapest, 27 November 1911
    (nos. 1–5); Ferenc Székelyhidy (tenor), Bartók, Vienna, 12 January
    1918 (nos. 6–8)
Village Scenes (Falun – Dedinské scény), five songs based on Slovak material,
  1924 (UE)
    First performance: Maria Basilides (contralto), Bartók, Budapest, 8
    December 1926
Twenty Hungarian Folksongs (Húsz magyar népdal), 1929 (UE)
    First performance: Maria Basilides (contralto), Bartók, Budapest, 30
    January 1930
'Debrecennek van egy vize', Hungarian song arranged from a number in *For
  Children*, ?1937 (in anthology published that year)
Ukrainian Folksongs, four songs for an incomplete cycle, 1945 (one in
  Demény's Hungarian edition of the letters)

7 Editions and arrangements

Concert versions for the piano of early Italian keyboard music, *c*.1926–8
  (Fischer):
    Benedetto Marcello: Sonata in B flat
    Michelangelo Rossi: Toccatas nos. 1–2, Tre correnti
    Azzolino Bernardino della Ciaia: Sonata in G
    Girolamo Frescobaldi: Toccata in G, Fugue in G minor
    Domenico Zipoli: Pastorale in C
Concert version for the piano of J.S. Bach's Trio Sonata no. 6 in G BWV 530,
  c.1930 (Rózsavölgyi es Társa)
Teaching editions for the piano of works by J.S. Bach, Beethoven, Chopin,
  Couperin, Haydn, Heller, Köhler, Mendelssohn, Mozart, Scarlatti,
  Schubert and Schumann, 1907–24

Appendix C
Personalia

Ady, Endre (1877–1919), Hungarian poet. He was one of the outstanding creative forces in Hungary during Bartók's early maturity, though the composer never knew him at all closely, despite the fact that they shared similar aims. Ady, like Bartók, was determined to create a distinctively Hungarian art, based on ancient Hungarian forms and metres, but aware of the most recent western European currents, which in his case meant symbolism of a vivid and flamboyant kind. In 1916 Bartók set five lyrics by him to make his most important set of art songs.

Arányi, Jelly d' (1893–1966), Hungarian violinist. She and her sister Adila (married name Fachiri) were friends of Bartók's from their common student days, she being a pupil of Hubay. Later he dedicated to her his two sonatas for violin and piano, which they played together in London in the early 1920s. In 1923 she settled in England.

Balázs, Béla (1884–1949), Hungarian poet and man of letters. Bartók's closest literary associate, he provided the libretto of *Duke Bluebeard's Castle* and the scenario of *The Wooden Prince*. His communist sympathies led him into exile in 1919, and he returned to Hungary only in 1945. He was a pioneer in giving films serious aesthetic attention.

Bartók, Béla (1855–88), the composer's father. He directed the agricultural college in Nagyszentmiklós, in which post he succeeded his own father at the age of twenty-one. A man of evident intellectual and artistic curiosity, he founded the local music league and played and composed for them.

Bartók, Béla, Jr (1910–), the composer's elder son. He was brought up by his mother after his parents divorced in 1923, remained in Hungary and trained as an engineer, working for the Hungarian State Railways in Budapest.

Bartók, Ditta (Edita), née Pásztory (1903–82), the composer's second wife. She studied with Bartók at the Academy of Music in Budapest and married him on 28 August 1923. Thereafter she gave up any possibility of a career as a pianist, until in 1938 she joined Bartók in giving the first performance of his Sonata for two pianos and percussion. After this he appeared with her regularly, and wrote other works for them; he also wrote his Third Piano Concerto for her as soloist. She returned to Hungary after his death, and frequently played and recorded his music. Bartók dedicated to her *Village Scenes*, his Piano Sonata and *Out of Doors*.

Bartók, Márta, nèe Ziegler (1893–1955), the composer's first wife. She studied with Bartók at the Academy of Music in Budapest and married him in August 1909. Bartók dedicated to her *Bluebeard's Castle* and two piano pieces. In 1923 they were divorced.

Bartók, Paula, née Voit (1857–1939), the composer's mother. Widowed at the age of thirty-one, she brought up the composer and his sister Elza by working as a teacher. The family settled in Bratislava in 1894, and she remained there after her children had left home. Some time in the 1930s, however, she moved to live with her son in Budapest. Her death was a severe blow to him.

Bartók, Péter (1924–), the composer's younger son, dedicatee of the first two books of *Mikrokosmos*. He left for New York after his parents, in 1942, served in the US Marines and stayed in America, where he worked as a sound engineer. He founded a company, Bartók Records, to republish his father's recordings and issue new recordings of Bartók's works.

Buşiţia, Ion (1875–1953), Romanian schoolteacher. In the summer of 1909 he accompanied Bartók on a folksong collecting tour in Bihar county. This saw the start of a deep friendship, chronicled in correspondence throughout the next three decades. Bartók dedicated the seven Romanian Folkdances to him.

Busoni, Ferruccio (1866–1924), Italian-German composer and pianist. He was impressed by Bartók's early piano music and invited him to Berlin to conduct a movement from the op. 4 Suite in 1909.

Debussy, Claude (1862–1918), French composer. Bartók got to know his music in 1907, and it had an enormous influence on him. The two composers must have met when Bartók visited Paris later and when Debussy came to Budapest in 1910, but little is known of their personal relationship.

Delius, Frederick (1862–1934), English composer. Bartók met him in 1910 and was for a short while hugely impressed, particularly by his *Mass of Life*.

Dent, Edward (1876–1957), English musicologist. He helped to found and was first chairman of the International Society for Contemporary Music, holding that post from 1922 to 1938. Bartók's interest in the society led him into contact with Dent, who was also professor of music at Cambridge and an authority on Mozart's operas.

Dille Denijs (1904–), Belgian musicologist. He got to know Bartók around the time he published his first book on the composer, in 1939. From 1961 until his retirement in 1971 he was director of the Bartók Archives in Budapest, in which capacity he was responsible for the publication of many early works and much documentary material.

Dohnányi, Ernő (1877–1960), Hungarian composer, pianist and conductor. He was a schoolfellow of Bartók's in Bratislava, and it was probably his example that led Bartók to decide to study in Budapest rather than in Vienna. His music, too, had a great influence on the young Bartók, and though Bartók outgrew this influence, Dohnányi was responsible as pianist or conductor for the premières of several of his junior colleague's works, including the Dance Suite.

Erkel, László (1844–96), Hungarian choral conductor and piano teacher. The son of the opera composer Ferenc Erkel (1810–93), he was Bartók's teacher in Bratislava.

Fábián, Felicitas (1884–1905). She was a fellow pupil with Bartók at the Academy of Music in Budapest, and his first love, to whom he addressed piano pieces and songs in 1900.

Freund, Etelka (1879–1977), Hungarian pianist. She studied with Busoni and in 1903 with Bartók, who during the few years thereafter wrote several important letters to her.

Geyer, Stefi (1888–1956), Hungarian violinist. A pupil of Hubay, she had an intimate friendship with Bartók in 1907–8, and he wrote his First Violin Concerto for her. In 1911 she moved to Vienna, and in 1919 to Zurich, where she married the composer and pianist Walter Schulthess. Bartók saw them on visits to Switzerland in the 1920s and 1930s.

Goodman, Benny (1909–), American jazz clarinettist. He commissioned *Contrasts*, which is dedicated to him and Szigeti.

Harsányi, Kálmán (1876–1929), Hungarian poet. Bartók set a poem of his in different solo and choral versions, and met him during the summer of 1904. They found they shared common ideas about the formation of a truly Hungarian art, but there seems to have been no lasting connection.

Hubay, Jenő (1858–1937), Hungarian violinist and composer. He conducted the first performance of Bartók's Rhapsody op. 1 but disapproved of later works. Bartók came into conflict with him when he was appointed director of the Academy of Music in Budapest in 1919.

Jurkovics, Irmy (1882–1945). A native of Bartók's own home town, she idolised the composer after his return visit there in 1903. He wrote important letters to her from Paris two years later.

Kerner, István (1867–1929), Hungarian conductor. Closely associated with the Budapest Philharmonic Society between 1900 and 1919, he conducted the first orchestral performance Bartók had, when *Kossuth* was played in 1904.

Kiriac-Georgescu, Dumitru (1866–1928), Romanian composer and conductor. He was one of Bartók's most important contacts in Romania: through his intervention Bartók's Bihar collection was published by the Academy of Sciences in Bucharest. As a composer himself he was interested in applying folksong modality.

Kodály, Emma, née Schlesinger, formerly Gruber (1863–1958), Hungarian musician and patroness. Her salon was a meeting-place for musicians in Budapest around the time Bartók was studying at the Academy of Music. He gained much from his attendance there, and dedicated to her his Rhapsody op. 1. In 1910 she married Kodály, and on that occasion Bartók dedicated the third of his *Sketches* to them.

Kodály, Zoltán (1882–1967), Hungarian composer and folklorist. He and Bartók met in 1905 and began almost at once to work together on folksong collecting. Both of them, too, were keen to draw creative inspiration from folk music, and Bartók lost no opportunity to play and praise his friend's works.

Koessler, Hans (1853–1926), German composer and teacher. A cousin of Reger's and stylistic adherent of Brahms, he was Bartók's composition teacher at the Academy of Music in Budapest. He seems to have thought little of his pupil's gifts.

Krohn, Ilmari (1867–1960), Finnish musicologist. His method of classifying folktunes, developed during the course of his work on Finnish material, was adapted by Bartók. He was also a composer, and author of detailed interpretations of the symphonies of Bruckner and Sibelius.

Kusevitzky, Serge (1874–1951), Russo-American conductor. He conducted the first performances of the orchestrated *Village Scenes* and of the Concerto for Orchestra, which he commissioned.

Lengyel, Menyhért (1880–1974), Hungarian dramatist. Bartók based *The Miraculous Mandarin* on a scenario he had published. Other works of his include *Typhoon* and a variety of other plays set in exotic locations.

Menuhin, Yehudi (1916–), American violinist. He commissioned the last work Bartók finished, his Sonata for solo violin.

Mihalovich, Ödön (1842–1929), Hungarian composer. He was director of the Academy of Music in Budapest from 1887 to 1919, and so throughout Bartók's time as a student there. His works include an operatic treatment of Wagner's scenario *Wieland der Schmied*.

Pósa, Lajos (1850–1914), Hungarian poet. A writer of folk-style simplicity to whom Bartók turned for the words of four songs in 1902.

Reinitz, Béla (1878–1943), Hungarian composer and critic. He recognised Bartók's genius early on, and headed a committee with Bartók and Kodály to supervise music during the period of the communist government in 1918–19. Later he was imprisoned and publicly humiliated, at which time Bartók dedicated to him the Ady songs op. 16.

Richter, Hans (1843–1916), Austro-Hungarian conductor. One of the first of the modern international conductors, he appeared regularly at Bayreuth, where he had conducted the first *Ring* in 1876, while also holding appointments with the London Symphony Orchestra (1904–11) and the Hallé Orchestra (1897–1911). In this last role he was responsible for Bartók's first appearance abroad as composer and pianist in 1904.

Sacher, Paul (1906–), Swiss conductor. He commissioned the Music for Strings, the Sonata for pianos and percussion, and the Divertimento, the last written while Bartók stayed with him at Saanen.

Schoenberg, Arnold (1874–1951), Austrian composer. Bartók played the first two pieces of his op. 11 in Budapest and Paris; Schoenberg included music by Bartók in the concerts of his Society for Private Musical Performances. There seems to have been no personal connection.

Strauss, Richard (1864–1949), German composer. Hearing his *Also sprach Zarathustra* in 1902 was a formative experience for Bartók, who made a piano transcription of *Ein Heldenleben*. The influence quickly waned, however, as a result of his work on folksong from 1904 onwards.

Stravinsky, Igor (1882–1971), Russian composer. He was the contemporary to whom Bartók felt closest, and by whom he was most deeply and continuously affected, as may be observed in the pounding orchestral chords of *The Miraculous Mandarin*, the percussive piano writing of the Sonata, the use of a *Les noces* ensemble in the Sonata for pianos and percussion, or the quotation from *The Firebird* in the Second Piano Concerto.

Szabó, Xavér Ferenc (1846–1911), Hungarian composer and teacher. He taught Bartók orchestration and score reading at the Academy of Music in Budapest.

Székely, Zoltán (1903–), Hungarian violinist. He studied with Hubay and Kodály, and gave several recitals with Bartók in the 1920s and 1930s. Bartók wrote his Second Rhapsody and Second Concerto for him.

Szigeti, Joseph (1892–1973), Hungarian violinist. He studied with Hubay and gave several recitals with Bartók; one in 1940, at the Library of Congress in Washington, DC, was recorded. Bartók wrote his First Rhapsody and *Contrasts* for him.

Tango, Egisto (1873–1951), Italian conductor. He worked at the Budapest Opera between 1912 and 1919, and was responsible there for the first performances of *Bluebeard's Castle* and *The Wooden Prince*, of which Bartók dedicated the latter to him.

Thomán, István (1862–1940), Hungarian pianist and teacher. A pupil of Liszt, he taught Bartók at the Academy of Music in Budapest, where Bartók succeeded him as professor in 1907. In 1938 Bartók played at a concert to mark his 75th birthday.

Vecsey, Ferenc (1893–1935), Hungarian violinist. Bartók accompanied him on an Iberian tour in 1906.

Vikár, Béla (1859–1945), Hungarian folklorist. Pioneer folksong collector in Hungary, whose recordings Bartók and Kodály used with their own in assembling a corpus of Hungarian folk music.

Waldbauer, Imre (1892–1953), Hungarian violinist. A pupil of Hubay, he gave recitals with Bartók, played the solo at the first performance of the *Two Portraits*, and founded a quartet which gave the first performances of all Bartók's first four quartets; the Second was dedicated to them. The Hungarian première of the Sixth, in 1946, was the occasion of their last concert: Waldbauer, together with the quartet's cellist Jenő Kerpely, then moved to the United States.

Appendix D
Bibliography

A comprehensive guide to the considerable body of literature on Bartók is contained in *The New Grove*. Here are listed only the more important volumes to have appeared in English.

1 Writings by Bartók

Hungarian Folk Music (Oxford University Press, London, 1931)

Serbo-Croation Folk Songs, with Albert B. Lord (Columbia University Press, New York, 1951)

Serbo-Croatian Heroic Songs, with Albert B. Lord (Harvard University Press, Cambridge, Massachusetts, and the Serbian Academy of Sciences, Belgrade, 1954)

Rumanian Folk Music, edited by Benjamin Suchoff (Martinus Nijhoff, The Hague, 1967–75)

Letters, edited by János Demény (Faber, London, 1971)

Essays, edited by Benjamin Suchoff (Faber, London, 1976)

Turkish Folk Music from Asia Minor, edited by Benjamin Suchoff (Princeton University Press, Princeton, New Jersey, 1976)

2 Documentary material

Documenta bartókiana (Budapest, 1964–)

Ferenc Bonis: *Béla Bartók: his Life in Pictures and Documents* (Corvina, Budapest, 1972, second edition 1981)

3 General monographs

Halsey Stevens: *The Life and Music of Béla Bartók* (Oxford University Press, New York, 1953, second edition 1964)

Józef Ujfalussy: *Béla Bartók* (Corvina, Budapest, 1971)

Ernő Lendvai: *Béla Bartók: an Analysis of his Music* (Kahn & Averill, London, 1971)

Lajos Lesznai: *Bartók* (Dent, London, 1973)

György Kroó: *A Guide to Bartók* (Corvina, Budapest, 1974)

Ernő Lendvai: *The Workshop of Bartók and Kodály* (Editio Musica, Budapest, 1983)

4 Collections of essays

Todd Crow, ed.: *Bartók Studies* (Detroit Reprints in Music, Detroit, Michigan, 1976)
Studia musicologica, xxiii (1981)

5 Specialised studies

Benjamin Suchoff: *Guide to Bartók's Mikrokosmos* (Boosey & Hawkes, London, 1957, second edition 1971)
János Kárpáti: *Bartók's String Quartets* (Corvina, Budapest, 1975)
John McCabe: *Bartók Orchestral Music* (BBC, London, 1974)
Stephen Walsh: *Bartók Chamber Music* (BBC, London, 1982)

Index

Ady, Endre 83, 204, 207
Agghazy, Karóly 2
Altdörfer, Christian 2
Arányi, Adila 8, 39, 207
Arányi, Jelly (d') 8, 39, 100, 110, 201, 207

Babbitt, Milton 187, 194, 196
Bach, Johann Sebastian 6, 36, 120, 125, 141, 172, 179, 181, 205
Backhaus, Wilhelm 35
Balázs, Béla 59, 71, 72, 73, 76, 82, 197, 207
Bánffy, Miklós Count 76
Bartók, Béla (father) 1, 191, 207
Bartók, Béla
  in Algeria 23, 69, 80, 81, 86, 194
  in America 28, 108, 131, 138, 171-2, 173-85, 186, 195, 196
  atheism 40, 183
  birth 1, 191
  as conductor 52, 199
  education 2-9, 191-3
  as folksong collector 15, 16-23, 26, 57, 87, 152, 193-4, 196
  as folksong student 22-3, 26-8, 30, 43, 69, 145, 152, 194, 195,
    196
  in Hungarian musical life 5, 6, 8, 13, 14, 17-18, 31, 52, 65, 66-7,
    69, 70, 76, 87, 95, 106, 120, 153, 194, 195, 196, 197, 198,
    199, 200, 201, 202, 203, 204, 205
  infancy 2, 191
  and the League of Nations 138-9, 145, 195
  in London 97, 108
  in Paris 35-6, 42, 97, 108, 193
  as pianist 3, 4-5, 7, 8, 9, 13, 14, 34, 67, 108-9, 110-14, 120, 138,
    145, 192, 193, 194, 195, 196, 198, 200, 201, 202, 203, 204,
    205